**C.Neil**

**Inquests Jack the Ripper**

28th April 2013
CreateSpace Independent
Publishing Platform

## Martha Tabram a.k.a. Emma Turner

Born: Martha White, May 10, 1849, at 17 Marshall Street, London Rd., Southwark Father: Charles Samuel White, a warehouseman Mother: Elisabeth (Dowsett) Brothers: Henry (twelve years older than Martha), Stephen (8 years older) Sisters: Esther (10 years older), Mary Ann (3 years older)

Martha's parents separated and in May of 1865 Charles was lodging alone in the house of Mrs. Rebecca Glover. The house was located at 31 Pitt Street, St. George's Row. His health was questionable, he suffered severe diarrhea in October and a surgeon was called to examine him. The surgeon found him troubled by his familiar situation and complaining of bad circulation and cold. According to his daughter Mary Ann, he also stated that he had a weak back and was unable to work. On October 11th his estranged wife, Elisabeth, visited him for the first time since their separation. Over the next few days she visited often and on the evening of November 15th, both she and her daughter Mary Ann had supper at his lodging. The meal consisted of bread, butter, and beer. According to his landlady, Mrs. Grover, he was cheerful that evening.

At approximately 10:00 PM, he rose to go to bed and while removing his waistcoat he fell to the floor and died. As there was no evidence of any thing suspicious, the death was ruled as coming from natural causes. He was 59 years old. On Christmas Day, 1869, Martha married Henry Samuel Tabram at Trinity Church in St. Mary's Parish, Newington. He was a foreman furniture packer. A short, well dressed man with iron gray hair, mustache and imperial. They had already been living together in Pleasant Place and moved to 20 Marshall Street in February 1871. The new house was very near by the house in which Martha was born. Martha had two sons by the marriage, Frederick John, born in February 1871 and Charles Henry, born in December of 1872. The marriage ended in 1875. Henry left due to Martha's heavy drinking. He gave her an allowance of twelve shillings per week for three years but reduced it to 2s 6d due to her pestering him in the streets for money. She had a warrant taken out against him and had him locked up. He had also learned that she was living with another man. At this time he refused to support her any further. Henry Turner was a carpenter with whom Martha lived, off and on, for twelve years. He is described as a short, dirty man who dressed in a slovenly manner. He was young and had a pale face, light moustache and imperial. Their relationship also appears to have been greatly effected by Martha's drinking. Turner stated at the inquest into her death: "Since she has been living with me, her character for sobriety was not good. If I give her money she generally spent it in drink." Martha was in the habit of staying out late at night, usually not returning before 11:00 PM and occasionally staying out all night. Her excuse was usually that she had been taken with hysterical fits and had been taken to the police station. Turner had witnessed these fits and stated that they usually came about due to drunkenness. In 1888 Turner was out of regular employment and making his living hawking cheap trinkets, menthol cones and needles and pins. The couple lodged in the house of Mrs. Mary Bousfield at 4 Star Place, Commercial Road. Bousfield described Martha as a person who would "rather have a glass of ale than a cup of tea." She also said, however, that she was not a perpetual drunk. The couple left their lodgings without notice and behind in the rent approximately 4 to 6 weeks prior to the murder. Perhaps out of guilt, Martha secretly returned one night and left the key to the lodging without seeing the landlady.

Turner left Martha for the last time in July of 1888. At the time of her death he was living at the Victoria working man's home on Commercial Street. She tried to carry on earning a living through selling trinkets and prostitution. It is very likely that whatever small amount of money she made was spent on drink. Indeed, Turner is quoted as saying "If I gave her money she generally spent it on drink. In fact it was always drink. When she took to drink, however, I usually left her to her own resources, and I can't answer to her conduct then." Her last known address was 19 George Street, Spitalfields (known as Satchell's Lodging House). Turner saw a destitute Martha for the last time on Leadenhall Street, near Aldgate pump on August 4, 1888. He gave her 1s 6d to buy trinkets for trade with which she might earn some sort of living. On Bank Holiday Monday, August 6th, Martha went out with Mary Ann Connelly, who was known as "Pearly Poll." They were seen throughout the evening in pubs in the company of a soldier or soldiers. According to Pearly Poll, she and Martha picked up two guardsmen, a Corporal and a Private in the Two Brewers public house and drank with them in several pubs including the White Swan on Whitechapel High Street. Some time around 11:45 PM Martha and Pearly Poll went separate ways. Martha with the Private into George Yard and Pearly Poll and the Corporal into Angel Alley. Both, obviously, for the purpose of having sex. 1:50 AM: Elizabeth Mahoney returned to her home in George Yard Buildings. At the time that she ascended the stairs to her flat she saw no one or anything unusual in the building.

2:00 AM: PC Thomas Barrett saw a young Grenadier Guardsman in Wentworth Street, the north end of George Yard. Barrett questioned his reason for being there and was told by the Guardsman that he was waiting for a "chum who went off with a girl."

3:30 AM: Alfred Crow returned to his lodging in George Yard Buildings and noticed what he thought was a homeless person sleeping on the first floor landing. As this was not an uncommon occurrence he continued on to bed.

John Reeves left his lodgings in the George Yard Buildings at 4:45 AM. By this time the light was improving inside the stairwell. Reeves also noticed the body on the first floor landing but he was also aware that it was lying in a pool of blood. Reeves went off to find a policeman.

He returned with PC Barrett. Although not yet identified, the body was that of Martha Tabram. The body was supine with the arms and hands by the side. The fingers were tightly clenched and the legs open in a manner to suggest that intercourse had taken place.

Others who testified at the inquest include Francis Hewitt,the superintendent of George Yard Buildings and Mrs. Mary Bousfield (also known as Luckhurst), Martha's former landlady at 4 Star Street.

The Post-Mortem: The post-mortem examination of Martha Tabram was held by Dr. Timothy Killeen (also spelled Keeling or Keleene) at 5:30 AM on the morning of August 7th. Tabram was described as a plump middle-aged woman, about 5'3" tall, dark hair and complexion. The time of death was estimated at about three hours before the examination (around 2:30-2:45 AM). In all, there were thirty-nine stab wounds including:

5 wounds (left lung)
2 wounds (right lung)
1 wound (heart)
5 wounds (liver)
2 wounds (spleen)
6 wounds (stomach)

According to Killeen, the focus of the wounds were the breasts, belly, and groin area. In his opinion, all but one of the wounds were inflicted by a right-handed attacker, and all but one seemed to have been the result of an "ordinary pen-knife." There was, however, one wound on the sternum which appeared to have been inflicted by a dagger or bayonet (thereby leading police to believe that a sailor was the perpetrator).

**Wearing at the time of her death: A black bonnet Long black jacket A dark green skirt Brown petticoat Stockings Spring sided boots showing considerable age**


## Inquest: Martha Tabram

**Alfred George Crow**, cabdriver, 35, George-yard-buildings, deposed that he got home at half-past 3 on Tuesday morning. As he was passing the first-floor landing he saw a body lying on the ground. He took no notice, as he was accustomed to seeing people lying about there. He did not then know whether the person was alive or dead. He got up at half-past 9, and when he went down the staircase the body was not there. Witness heard no noise while he was in bed.

**John S. Reeves**, of 37, George-yard-buildings, a waterside labourer, said that on Tuesday morning he left home at a quarter to 5 to seek for work. When he reached the first-floor landing he found the deceased lying on her back in a pool of blood. He was frightened, and did not examine her, but at once gave information to the police. He did not know the deceased. The deceased's clothes were disarranged, as though she had had a struggle with some one. Witness saw no footmarks on the staircase, nor did he find a knife or other weapon.

**Police-constable Thomas Barrett**, 226 H, said that the last witness called his attention to the body of the deceased. He sent for a doctor, who pronounced life extinct.

**Dr. T. R. Killeen**, of 68, Brick-lane, said that he was called to the deceased, and found her dead. She had 39 stabs on the body. She had been dead some three hours. Her age was about 36, and the body was very well nourished. Witness had since made a post-mortem examination of the body. The left lung was penetrated in five places, and the right lung was penetrated in two places. The heart, which was rather fatty, was penetrated in one place, and that would be sufficient to cause death. The liver was healthy, but was penetrated in five places, the spleen was penetrated in two places, and the stomach, which was perfectly healthy, was penetrated in six places. The witness did not think all the wounds were inflicted with the same instrument. The wounds generally might have been inflicted by a knife, but such an instrument could not have inflicted one of the wounds, which went through the chest-bone. His opinion was that one of the wounds was inflicted by some kind of dagger, and that all of them were caused during life.

**The Coroner** said he was in hopes that the body would be identified, but three women had identified it under three different names. He therefore proposed to leave that question open until the next occasion. The case would be left in the hands of Detective-Inspector Reid, who would endeavor to discover the perpetrator of this dreadful murder. It was one of the most dreadful murders any one could imagine. The man must have been a perfect savage to inflict such a number of wounds on a defenseless woman in such a way. The inquiry would be adjourned for a fortnight.

The case was then adjourned.

---

## Day 2, Thursday, August 23, 1888
(*The Times*, August 24, 1888)

Yesterday afternoon [23 Aug] Mr. George Collier, the Deputy Coroner for the South-Eastern Division of Middlesex, resumed his inquiry at the Working Lads' Institute, Whitechapel-road, respecting the death of the woman who was found dead at George-yard-buildings, on the early morning of Tuesday, the 7th inst., with no less than 39 wounds on various parts of her body. The body has been identified as that of Martha Tabram, aged 39 or 40 years, the wife of a foreman packer at a furniture warehouse.

**Henry Samuel Tabram**, 6, River-terrace, East Greenwich, husband of the deceased woman, said he last saw her alive about 18 months ago, in the Whitechapel-road. They had been separated for 13 years, owing to her drinking habits. She obtained a warrant against him. For some part of the time witness allowed her 12s. a week, but in consequence of her annoyance he stopped this allowance ten years ago, since which time he had made it half-a-crown a week, as he found she was living with a man.

**Henry Turner**, a carpenter, staying at the Working Men's Home, Commercial-street, Spitalfields, stated that he had been living with the woman Tabram as his wife for about nine years. Two or three weeks previously to this occurrence he ceased to do so. He had left her on two or three occasions in consequence of her drinking habits, but they had come together again. He last saw her alive on Saturday, the 4th inst., in Leadenhall-street. He then gave her 1s. 6d. to get some stock. When she had money she spent it in drink. While living with witness deceased's usual time for coming home was about 11 o'clock. As far as he knew she had no regular companion and he did not know that she walked the streets. As a rule he was, he said, a man of sober habits, and when the deceased was sober they usually got on well together.
By Inspector Reid. - At times the deceased had stopped out all night. After those occasions she told him she had been taken in a fit and was removed to the police-station or somewhere else.
By the Coroner. - He knew she suffered from fits, but they were brought on by drink.

**Mrs. Mary Bousfield**, wife of a wood cutter, residing at 4, Star-place, Commercial-road, knew the deceased by the name of Turner. She was formerly a lodger in her house with the man Turner. Deceased would rather have a glass of ale than a cup of tea, but she was not a woman who got continually drunk, and she never brought home any companions with her. She left without giving notice, and owed two weeks' rent.

**Mrs. Ann Morris**, a widow, of 23, Lisbon-street, E., said she last saw the deceased, who was her sister-in-law, at about 11 o'clock on Bank Holiday night in the Whitechapel-road. She was then about to enter a public house.

**Mary Ann Connolly** ("Pearly Poll"), who at the suggestion of Inspector Reid was cautioned in the usual manner before being sworn, stated she had been for the last two nights living at a lodging house in Dorset-street, Spitalfields. Witness was a single woman. She had known the woman Tabram for about four or five months. She knew her by the name of Emma. She last saw her alive on Bank Holiday night, when witness was with her about three-quarters of an hour, and they separated at a quarter to 12. Witness was with Tabram and two soldiers - one private and one corporal. She did not know what regiment they belonged to, but they had white bands round their caps. After they separated, Tabram went away with the private, and witness accompanied the corporal up Angel-alley. There was no quarrelling between any of them. Witness had been to the barracks to identify the soldiers, and the two men she picked out were, to the best of her belief, the men she and Tabram were with. The men at the Wellington Barracks were paraded before witness. One of the men picked out by witness turned out not to be a corporal, but he had stripes on his arm.

By Inspector Reid. - Witness heard of the murder on the Tuesday. Since the occurrence witness had threatened to drown herself, but she only said it for a lark. She stayed away two days and two nights, and she only said that when asked where she was going. She knew the police were looking after her, but she did not let them know her whereabouts. By a juryman. - The woman Tabram was not drunk. They were, however, drinking at different houses for about an hour and three-quarters. They had ale and rum.

**Detective-Inspector Reid** made a statement of the efforts made by the police to discover the perpetrator of the murder. Several persons had stated that they saw the deceased woman on the previous Sunday with a corporal, but when all the corporals and privates at the Tower and Wellington Barracks were paraded before them they failed to identify the man. The military authorities afforded every facility to the police. "Pearly Poll" picked out two men belonging to the Cold stream Guards at the Wellington Barracks. One of those men had three good conduct stripes, and he was proved beyond doubt to have been with his wife from 8 o'clock on the Monday night until 6 o'clock the following morning. The other man was also proved to have been in barracks at five minutes past 10 on Bank Holiday night. The police would be pleased if anyone would give them information of having seen anyone with the deceased on the night of Bank Holiday.

**Henry Samuel Tabram**, of 6, River-terrace, East Greenwich, stated that he was a foreman packer in a furniture warehouse. He identified the body as that of his wife. Her name was Martha Tabram, and she was thirty-nine years of age. He last saw her alive eighteen months ago in the Whitechapel-road. Witness had been separated from her thirteen years.

**Henry Turner**, who stated that he lived at the Working Men's Home, Commercial-street, deposed that he was a carpenter by trade, but latterly he had got his living as a hawker. Up till three weeks previous to this affair he was living with the deceased. They had lived together on and off for nine years. She used to get her living, like himself, as a street hawker. He last saw her alive on the Saturday before her death, when they met accidentally in Leadenhall-street. She said she had got no money, so witness gave her some to buy stock with. Deceased was a woman who, when she had the money, would get drunk with it.

**Mary Bousfiled**, 4, Star-place, Commercial-road, deposed that Turner and the deceased lived at her house till three weeks before her death. Turner was very good to her, and helped to support two children she had by her husband.

**Ann Morris**, 23, Lisburn-street, E., a widow, deposed that she was the sister-in-law of the deceased. Witness last saw her alive on Bank Holiday, as she was entering the White Swan public-house in Whitechapel-road. Deceased then appeared to be sober. She was alone when she entered the bar.

**Mary Ann Connelly** said she had known the deceased for four or five months under the name of Emma. The last time she saw her alive was on Bank Holiday, at the corner of George-yard, Whitechapel. They went to a public-house together, and parted about 11.45. They were accompanied by two soldiers, one a private and the other a corporal. She did not know to what regiment they belonged, but they had white bands round their caps. Witness did not know if the corporal had any side arms. They picked up with the soldiers together, and entered several public-houses, where they drank. When they separated, the deceased went away with the private. They went up George-yard, while witness and the corporal went up Angel-alley. Before they parted witness and the corporal had a quarrel and he hit her with a stick. She did not hear deceased have any quarrel. Witness never saw the deceased again alive. -

**The Coroner**, in summing up, said that the crime was one of the most brutal that had occurred for some years. For a poor defenseless woman to be outraged and stabbed in the manner which this woman had been was almost beyond belief. They could only come to one conclusion, and that was that the deceased was brutally and cruelly murdered.

# Mary Ann Nichols

Born Mary Ann Walker on August 26, 1845 in Dawes Court, Shoe Lane, off Fleet Street. She was christened in or some years before 1851. At the time of her death the East London Observer guessed her age at 30-35. At the inquest her father said "she was nearly 44 years of age, but it must be owned that she looked ten years younger." Features 5'2" tall; brown eyes; dark complexion; brown hair turning grey; five front teeth missing , her teeth are slightly discolored. She is described as having small, delicate features with high cheekbones and grey eyes. She has a small scar on her forehead from a childhood injury. She is described by Emily Holland as "a very clean woman who always seemed to keep to herself." The doctor at the post mortem remarked on the cleanliness of her thighs. She is also an alcoholic.  History Father: Edward Walker (Blacksmith, formerly a locksmith). He has gray hair and beard and, as a smithy, was probably powerfully built. At the time of Polly's death he is living at 16 Maidswood Rd., Camberwell. Mother: Caroline. Polly married William Nichols on January 16, 1864. She would have been about 22 years old. The marriage is performed by Charles Marshall, Vicar of Saint Bride's Parish Church and witnessed by Seth George Havelly and Sarah Good. William Nichols is in the employ of Messrs. Perkins, Bacon & Co., Whitefriars Rd. and living at Cogburg Rd. off Old Kent Road at the time of his wife's death. The couple have five children. Edward John, born 1866; Percy George, 1868; Alice Esther, 1870; Eliza Sarah, 1877 and Henry Alfred born in 1879. The oldest, 21 in 1888, is living with his grandfather (Polly's father) at the time of her death. He had left home in 1880 according to his father, on his own accord. The other children continued to live with Nichols. William and Polly briefly lodged in Bouverie Street then moved in with her father at 131 Trafalgar Street for about ten years. They spend six years, (no dates) at No. 6 D block, Peabody Buildings, Stamford Street, Blackfriars Rd. There they are paying a rent of 5 shillings, 6 pence per week. If Peabody Buildings is their last address then they would have lived there from 1875-1881, with her father from 1865 to 1875. Polly separated from Nichols for the final time in 1881. It was the last of many separations during 24 years of marriage. In 1882, William found out that his wife was living as a prostitute and discontinued support payments to her. (Sugden: she is living with another man, probably Thomas Dew). Parish authorities tried to collect maintenance money from him. He countered that she had deserted him leaving him with the children. He won his case after establishing that she was living as a common prostitute. At the time of her death, he had not seen his wife in three years. Polly's father spread the story that the separation had come about due to William having an affair with the nurse who took care of Polly during her last confinement. William does not deny that he had an affair but states that it was not the cause of her leaving. "The woman left me four or five times, if not six." He claims that the affair took place after

Polly left. There is obvious disharmony in the family as the eldest son would have nothing to do with his father at his mother's funeral. After the separation, Polly begins a sad litany of moving from workhouse to workhouse. 3/24/83-5/21/83 -- She is living with her father in Camberwell. He testifies at the inquest into her death that she was "a dissolute character and drunkard whom he knew would come to a bad end." He found her not a sober person but not in the habit of staying out late at night. Her drinking caused friction and they argued. He claims that he had not thrown her out but she left the next morning. /2/83-10/26/87 -- She is said to have been living with a man named Thomas Dew, a blacksmith, with a shop in York Mews, 15 York St., Walworth. In June 1886 she had attended the funeral of her brother who had been burned to death by the explosion of a paraffin lamp. It was remarked by the family that she was respectably dressed. 10/25/87 -- She spends one day in St. Giles Workhouse, Endell Street. 10/26/87-12/2/87 -- Strand Workhouse, Edmonton 12/2/87-12/19/87 -- Lambeth Workhouse On 12/2/87 It is said that she was caught "sleeping rough (in the open)" in Trafalgar Square. She was found to be destitute and with no means of sustenance and was sent on to Lambeth Workhouse. 12/19/87-12/29/87 -- Lambeth Workhouse 1/4/88-4/16/88 -- Mitcham Workhouse, Holborn and Holborn Infirmary. 4/16/88-5/12/88 -- Lambeth Workhouse. It is in Lambeth Workhouse that she meets Mary Ann Monk who will eventually identify Polly's body for the police. Monk is described as a young woman with a "Haughty air and flushed face." Polly has another friend in the Lambeth Workhouse, a Mrs. Scorer. She had been separated from her husband James Scorer, an assistant salesman in Spitalfields Market, for eleven years. He claimed that he knew Polly by sight but was unable to identify the body at the mortuary. On 12 May she left Lambeth to take a position as a domestic servant in the home of Samuel and Sarah Cowdry. This was common practice at the time for Workhouses to find domestic employment for female inmates. The Cowdry's live at "Ingleside", Rose Hill Rd, Wandsworth. Samuel (b. 1827)is the Clerk of Works in the Police Department. Sarah is one year younger than her husband. They are described as upright people. Both are religious and both are teetotaler.

Polly writes her father:

"I just right to say you will be glad to know that I am settled in my new place, and going all right up to now. My people went out yesterday and have not returned, so I am left in charge. It is a grand place inside, with trees and gardens back and front. All has been newly done up. They are teetotalers and religious so I ought to get on. They are very nice people, and I have not too much to do. I hope you are all right and the boy has work. So good bye for the present.

from yours truly, Polly Answer soon, please, and let me know how you are."

Walker replies to the letter but does not hear back. She works for two months and then left while stealing clothing worth three pounds, ten shillings. 8/1/88-8/2/88 -- Grays Inn Temporary Workhouse Last Addresses Wilmott's Lodging House at 18 Thrawl Street, Spitalfields. There she shares a room with four women including Emily Holland. The room is described as being surprisingly neat. The price of the room is 4d per night. On 8/24/88 Polly moves to a lodging house known as the White House at 56 Flower and Dean Street. In this doss-house men are allowed to share a bed with a woman.

Thursday, August 30 through Friday, August 31, 1888.

Heavy rains have ushered out one of the coldest and wettest summers on record. On the night of August 30, the rain was sharp and frequent and was accompanied by peals of thunder and flashes of lightning. the sky on that night was turned red by the occasion of two dock fires.

11:00 PM -- Polly is seen walking down Whitechapel Road, she is probably soliciting trade.

12:30 AM -- She is seen leaving the Frying Pan Public House at the corner of Brick Lane and Thrawl Street. She returns to the lodging house at 18 Thrawl Street.

1:20 or 1:40 AM -- She is told by the deputy to leave the kitchen of the lodging house because she could not produce her doss money. Polly, on leaving, asks him to save a bed for her. " Never Mind!" She says, "I'll soon get my doss money. See what a jolly bonnet I've got now." She indicates a little black bonnet which no one had seen before.

2:30 AM -- She meets Emily Holland, who was returning from watching the Shadwell Dry Dock fire, outside of a grocer's shop on the corner of Whitechapel Road and Osborn Street. Polly had come down Osborn Street. Holland describes her as "very drunk and staggered against the wall." Holland calls attention to the church clock striking 2:30. Polly tells Emily that she had had her doss money three times that day and had drunk it away. She says she will return to Flower and Dean Street where she could share a bed with a man after one more attempt to find trade. "I've had my doss money three times today and spent it." She says, "It won't be long before I'm back." The two women talk for seven or eight minutes. Polly leaves walking east down Whitechapel Road.

PC Neil discovers Nichols' body in Buck's Row.

3:15 AM -- PC John Thain, 96J, passes down Buck's Row on his beat. He sees nothing unusual. At approximately the same time Sgt. Kerby passes down Buck's Row and reports the same.

3:40 or 3:45 AM -- Polly Nichols' body is discovered in Buck's Row by Charles Cross, a carman, on his way to work at Pickfords in the City Road., and Robert Paul who joins him at his request. "Come and look over here, there's a woman." Cross calls to Paul. Cross believes she is dead. Her hands and face are cold but the arms above the elbow and legs are still warm. Paul believes he feels a faint heartbeat. "I think she's breathing," he says "but it is little if she is." The two men agree that they do not want to be late for work and after arranging Nichols' skirts to give her some decency, decide to alert the first police officer they meet on their way. They eventually meet PC Jonas Mizen at the junction of Hanbury Street and Baker's Row and tell him of their find. In the meantime, Nichols' body has been found by PC John Neil, 97J. He signals to PC Thain who then joins him and the two are soon joined by Mizen. Thain calls for Dr. Rees Ralph Llewellyn, who resides nearby. The two return a few minutes later (around 3:50 A.M.) and Dr. Llewellyn pronounces life to have been extinct "but a few minutes." Buck's Row is ten minutes walk from Osborn Street. The only illumination is from a single gas lamp at the far end of the street. Polly's body is found across from Essex Wharf and the Brown and Eagle Wool Warehouse and Schneiders Cap Factory in a gateway entrance to Brown's stableyard between a board school (to the west) and terrace houses (cottages) belonging to better class tradesmen. She is almost underneath the window of Mrs. Emma Green, a light sleeper, who lives in the first house next to the stable gates. Her house is called the 'New Cottage'. She is a widower with two sons and a daughter living with her. That night, one son goes to bed at 9:00 PM, the other follows at 9:45. Mrs. Green and her daughter shared a first floor room at the front of the house. They went to bed at approximately 11:00 PM. She claims she slept undisturbed by any unusual sound until she was awakened by the police. Opposite New Cottage lives Walter Purkiss, the manager of Essex Wharf with his wife, children and a servant. He and his wife went to bed at 11:00 and 11:15 respectively. Both claimed to have been awake at various times in the night and heard nothing. Polly Nichols' body is identified by Lambeth Workhouse inmate Mary Ann Monk and the identification confirmed by William Nichols. An inventory of her clothes is taken by Inspector John Spratling at the mortuary. She was wearing: (overall impression -- shabby and stained)

Black Straw bonnet trimmed with black velvet Reddish brown ulster with seven large brass buttons bearing the pattern of a woman on horseback accompanied by a man.

Brown linsey frock White flannel chest cloth Black ribbed wool stockings Two petticoats, one gray wool, one flannel. Both stenciled on bands "Lambeth Workhouse" Brown stays (short) Flannel drawers Men's elastic (spring) sided boots with the uppers cut and steel tips on the heels Possessions: Comb White pocket handkerchief Broken piece of mirror (a prized possession in a lodging house) Observations of Dr. Rees Ralph Llewellyn upon arrival at Bucks row at 4:00 AM on the morning of August 31st. After only a brief examination of the body he pronounced Polly Nichols dead. He noted that there was a wine glass and a half of blood in the gutter at her side but claimed that he had no doubt that she had been killed where she lay.

Inquest testimony as reported in The Times:

"Five teeth were missing, and there was a slight laceration of the tongue. There was a bruise running along the lower part of the jaw on the right side of the face. That might have been caused by a blow from a fist or pressure from a thumb. There was a circular bruise on the left side of the face which also might have been inflicted by the pressure of the fingers. On the left side of the neck, about 1 in. below the jaw, there was an incision about 4 in. in length, and ran from a point immediately below the ear. On the same side, but an inch below, and commencing about 1 in. in front of it, was a circular incision, which terminated at a point about 3 in. below the right jaw. That incision completely severed all the tissues down to the vertebrae. The large vessels of the neck on both sides were severed. The incision was about 8 in. in length. the cuts must have been caused by a long-bladed knife, moderately sharp, and used with great violence. No blood was found on the breast, either of the body or the clothes. There were no injuries about the body until just about the lower part of the abdomen. Two or three inches from the left side was a wound running in a jagged manner. The wound was a very deep one, and the tissues were cut through. There were several incisions running across the abdomen. There were three or four similar cuts running downwards, on the right side, all of which had been caused by a knife which had been used violently and downwards. the injuries were form left to right and might have been done by a left handed person. All the injuries had been caused by the same instrument."

Inspector Joseph Helson, J-division, is notified of the murder at 6.45am and at the mortuary he is shown the body and the extent of the mutilations. With all of her faults Nichols seems to have been well-liked by all who knew her. At the inquest her father says, "I don't think she had any enemies, she was too good for that."

# Inquest: Mary Ann "Polly" Nichols

Day 1, Saturday, September 1, 1888

(The Daily Telegraph, Monday, September 3, 1888, Page 3)

On Saturday [1 Sep] Mr. Wynne E. Baxter, the coroner for South-East Middlesex, opened an inquiry at the Working Lads' Institute, Whitechapel-road, into the circumstances attending the death of a woman supposed to be Mary Ann Nicholls, who was discovered lying dead on the pavement in Buck's-row, Baker's-row, Whitechapel, early on Friday morning. Her throat was cut, and she had other terrible injuries.

Inspector Helston, who has the case in hand, attended, with other officers, on behalf of the Criminal Investigation Department.

Edward Walker deposed: I live at 15, Maidwell-street, Albany-road, Camberwell, and have no occupation. I was a smith when I was at work, but I am not now. I have seen the body in the mortuary, and to the best of my belief it is my daughter; but I have not seen her for three years. I recognize her by her general appearance and by a little mark she has had on her forehead since she was a child. She also had either one or two teeth out, the same as the woman I have just seen. My daughter's name was Mary Ann Nicholls, and she had been married twenty-two years. Her husband's name is William Nicholls, and he is alive. He is a machinist. They have been living apart about seven or eight years. I last heard of her before Easter. She was forty-two years of age.

The Coroner: How did you see her?

Witness: She wrote to me.

The Coroner: Is this letter in her handwriting?

Witness: Yes, that is her writing. The letter, which was dated April 17, 1888, was read by the Coroner, and referred to a place which the deceased had gone to at Wandsworth.

The Coroner: When did you last see her alive?

Witness: Two years ago last June.

The Coroner: Was she then in a good situation?

Witness: I don't know. I was not on speaking terms with her. She had been living with me three or four years previously, but thought she could better herself, so I let her go.

The Coroner: What did she do after she left you?

Witness: I don't know.

The Coroner: This letter seems to suggest that she was in a decent situation.

Witness: She had only just gone there.

The Coroner: Was she a sober woman?

Witness: Well, at times she drank, and that was why we did not agree.

The Coroner: Was she fast?

Witness: No; I never heard of anything of that sort. She used to go with some young women and men that she knew, but I never heard of anything improper.

The Coroner: Have you any idea what she has been doing lately?

Witness: I have not the slightest idea.

The Coroner: She must have drunk heavily for you to turn her out of doors?

Witness: I never turned her out. She had no need to be like this while I had a home for her.

The Coroner: How is it that she and her husband were not living together?

Witness: When she was confined her husband took on with the young woman who came to nurse her, and they parted, he living with the nurse, by whom he has another family.

The Coroner: Have you any reasonable doubt that this is your daughter?

Witness: No, I have not. I know nothing about her acquaintances, or what she had been doing for a living. I had no idea she was over here in this part of the town. She has had five children, the eldest being twenty-one years old and the youngest eight or nine years. One of them lives with me, and the other four are with their father.

The Coroner: Has she ever lived with anybody since she left her husband?

Witness: I believe she was once stopping with a man in York-street, Walworth. His name was Drew, and he was a smith by trade. He is living there now, I believe. The parish of Lambeth summoned her husband for the keep of the children, but the summons was dismissed, as it was proved that she was then living with another man. I don't know who that man was.

The Coroner: Was she ever in the workhouse?

Witness: Yes, sir; Lambeth Workhouse, in April last, and went from there to a situation at Wandsworth.

By the Jury: The husband resides at Coburg-road, Old Kent-road. I don't know if he knows of her death.

Coroner: Is there anything you know of likely to throw any light upon this affair?

Witness: No; I don't think she had any enemies, she was too good for that.


John Neil, police-constable, 97J, said: Yesterday morning I was proceeding down Buck's-row, Whitechapel, going towards Brady-street. There was not a soul about. I had been round there half an hour previously, and I saw no one then. I was on the right-hand side of the street, when I noticed a figure lying in the street. It was dark at the time, though there was a street lamp shining at the end of the row. I went across and found deceased lying outside a gateway, her head towards the east. The gateway was closed. It was about nine or ten feet high, and led to some stables. There were houses from the gateway eastward, and the School Board school occupies the westward. On the opposite side of the road is Essex Wharf. Deceased was lying lengthways along the street, her left hand touching the gate. I examined the body by the aid of my lamp, and noticed blood oozing from a wound in the throat. She was lying on her back, with her clothes disarranged. I felt her arm, which was quite warm from the joints upwards. Her eyes were wide open. Her bonnet was off and lying at her side, close to the left hand. I heard a constable passing Brady-street, so I called him. I did not whistle. I said to him, "Run at once for Dr. Llewellyn," and, seeing another constable in Baker's-row, I sent him for the ambulance. The doctor arrived in a very short time. I had, in the meantime, rung the bell at Essex Wharf, and asked if any disturbance had been heard. The reply was "No." Sergeant Kirby came after, and he knocked. The doctor looked at the woman and then said, "Move her to the mortuary. She is dead, and I will make a further examination of her." We placed her on the ambulance, and moved her there. Inspector Spratley came to the mortuary, and while taking a description of the deceased turned up her clothes, and found that she was disemboweled. This had not been noticed by any of them before. On the body was found a piece of comb and a bit of looking-glass. No money was found, but an unmarked white handkerchief was found in her pocket.

The Coroner: Did you notice any blood where she was found?

Witness: There was a pool of blood just where her neck was lying. It was running from the wound in her neck.

The Coroner: Did you hear any noise that night?

Witness: No; I heard nothing. The farthest I had been that night was just through the Whitechapel-road and up Baker's-row. I was never far away from the spot.

The Coroner: Whitechapel-road is busy in the early morning, I believe. Could anybody have escaped that way?

Witness: Oh yes, sir. I saw a number of women in the main road going home. At that time any one could have got away.

The Coroner: Some one searched the ground, I believe?

Witness: Yes; I examined it while the doctor was being sent for.

Inspector Spratley: I examined the road, sir, in daylight.

A Juryman (to witness): Did you see a trap in the road at all?

Witness: No.

A Juryman: Knowing that the body was warm, did it not strike you that it might just have been laid there, and that the woman was killed elsewhere?

Witness: I examined the road, but did not see the mark of wheels. The first to arrive on the scene after I had discovered the body were two men who work at a slaughterhouse opposite. They said they knew nothing of the affair, and that they had not heard any screams. I had previously seen the men at work. That would be about a quarter-past three, or half an hour before I found the body.

Henry Llewellyn, surgeon, said: On Friday morning I was called to Buck's-row about four o'clock. The constable told me what I was wanted for. On reaching Buck's-row I found the deceased woman lying flat on her back in the pathway, her legs extended. I found she was dead, and that she had severe injuries to her throat. Her hands and wrists were cold, but the body and lower extremities were warm. I examined her chest and felt the heart. It was dark at the time. I believe she had not been dead more than half-an-hour. I am quite certain that the injuries to her neck were not self-inflicted. There was very little blood round the neck. There were no marks of any struggle or of blood, as if the body had been dragged. I told the police to take her to the mortuary, and I would make another examination. About an hour later I was sent for by the Inspector to see the injuries he had discovered on the body. I went, and saw that the abdomen was cut very extensively. I have this morning made a post-mortem examination of the body. I found it to be that of a female about forty or forty-five years. Five of the teeth are missing, and there is a slight laceration of the tongue. On the right side of the face there is a bruise running along the lower part of the jaw. It might have been caused by a blow with the fist or pressure by the thumb. On the left side of the face there was a circular bruise, which also might have been done by the pressure of the fingers. On the left side of the neck, about an inch below the jaw, there was an incision about four inches long and running from a point immediately below the ear. An inch below on the same side, and commencing about an inch in front of it, was a circular incision terminating at a point about three inches below the right jaw. This incision completely severs all the tissues down to the vertebrae. The large vessels of the neck on both sides were severed. The incision is about eight inches long. These cuts must have been caused with a long-bladed knife, moderately sharp, and used with great violence. No blood at all was found on the breast either of the body or clothes. There were no injuries about the body till just about the lower part of the abdomen. Two or three inches from the left side was a wound running in a jagged manner. It was a very deep wound, and the tissues were cut through. There were several incisions running across the abdomen. On the right side there were also three or four similar cuts running downwards. All these had been caused by a knife, which had been used violently and been used downwards. The wounds were from left to right, and might have been done by a left-handed person. All the injuries had been done by the same instrument.


Day 2, Monday, September 3, 1888

(The Daily Telegraph, Tuesday, September 4, 1888, Page 2)


Mr. Wynne E. Baxter, the coroner for South-East Middlesex, yesterday [3 Sep] resumed his inquiry at the Working Lads' Institute, Whitechapel-road, into the circumstances attending the death of the woman Mary Ann Nicholls, who was discovered lying dead on the pavement in Buck's-row, Baker's-row, Whitechapel, early on Friday morning last.

Inspectors Helston and Aberline attended for the police; whilst Detective- sergeant Enright, of Scotland-year, was also in attendance.

Inspector John Spratling, J Division, deposed that he first heard of the murder about half-past four on Friday morning, while he was in Hackney-road. He proceeded to Buck's-row, where he saw Police-constable Thain, who showed him the place where the deceased had been found. He noticed a blood stain on the footpath. The body of deceased had been removed to the mortuary in Old Montague- street, where witness had an opportunity of preparing a description. The skin presented the appearance of not having been washed for some time previous to the murder. On his arrival Dr. Llewellyn made an examination of the body which lasted about ten minutes.

Witness said he next saw the body when it was stripped.

Detective-sergeant Enright: That was done by two of the workhouse officials.

The Coroner: Had they any authority to strip the body?

Witness: No, sir; I gave them no instructions to strip it. In fact, I told them to leave it as it was.

The Coroner: I don't object to their stripping the body, but we ought to have evidence about the clothes.

Sergeant Enright, continuing, said the clothes, which were lying in a heap in the yard, consisted of a reddish-brown ulster, with seven large brass buttons, and a brown dress, which looked new. There were also a woollen and a flannel petticoat, belonging to the workhouse. Inspector Helson had cut out pieces marked "P. R., Princes-road," with a view to tracing the body. There was also a pair of stays, in fairly good condition, but witness did not notice how they were adjusted.

The Coroner said he considered it important to know the exact state in which the stays were found.

On the suggestion of Inspector Aberline, the clothes were sent for.

The Foreman of the jury asked whether the stays were fastened on the body.

Inspector Spratling replied that he could not say for certain. There was blood on the upper part of the dress body, and also on the Ulster, but he only saw a little on the under-linen, and that might have happened after the removal of the body from Buck's-row. The clothes were fastened when he first saw the body. The stays did not fit very tightly, for he was able to see the wounds without unfastening them. About six o'clock that day he made an examination at Buck's- row and Brady-street, which ran across Baker's-row, but he failed to trace any marks of blood. He subsequently examined, in company with Sergeant Godley, the East London and District Railway lines and embankment, and also the Great Eastern Railway yard, without, however, finding any traces. A watchman of the Great Eastern Railway, whose box was fifty or sixty yards from the spot where the body was discovered, heard nothing particular on the night of the murder.

Witness also visited half a dozen persons living in the same neighborhood, none of whom had noticed anything at all suspicious. One of these, Mrs. Purkiss, had not gone to bed at the time the body of deceased was found, and her husband was of opinion that if there had been any screaming in Buck's-row they would have heard it. A Mrs. Green, whose window looked out upon the very spot where the body was discovered, said nothing had attracted her attention on the morning of Friday last.

Replying to a question from one of the jury, witness stated that Constable Neil was the only one whose duty it was to pass through Buck's-row, but another constable passing along Broad-street from time to time would be within hearing distance.

In reply to a juryman, witness said it was his firm belief that the woman had her clothes on at the time she was murdered.

Henry Tomkins, horse-slaughterer, 12, Coventry-street, Bethnal-green, was the next witness. He deposed that he was in the employ of Messrs. Barber, and was working in the slaughterhouse, Winthrop-street, from between eight and nine o'clock on Thursday evening till twenty minutes past four on Friday morning. He and his fellow workmen usually went home upon finishing their work, but on that morning they did not do so. They went to see the dead woman, Police-constable Thain having passed the slaughterhouse at about a quarter-past four, and told them that a murder had been committed in Buck's-row. Two other men, James Mumford and Charles Britten, had been working in the slaughterhouse. He (witness) and Britten left the slaughterhouse for one hour between midnight and one o'clock in the morning, but not afterwards till they went to see the body. The distance from Winthrop-street to Buck's-row was not great.

The Coroner: Is your work noisy?

Witness: No, sir, very quiet.

The Coroner: Was it quiet on Friday morning, say after two o'clock?

Witness: Yes, sir, quite quiet. The gates were open and we heard no cry.

The Coroner: Did anybody come to the slaughterhouse that night?

Witness: Nobody passed except the policeman.

The Coroner: Are there any women about there?

Witness: Oh! I know nothing about them, I don't like 'em.

The Coroner: I did not ask you whether you like them; I ask you whether there were any about that night.

Witness: I did not see any.

The Coroner: Not in Whitechapel-road?

Witness: Oh, yes, there, of all sorts and sizes; its a rough neighborhood, I can tell you.

Witness, in reply to further questions, said the slaughter-house was too far away from the spot where deceased was found for him to have heard if anybody had called for assistance. When he arrived at Buck's-row the doctor and two or three policemen were there. He believed that two other men, whom he did not know, were also there. He waited till the body was taken away, previous to which about a dozen men came up. He heard no statement as to how the deceased came to be in Buck's-row.

The Coroner: Have you read any statement in the newspapers that there were two people, besides the police and the doctor, in Buck's-row, when you arrived?

Witness: I cannot say, sir.

The Coroner: Then you did not see a soul from one o'clock on Friday morning till a quarter-past four, when the policeman passed your slaughterhouse?

Witness: No, sir.

A Juryman: Did you hear any vehicle pass the slaughterhouse? - No, sir.

[Juryman?] Would you have heard it if there had been one? - Yes, sir.

[Juryman?] Where did you go between twenty minutes past twelve and one o'clock? - I and my mate went to the front of the road.

[Juryman?] Is not your usual hour for leaving off work six o'clock in the morning, and not four? - No; it is according to what we have to do. Sometimes it is one time and sometimes another.

[Juryman?] What made the constable come and tell you about the murder? - He called for his cape.

Inspector Jos. Helson deposed that he first received information about the murder at a quarter before seven on Friday morning. He afterwards went to the mortuary, where he saw the body with the clothes still on it. The dress was fastened in front, with the exception of a few buttons, the stays, which were attached with clasps, were also fastened. He noticed blood on the hair, and on the collars of the dress and ulster, but not on the back of the skirts. There were no cuts in the clothes, and no indications of any struggle having taken place. The only suspicious mark discovered in the neighborhood of Buck's-row was in Broad-street, where there was a stain which might have been blood.

Witness was of opinion that the body had not been carried to Buck's-row, but that the murder was committed on the spot.

Police-constable Mizen said that at a quarter to four o'clock on Friday morning he was at the crossing, Hanbury-street, Baker's-row, when a carman who passed in company with another man informed him that he was wanted by a policeman in Buck's-row, where a woman was lying. When he arrived there Constable Neil sent him for the ambulance. At that time nobody but Neil was with the body.

Chas. Andrew Cross, car man, said he had been in the employment of Messrs. Pickford and Co. for over twenty years. About half-past three on Friday he left his home to go to work, and he passed through Buck's-row. He discerned on the opposite side something lying against the gateway, but he could not at once make out what it was. He thought it was a tarpaulin sheet. He walked into the middle of the road, and saw that it was the figure of a woman. He then heard the footsteps of a man going up Buck's-row, about forty yards away, in the direction that he himself had come from. When he came up witness said to him, "Come and look over here; there is a woman lying on the pavement." They both crossed over to the body, and witness took hold of the woman's hands, which were cold and limp. Witness said, "I believe she is dead." He touched her face, which felt warm. The other man, placing his hand on her heart, said "I think she is breathing, but very little if she is." Witness suggested that they should give her a prop, but his companion refused to touch her. Just then they heard a policeman coming. Witness did not notice that her throat was cut, the night being very dark. He and the other man left the deceased, and in Baker's-row they met the last witness, whom they informed that they had seen a woman lying in Buck's-row. Witness said, "She looks to me to be either dead or drunk; but for my part I think she is dead." The policeman said, "All right," and then walked on. The other man left witness soon after. Witness had never seen him before.

Replying to the coroner, witness denied having seen Police-constable Neil in Buck's-row. There was nobody there when he and the other man left. In his opinion deceased looked as if she had been outraged and gone off in a swoon; but he had no idea that there were any serious injuries.

The Coroner: Did the other man tell you who he was?

Witness: No, sir; he merely said that he would have fetched a policeman, only he was behind time. I was behind time myself.

A Juryman: Did you tell Constable Mizen that another constable wanted him in Buck's-row?

Witness: No, because I did not see a policeman in Buck's-row.

Wm. Nicholls [Nichols], printer's machinist, Coburg-road, Old Kent-road, said deceased was his wife, but they had lived apart for eight years. He last saw her alive about three years ago, and had not heard from her since. He did not know what she had been doing in the meantime.

A Juryman: It is said that you were summoned by the Lambeth Union for her maintenance, and you pleaded that she was living with another man. Was he the blacksmith whom she had lived with?

Witness: No; it was not the same; it was another man. I had her watched.

Witness further deposed that he did not leave his wife, but that she left him of her own accord. She had no occasion for so doing. If it had not been for her drinking habits they would have got on all right together.

Emily Holland, a married woman, living at 18, Thrawl-street, said deceased had stayed at her lodgings for about six weeks, but had not been there during the last ten days or so. About half-past two on Friday morning witness saw deceased walking down Osborne-street, Whitechapel-road. She was alone, and very much the worse for drink. She informed witness that where she had been living they would not allow her to return because she could not pay for her room. Witness persuaded her to go home. She refused, adding that she had earned her lodging money three times that day. She then went along the Whitechapel-road. Witness did not know in what way she obtained a living. She always seemed to her to be a quiet woman, and kept very much to herself.

In reply to further questions witness said she had never seen deceased quarrel with anybody. She gave her the impression of being weighed down by some trouble. When she left the witness at the corner of Osborne-street, she said she would soon be back.

Mary Ann Monk was the last witness examined. She deposed to having seen deceased about seven o'clock entering a public-house in the New Kent-road. She had seen her before in the workhouse, and had no knowledge of her means of livelihood.

The inquiry was then adjourned until Sept. 17.

Day 3, Monday, September 17, 1888

(The Daily Telegraph, Tuesday, September 18, 1888, Page 2)

Yesterday [17 Sep], at the Working Lads' Institute, Whitechapel-road, Mr. Wynne Baxter, coroner for the North-Eastern District of Middlesex, resumed his inquiry relative to the death of Mary Ann Nicholls, the victim of the Buck's-row tragedy, on Friday morning, Aug. 31.

Dr. Llewellyn, recalled, said he had re-examined the body and there was no part of the viscera missing.

Emma Green, who lives in the cottage next to the scene of the murder in Buck's- row, stated that she had heard no unusual sound during the night.

By the Jury: Rough people often passed through the street, but she knew of no disorderly house in Buck's-row, all the houses being occupied by hardworking folk.

Thomas Ede, a signalman in the employ of the East London Railway Company, said he saw a man with a knife on the morning of the 8th.

The coroner was of opinion that this incident could have no reference to the present inquiry, as the 8th was the day of the Hanbury-street murder. He would, however, accept the evidence.

Witness then said: On Saturday, the 8th inst., at noon, I was coming down the Cambridge-heath-road, and when near the Forester's Arms I saw a man on the other side of the street. His peculiar appearance made me take notice of him. He seemed to have a wooden arm. I watched him until level with the Forester's Arms, and then he put his hand to his trouser's pocket, and I saw about four inches of a knife. I followed him, but he quickened his pace, and I lost sight of him.

Inspector Helson, in reply to the coroner, stated that the man had not been found.

Witness described the man as 5 ft. 8 in. high, about thirty-five years of age, with a dark moustache and whiskers. He wore a double-peaked cap, a short dark brown jacket, and a pair of clean white overalls over dark trousers. The man walked as though he had a stiff knee, and he had a fearful look about the eyes. He seemed to be a mechanic.

By the Jury: He was not a muscular man.

Walter Purkess [Purkiss], manager, residing at Essex Wharf, deposed that his house fronted Buck's-row, opposite the gates where deceased was discovered. He slept in the front room on the second floor and had heard no sound, neither had his wife.

Alfred Malshaw [Mulshaw], a night watchman in Winthorpe-street, had also heard no cries or noise. He admitted that he sometimes dozed.

The Coroner: I suppose your watching is not up to much?

The Witness: I don't know. It is thirteen long hours for 3s and find your own coke. (Laughter.)

By the Jury: In a straight line I was about thirty yards from the spot where the deceased was found.

Police-constable John Thail [Thain] stated that the nearest point on his beat to Buck's- row was Brady-street. He passed the end every thirty minutes on the Thursday night, and nothing attracted his attention until 3.45 a.m., when he was signalled by the flash of the lantern of another constable (Neale). He went to him, and found Neale standing by the body of the deceased, and witness was despatched for a doctor. About ten minutes after he had fetched the surgeon he saw two workmen standing with Neale. He did not know who they were. The body was taken to the mortuary, and witnessed remained on the spot. Witness searched Essex Wharf, the Great Eastern Railway arches, the East London Railway line, and the District Railway as far as Thames-street, and detected no marks of blood or anything of a suspicious character.

By the Jury: When I went to the horse-slaughterer's for my cape I did not say that I was going to fetch a doctor, as a murder had been committed. Another constable had taken my cape there.

By the Coroner: There were one or two working men going down Brady-street shortly before I was called by Neale.

Robert Baul [Paul], 30, Forster-street, Whitechapel, carman, said as he was going to work at Cobbett's-court, Spitalfields, he saw in Buck's-row a man standing in the middle of the road. As witness drew closer he walked towards the pavement, and he (Baul) stepped in the roadway to pass him. The man touched witness on the shoulder and asked him to look at the woman, who was lying across the gateway. He felt her hands and face, and they were cold. The clothes were disarranged, and he helped to pull them down. Before he did so he detected a slight movement as of breathing, but very faint. The man walked with him to Montague-street, and there they saw a policeman. Not more than four minutes had elapsed from the time he first saw the woman. Before he reached Buck's-row he had seen no one running away.

Robert Mann, the keeper of the mortuary, said the police came to the workhouse, of which he was an inmate. He went, in consequence, to the mortuary at five a.m. He saw the body placed there, and then locked the place up and kept the keys. After breakfast witness and Hatfield, another inmate of the workhouse, undressed the woman.

[Coroner] The police were not present? - No; there was no one present. Inspector Helson was not there.

[Coroner] Had you been told not to touch it? - No.

[Coroner] Did you see Inspector Helson? - I can't say.

[Coroner] Was he present? - I can't say.

[Coroner] I suppose you do not recollect whether the clothes were torn? - They were not torn or cut.

[Coroner] You cannot describe where the blood was? - No, sir; I cannot.

[Coroner] How did you get the clothes off? - Hatfield had to cut them down the front.

A Juryman: Was the body undressed in the mortuary or in the yard? - In the mortuary.

The Coroner: It appears the mortuary-keeper is subject to fits, and neither his memory nor statements are reliable.

James Hatfield, an inmate of the Whitechapel Workhouse, said he accompanied Mann, the last witness, to the mortuary, and undressed the deceased. Inspector Helson was not there.

[Coroner] Who was there? - Only me and my mate.

[Coroner] What did you take off first? - An ulster, which I put aside on the ground. We then took the jacket off, and put it in the same place. The outside dress was loose, and we did not cut it. The bands of the petticoats were cut, and I then tore them down with my hand. I tore the chemise down the front. There were no stays.

[Coroner] Who gave you instructions to do all this? - No one gave us any. We did it to have the body ready for the doctor.

[Coroner] Who told you a doctor was coming? - I heard someone speak about it.

[Coroner] Was any one present whilst you were undressing the body? - Not as I was aware of.

[Coroner] Having finished, did you make the post-mortem examination? - No, the police came.

[Coroner] Oh, it was not necessary for you to go on with it! The police came? - Yes, they examined the petticoats, and found the words "Lambeth Workhouse" on the bands.

[Coroner] It was cut out? - I cut it out.

[Coroner] Who told you to do it? - Inspector Helson.

[Coroner] Is that the first time you saw Inspector Helson on that morning? - Yes; I arrived at about half-past six.

[Coroner] Would you be surprised to find that there were stays? - No.

[Coroner] A juryman: Did not you try the stays on in the afternoon to show me how short they were. - I forgot it.

The Coroner: He admits that his memory is bad.

Witness: Yes.

The Coroner: We cannot do more. (To the police): There was a man who passed down Buck's-row when the doctor was examining the body. Have you heard anything of him?

Inspector Abberline: We have not been able to find him. Inspector Spratley, J Division, stated he had made inquiries in Buck's-row, but not at all of the houses.

The Coroner: Then that will have to be done.

Witness added [Spratling] that he made inquiries at Green's, the wharf, Snider's factory, and also at the Great Eastern wharf, and no one had heard anything unusual on the morning of the murder. He had not called at any of the houses in Buck's-row, excepting at Mrs. Green's. He had seen the Board School keeper.

The Coroner: Is there not a gentleman at the G.E. Railway? I thought we should have had him here.

Witness: I saw him that morning, but he said he had heard nothing.

The witness added that when at the mortuary he had given instructions that the body was not to be touched.

The Coroner: Is there any other evidence?

Inspector Helson: No, not at present.

The Foreman thought that, had a reward been offered by the Government after the murder in George-yard, very probably the two later murders would not have been perpetrated. It mattered little into whose hands the money went so long as they could find out the monster in their midst, who was terrorising everybody and making people ill. There were four horrible murders remaining undiscovered.

The Coroner considered that the first one was the worst, and it had attracted the least attention.

The Foreman intimated that he would be willing to give £25 himself, and he hoped that the Government would offer a reward. These poor people had souls like anybody else.

The Coroner understood that no rewards were now offered in any case. It mattered not whether the victims were rich or poor. There was no surety that a rich person would not be the next.

The Foreman: If that should be, then there will be a large reward.

Inspector Helson, in reply to the coroner, said rewards had been discontinued for years.

The inquiry was then adjourned until Saturday.

Day 4, Saturday, September 22, 1888

(The Daily Telegraph, Monday, September 24, 1888, Page 3)

On Saturday [22 Sep] Mr. Wynne E. Baxter resumed the inquest upon the body of Mary Ann Nicholls, aged forty-seven, the victim in the Buck's-row murder, one of the series of Whitechapel tragedies. The inquiry was held at the Working Lads' Institute.

Signalman Eades was recalled to supplement his previous evidence to the effect that he had seen a man named John James carrying a knife near the scene of the murder. It transpired, however, that this man is a harmless lunatic who is well known in the neighbourhood.

The Coroner then summed up. Having reviewed the career of the deceased from the time she left her husband, and reminded the jury of the irregular life she had led for the last two years, Mr. Baxter proceeded to point out that the unfortunate woman was last seen alive at half-past two o'clock on Saturday morning, Sept 1, by Mrs. Holland, who knew her well. Deceased was at that time much the worse for drink, and was endeavouring to walk eastward down Whitechapel. What her exact movements were after this it was impossible to say; but in less than an hour and a quarter her dead body was discovered at a spot rather under three-quarters of a mile distant. The time at which the body was found cannot have been far from 3.45 a.m., as it is fixed by so many independent data. The condition of the body appeared to prove conclusively that the deceased was killed on the exact spot in which she was found. There was not a trace of blood anywhere, except at the spot where her neck was lying, this circumstance being sufficient to justify the assumption that the injuries to the throat were committed when the woman was on the ground, whilst the state of her clothing and the absence of any blood about her legs suggested that the abdominal injuries were inflicted whilst she was still in the same position. Coming to a consideration of the perpetrator of the murder, the Coroner said: It seems astonishing at first thought that the culprit should have escaped detection, for there must surely have been marks of blood about his person. If, however, blood was principally on his hands, the presence of so many slaughter-houses in the neighborhood would make the frequenters of this spot familiar with blood- stained clothes and hands, and his appearance might in that way have failed to attract attention while he passed from Buck's-row in the twilight into Whitechapel-road, and was lost sight of in the morning's market traffic. We cannot altogether leave unnoticed the fact that the death that you have been investigating is one of four presenting many points of similarity, all of which have occurred within the space of about five months, and all within a very short distance of the place where we are sitting. All four victims were women of middle age, all were married, and had lived apart from their husbands in consequence of intemperate habits, and were at the time of their death leading an irregular life, and eking out a miserable and precarious existence in common lodging-houses. In each case there were abdominal as well as other injuries. In each case the injuries were inflicted after midnight, and in places of public resort, where it would appear impossible but that almost immediate detection should follow the crime, and in each case the inhuman and dastardly criminals are at large in society. Emma Elizabeth Smith, who received her injuries in Osborn-street on the early morning of Easter Tuesday, April 3, survived in the London Hospital for upwards of twenty-four hours, and was able to state that she had been followed by some men, robbed and mutilated, and even to describe imperfectly one of them. Martha Tabram was found at three a.m. on Tuesday, Aug. 7, on the first floor landing of George-yard-buildings, Wentworth-street, with thirty-nine punctured wounds on her body. In addition to these, and the case under your consideration, there is the case of Annie Chapman, still in the hands of another jury. The instruments used in the two earlier cases are dissimilar. In the first it was a blunt instrument, such as a walking-stick; in the second, some of the wounds were thought to have been made by a dagger; but in the two recent cases the instruments suggested by the medical witnesses are not so different. Dr. Llewellyn says the injuries on Nicholls could have been produced by a strong bladed instrument, moderately sharp. Dr. Phillips is of opinion that those on Chapman were by a very sharp knife, probably with a thin, narrow blade, at least six to eight inches in length, probably longer. The similarity of the injuries in the two cases is considerable. There are bruises about the face in both cases; the head is nearly severed from the body in both cases; there are other dreadful injuries in both cases; and those injuries, again, have in each case been performed with anatomical knowledge. Dr. Llewellyn seems to incline to the opinion that the abdominal injuries were first, and caused instantaneous death; but, if so, it seems difficult to understand the object of such desperate injuries to the throat, or how it comes about that there was so little bleeding from the several arteries, that the clothing on the upper surface was not stained, and, indeed, very much less bleeding from the abdomen than from the neck. Surely it may well be that, as in the case of Chapman, the dreadful wounds to the throat were inflicted first and the others afterwards. This is a matter of some importance when we come to consider what possible motive there can be for all this ferocity. Robbery is out of the question; and there is nothing to suggest jealousy; there could not have been any quarrel, or it would have been heard. I suggest to you as a possibility that these two women may have been murdered by the same man with the same object, and that in the case of Nicholls the wretch was disturbed before he had accomplished his object, and having failed in the open street he tries again, within a week of his failure, in a more secluded place. If this should be correct, the audacity and daring is equal to its maniacal fanaticism and abhorrent wickedness. But this surmise may or may not be correct, the suggested motive may be the wrong one; but one thing is very clear - that a murder of a most atrocious character has been committed.

The jury, after a short consultation, returned a verdict of wilful murder against some person or persons unknown.

# Annie Chapman aka Dark Annie, Annie Siffey

Born: Annie Eliza Smith in September 1841. Father: George Smith of Harrow Road. Described on the marriage certificate as a Private, 2nd Battalion of Lifeguards. At the time of his death he was listed as a servant. Mother: Ruth Chapman of Market Street. Annie's parents were married on February 22, 1842, 6 months after Annie was born. The marriage took place in Paddington. She had three sisters, Emily Latitia (b.1844), Georgina (b.1856) and Mirium Ruth (b.1858). A brother, Fountain Smith was born in 1861. The sisters appeared not to get along with Annie.

Description: 5' tall 47 years old at time of death Pallid complexion Blue eyes Dark brown wavy hair Excellent teeth (possibly two missing in lower jaw) Strongly built (stout) Thick nose She was under-nourished and suffering from a chronic disease of the lungs (tuberculosis) and brain tissue. It is said that she was dying (these could also be symptoms of syphilis). Although she has a drinking problem she is not described as an alcoholic. Her friend Amelia Palmer described her as "sober, steady going woman who seldom took any drink." She was, however, known to have a taste for rum.

History: Annie and John Chapman, c.1869 (Chapman family/Neal Shelden) Annie married John Chapman, a coachman, on May 1, 1869. She was 28 at the time of her marriage.

Their residence on the marriage certificate is listed as 29 Montpelier Place, Brompton. This is also where her mother lived until her (mother's) death in 1893. In 1870 they moved to 1 Brook Mews in Bayswater and then in 1873 to 17 South Bruton Mews, Berkeley Square. In 1881 they moved to Windsor where John took a job as a domestic coachman. The couple had three children. Emily Ruth Chapman, born 1870, Annie Georgina Chapman, born 1873 and John Alfred Chapman, born in 1880. John was a cripple and sent to a home and Emily Ruth died of meningitis at the age of twelve. Annie and John separated by mutual consent in 1884 or 1885. The reason is uncertain. A police report says it was because of her "drunken and immoral ways." She was arrested several times in Windsor for drunkenness and it is believed her husband was also a heavy drinker. John Chapman semi-regularly paid his wife 10 shillings per week by Post Office order until his death on Christmas day in 1886. At the time of his death he was living at Grove Road, Windsor. He died of cirrhosis of the liver and dropsy. Annie found out about his death through her brother-in-law who lived in Oxford Street, Whitechapel. On telling Amelia Palmer about it she cried. Palmer said that even two years later she seemed downcast when speaking of her children and how "since the death of her husband she seemed to have given away all together." Sometime during 1886 she was living with a sieve maker named John Sivvey (unknown whether this is a nickname or not) at the common lodging house at 30 Dorset Street,

Spitalfields. He left her soon after her husband's death, probably when the money stopped coming. He moved to Notting Hill. From May or June 1888, Annie was living consistently at Crossingham's Lodging House at 35 Dorset Street, Spitalfields, which catered for approximately 300 people. The deputy was Timothy Donovan. More recently, Annie had been having a relationship with Edward Stanley, a bricklayer's mate, known as the Pensioner. At the time of Annie's death he was living at 1 Osborn Place, Whitechapel. He claimed to be a member of the military but later admitted that he was not and was not drawing a pension from any military unit. Stanley and Annie spent weekends together at Crossingham's. Stanley instructed Donovan to turn Annie away if she tried to enter with another man. He often paid for Annie's bed as well as that of Eliza Cooper. They spent Saturdays and Sundays together, parting between 1:00 and 3:00 AM on Sundays. Stanley said that he had known Annie in Windsor., Annie didn't take to prostitution until after her husband's death. Prior to that she lived off the allowance he sent her and worked doing crochet-work and selling flowers. In mid to late August of 1888 she ran into her brother Fountain Smith on Commercial Road. She said she was hard up but would not tell him where she was living. He gave her 2 shillings.

Saturday, September 1, 1888

Edward Stanley returns after having been away since August 6. He meets Annie at the corner of Brushfield Street. Sometime close to this date, Annie has a fight with Eliza Cooper. The fight has several different tellings but all revolve around Edward Stanley. An argument breaks out in the Britannia Public House between Eliza Cooper and Annie. Also present are Stanley and Harry the Hawker. Cooper is Annie's rival for the affections of Stanley. Cooper struck her, giving her a black eye and bruising her breast.

The cause is alternately given as: Chapman noticed Cooper palming a florin belonging to Harry, who was drunk, and replacing it with a penny. Chapman mentions this to Harry and otherwise calls attention to

Cooper's deceit. Cooper says she struck Annie in the pub on September 2nd.

Amelia Palmer says that Annie told her the argument took place at the pub but the fisticuffs took place at the lodging house, later.

John Evans, night watchman at the lodging house says the fight broke out in the lodging house on September 6th. Cooper also says that the fight was not over Harry but over soap which Annie had borrowed for the Pensioner and not returned. In one version of the story, Annie is to have thrown a half penny at Cooper and slapped her in the face saying "Think yourself lucky I did not do more."

Donovan states that on August 30th he noticed she had a black eye. "Tim, this is lovely, aint it." She is to have said to him. Stanley noticed that she had a black eye on the evening of September 2nd and on the 3rd Annie showed her bruises to Amelia Palmer. Donovan will tell the inquest into her death that she was not at the lodging house during the week prior to her death. So it appears from the bulk of the evidence that the fight took place in the last few days of August and probably in the lodging house.

Chapman says that she may have to go to the infirmary but there is no record of any woman being admitted to either Whitechapel or Spitalfields workhouse infirmaries. She may have picked up medication though.

Monday, September 3: She meets Amelia Palmer in Dorset Street. "How did you get that?" asks Palmer, noticing the bruise on her right temple. By way of answer, Annie opened her dress. "Yes," Annie said "look at my chest." Annie complains of feeling unwell and says she may go see her sister. "If I can get a pair of boots from my sister," she says "I may go hop picking."

Tuesday, September 4: Amelia Palmer again sees Annie near Christ Church. Chapman again complains she is feeling ill and says she may go the casual ward for a day or two. She says she has had nothing to eat or drink all day. Palmer gives her 2d for tea and warns her not to spend it on rum.

Wednesday-Thursday, September 5-6: Possibly she is in the casual ward although there are no records to support the assumption. However, following her death, Donovan finds a bottle of medicine in her room.


Friday, September 7, Saturday, September 8th: 5:00 PM: Amelia Palmer again sees Annie in Dorset Street. Chapman is sober and Palmer asks her if she is going to Stratford (believed to be the territory where Annie plied her trade). Annie says she is too ill to do anything. Farmer left but returned a few minutes later only to find Chapman not having moved. It's no use my giving way," Annie says "I must pull myself together and go out and get some money or I shall have no lodgings."

11:30 PM: Annie returns to the lodging house and asks permission to go into the kitchen.

12:10 AM: Frederick Stevens, also a lodger at Crossingham's says he drank a pint of beer with Annie who was already slightly the worse for drink. He states that she did not leave the lodging house until 1:00 AM.

12:12 AM: William Stevens (a printer), another lodger, enters the kitchen and sees Chapman. She says that she has been to Vauxhall to see her sister, that she went to get some money and that her family had given her 5 pence. (If this is so, she spent it on drink.) Stevens sees her take a broken box of pills from her pocket. The box breaks and she takes a torn piece of envelope from the mantelpiece and places the pills in it. Chapman leaves the kitchen. Stevens thinks she has gone to bed. It appears obvious that she did pick up medication at the casual ward. The lotion found in her room may have brought up there at this time. This would re-enforce Stevens' impression that she had gone to bed. She certainly shows every sign of intending to return to Crossingham's.

1:35 AM: Annie returns to the lodging house again. She is eating a baked potato. John Evans, the night watchman, has been sent to collect her bed money. She goes upstairs to see Donovan in his office. "I haven't sufficient money for my bed," she tells him, "but don't let it. I shall not be long before I'm in." Donovan chastises her, "You can find money for your beer and you can't find money for your bed." Annie is not dismayed. She steps out of the office and stands in the doorway for two or three minutes. "Never mind, Tim." she states, "I'll soon be back." And to Evans she says, "I won't be long, Brummy (his nickname). See that Tim keeps the bed for me." Her regular bed in the lodging house is number 29. Evans sees her leave and enter Little Paternoster Row going in the direction of Brushfield Street and then turn towards Spitalfields Market.

4:45 AM: Mr. John Richardson enters the backyard of 29 Hanbury St. on his way to work, and sits down on the steps to remove a piece of leather which was protruding from his boot. Although it was quite dark at the time, he was sitting no more than a yard away from where the head of Annie Chapman would have been had she already been killed. He later testified to have seen nothing of extraordinary nature.

5:30 AM: Elizabeth Long sees Chapman with a man, hard against the shutters of 29 Hanbury Street. they are talking. Long hears the man say "Will you?" and Annie replies "Yes." Long is certain of the time as she had heard the clock on the Black Eagle Brewery, Brick Lane, strike the half hour just as she had turned onto the street. The woman (Chapman) had her back towards Spitalfields Market and, thus, her face towards Long. The man had his back towards Long.

A few moments after the Long sighting, Albert Cadosch, a young carpenter living at 27 Hanbury Street walks into his back yard probably to use the outhouse. Passing the five foot tall wooden fence which separates his yard from that of number 29, he hears voices quite close.

The only word he can make out is a woman saying "No!" He then heard something falling against the fence.

Annie's body was discovered a little before 6.00am by John Davis, a carman who lived on the third floor of No.29 with his family. After alerting James Green, James Kent and Henry Holland in Hanbury Street, Davis went to Commercial Street Police Station before returning to No.29.

Annie's Clothes and Possessions: Long black figured coat that came down to her knees. Black skirt

Brown bodice Another bodice 2 petticoats A large pocket worn under the skirt and tied about the waist with strings (empty when found) Lace up boots Red and white striped woolen stockings Neckerchief, white with a wide red border (folded tri-corner and knotted at the front of her neck. she is wearing the scarf in this manner when she leaves Crossingham's) Had three recently acquired brass rings on her middle finger (missing after the murder) Scrap of muslin One small tooth comb One comb in a paper case Scrap of envelope she had taken form the mantelpiece of the kitchen containing two pills. It bears the seal of the Sussex Regiment. It is postal stamped "London, 28,Aug., 1888" inscribed is a partial address consisting of the letter M, the number 2 as if the beginning of an address and an S.

Dr. George Bagster Phillips describes the body of Annie Chapman as he saw it at 6:30 AM in the back yard of the house at 29 Hanbury Street. This is inquest testimony.

"The left arm was placed across the left breast. The legs were drawn up, the feet resting on the ground, and the knees turned outwards. The face was swollen and turned on the right side. The tongue protruded between the front teeth, but not beyond the lips. The tongue was evidently much swollen. The front teeth were perfect as far as the first molar, top and bottom and very fine teeth they were. The body was terribly mutilated...the stiffness of the limbs was not marked, but was evidently commencing. He noticed that the throat was dissevered deeply.; that the incision through the skin were jagged and reached right round the neck...On the wooden paling between the yard in question and the next, smears of blood, corresponding to where the head of the deceased lay, were to be seen. These were about 14 inches from the ground, and immediately above the part where the blood from the neck lay. He should say that the instrument used at the throat and abdomen was the same. It must have been a very sharp knife with a thin narrow blade, and must have been at least 6 in. to 8 in. in length, probably longer. He should say that the injuries could not have been inflicted by a bayonet or a sword bayonet. They could have been done by such an instrument as a medical man used for post-mortem purposes, but the ordinary surgical cases might not contain such an instrument. Those used by the slaughtermen, well ground down, might have caused them. He thought the knives used by those in the leather trade would not be long enough in the blade. There were indications of anatomical knowledge...he should say that the deceased had been dead at least two hours, and probably more, when he first saw her; but it was right to mention that it was a fairly cool morning, and that the body would be more apt to cool rapidly from its having lost a great quantity of blood. There was no evidence...of a struggle having taken place. He was positive the deceased entered the yard alive... A handkerchief was round the throat of the deceased when he saw it early in the morning. He should say it was not tied on after the throat was cut."

Report following the post mortem examination:

"He noticed the same protrusion of the tongue. There was a bruise over the right temple. On the upper eyelid there was a bruise, and there were two distinct bruises, each the size of a man's thumb, on the forepart of the top of the chest. The stiffness of the limbs was now well marked. There was a bruise over the middle part of the bone of the right hand. There was an old scar on the left of the frontal bone. The stiffness was more noticeable on the left side, especially in the fingers, which were partly closed. There was an abrasion over the ring finger, with distinct markings of a ring or rings. The throat had been severed as before described. the incisions into the skin indicated that they had been made from the left side of the neck. There were two distinct clean cuts on the left side of the spine. They were parallel with each other and separated by about half an inch. The muscular structures appeared as though an attempt had made to separate the bones of the neck. There were various other mutilations to the body, but he was of the opinion that they occurred subsequent to the death of the woman, and to the large escape of blood from the division of the neck.


The deceased was far advanced in disease of the lungs and membranes of the brain, but they had nothing to do with the cause of death. The stomach contained little food, but there was not any sign of fluid. There was no appearance of the deceased having taken alcohol, but there were signs of great deprivation and he should say she had been badly fed. He was convinced she had not taken any strong alcohol for some hours before her death. The injuries were certainly not self-inflicted. The bruises on the face were evidently recent, especially about the chin and side of the jaw, but the bruises in front of the chest and temple were of longer standing - probably of days. He was of the opinion that the person who cut the deceased throat took hold of her by the chin, and then commenced the incision from left to right. He thought it was highly probable that a person could call out, but with regard to an idea that she might have been gagged he could only point to the swollen face and the protruding tongue, both of which were signs of suffocation. The abdomen had been entirely laid open: the intestines, severed from their mesenteric attachments, had been lifted out of the body and placed on the shoulder of the corpse; whilst from the pelvis, the uterus and its appendages with the upper portion of the vagina and the posterior two thirds of the bladder, had been entirely removed. No trace of these parts could be found and the incisions were cleanly cut, avoiding the rectum, and dividing the vagina low enough to avoid injury to the cervix uteri. Obviously the work was that of an expert- of one, at least, who had such knowledge of anatomical or pathological examinations as to be enabled to secure the pelvic organs with one sweep of the knife, which must therefore must have at least 5 or 6 inches in length, probably more. The appearance of the cuts confirmed him in the opinion that the instrument, like the one which divided the neck, had been of a very sharp character. The mode in which the knife had been used seemed to indicate great anatomical knowledge. He thought he himself could not have performed all the injuries he described, even without a struggle, under a quarter of an hour. If he had down it in a deliberate way such as would fall to the duties of a surgeon it probably would have taken him the best part of an hour."

## Inquest: Annie Chapman

Day 1, Monday, September 10, 1888

(The Daily Telegraph, Tuesday, September 11, 1888, Page 3)

At the Working Lads' Institute, Whitechapel-road, yesterday morning [10 Sep], Mr. Wynne Baxter opened an inquiry into the circumstances attending the death of Annie Chapman, a widow, whose body was found horribly mutilated in the back yard of 29, Hanbury-street, Spitalfields, early on Saturday morning. The jury viewed the corpse at the mortuary in Montague-street, but all evidences of the outrage to which the deceased had been subjected were concealed. The clothing was also inspected, and subsequently the following evidence was taken.

John Davies [Davis] deposed: I am a carman employed at Leadenhall Market. I have lodged at 29, Hanbury-street for a fortnight, and I occupied the top front room on the third floor with my wife and three sons, who live with me. On Friday night I went to bed at eight o'clock, and my wife followed about half an hour later. My sons came to bed at different times, the last one at about a quarter to eleven. There is a weaving shed window, or light across the room. It was not open during the night. I was awake from three a.m. to five a.m. on Saturday, and then fell asleep until a quarter to six, when the clock at Spitalfields Church struck. I had a cup of tea and went downstairs to the back yard. The house faces Hanbury-street, with one window on the ground floor and a front door at the side leading into a passage which runs through into the yard. There is a back door at the end of this passage opening into the yard. Neither of the doors was able to be locked, and I have never seen them locked. Any one who knows where the latch of the front door is could open it and go along the passage into the back yard.

[Coroner] When you went into the yard on Saturday morning was the yard door open or shut? - I found it shut. I cannot say whether it was latched - I cannot remember. I have been too much upset. The front street door was wide open and thrown against the wall. I was not surprised to find the front door open, as it was not unusual. I opened the back door, and stood in the entrance.

[Coroner] Will you describe the yard? - It is a large yard. Facing the door, on the opposite side, on my left as I was standing, there is a shed, in which Mrs. Richardson keeps her wood. In the right-hand corner there is a closet. The yard is separated from the next premises on both sides by close wooden fencing, about 5 ft. 6 in. high.

The Coroner: I hope the police will supply me with a plan. In the country, in cases of importance, I always have one.Inspector Helson:

[Insp Helosn] We shall have one at the adjourned hearing.

The Coroner: Yes; by that time we shall hardly require it.

Examination resumed: There was a little recess on the left. From the steps to the fence is about 3 ft. There are three stone steps, unprotected, leading from the door to the yard, which is at a lower level than that of the passage. Directly I opened the door I saw a woman lying down in the lefthand recess, between the stone steps and the fence. She was on her back, with her head towards the house and her legs towards the wood shed. The clothes were up to her groins. I did not go into the yard, but left the house by the front door, and called the attention of two men to the circumstances. They work at Mr. Bailey's, a packing-case maker, of Hanbury-street. I do not know their names, but I know them by sight.

The Coroner: Have the names of these men been ascertained?

Inspector Chandler: I have made inquiries, but I cannot find the men.

The Coroner: They must be found.

Davies: They work at Bailey's; but I could not find them on Saturday, as I had my work to do.

The Coroner: Your work is of no consequence compared with this inquiry.

Davies: I am giving all the information I can.

The Coroner (to witness): You must find these men out, either with the assistance of the police or of my officer.

Examination resumed: Mr Bailey's is three doors off 29, Hanbury-street, on the same side of the road. The two men were waiting outside the workshop. They came into the passage, and saw the sight. They did not go into the yard, but ran to find a policeman. We all came out of the house together. I went to the Commercial-street Police-station to report the case. No one in the house was informed by me of what I had discovered. I told the inspector at the police-station, and after a while I returned to Hanbury-street, but did not re-enter the house. As I passed I saw constables there.

[Coroner] Have you ever seen the deceased before? - No.

[Coroner] Were you the first down in the house that morning? - No; there was a lodger named Thompson, who was called at half-past three.

[Coroner] Have you ever seen women in the passage? - Mrs. Richardson has said there have been. I have not seen them myself. I have only been in the house a fortnight.

[Coroner] Did you hear any noise that Saturday morning? - No, sir.

Amelia Palmer, examined, stated: I live at 35, Dorset-street, Spitalfields, a common lodging-house. Off and on I have stayed there three years. I am married to Henry Palmer, a dock labourer. He was foreman, but met with an accident at the beginning of the year. I go out charing. My husband gets a pension, having been in the Army Reserve. I knew the deceased very well, for quite five years. I saw the body on Saturday at the mortuary, and am quite sure that it is that of Annie Chapman. She was a widow, and her husband, Frederick Chapman, was a veterinary surgeon in Windsor. He died about eighteen months ago. Deceased had lived apart from him for about four years or more. She lived in various places, principally in common lodging-houses in Spitalfields. I never knew her to have a settled home.

[Coroner] Has she lived at 30, Dorset-street? - Yes, about two years ago, with a man who made wire sieves, and at that time she was receiving 10s a week from her husband by post-office order, payable to her at the Commercial-road. This payment stopped about eighteen months ago, and she then found, on inquiry of some relative, that her husband was dead. I am under the impression that she ascertained this fact either from a brother or sister of her husband in Oxford-street, Whitechapel. She was nick-named, "Mrs. Sivvy," because she lived with the sieve-maker. I know the man perfectly well, but don't know his name. I saw him last about eighteen months ago, in the City, and he told me that he was living at Notting-hill. I saw deceased two or three times last week. On Monday she was standing in the road opposite 35, Dorset-street. She had been staying there, and had no bonnet on. She had a bruise on one of her temples - I think the right. I said, "How did you get that?" She said, "Yes, look at my chest." Opening her dress, she showed me a bruise. She said, "Do you know the woman?" and gave some name which I do not remember. She made me understand that it was a woman who goes about selling books. Both this woman and the deceased were acquainted with a man called "Harry the Hawker." Chapman told me that she was with some other man, Ted Stanley, on Saturday, Sept. 1. Stanley is a very respectable man. Deceased said she was with him at a beer-shop, 87, Commercial-street, at the corner of Dorset-street, where "Harry the Hawker" was with the woman. This man put down a two shilling piece and the woman picked it up and put down a penny. There was some feeling in consequence and the same evening the book-selling woman met the deceased and injured her in the face and chest. When deceased told me this, she said she was living at 35, Dorset-street. On the Tuesday afternoon I saw Chapman again near to Spitalfields Church. She said she felt no better, and she should go into the casual ward for a day or two. I remarked that she looked very pale, and asked her if she had had anything to eat. She replied, "No, I have not had a cup of tea to-day." I gave her two-pence to get some, and told her not to get any rum, of which she was fond. I have seen her the worse for drink.

[Coroner] What did she do for a living? - She used to do crochet work, make antimaccassars, and sell flowers. She was out late at night at times. On Fridays she used to go to Stratford to sell anything she had. I did not see her from the Tuesday to the Friday afternoon, 7th inst., when I met her about five o'clock in Dorset-street. She appeared to be perfectly sober. I said, "Are you going to Stratford to-day?" She answered, "I feel too ill to do anything." I left her immediately afterwards, and returned about ten minutes later, and found her in the same spot. She said, "It is of no use my going away. I shall have to go somewhere to get some money to pay my lodgings." She said no more, and that was the last time that I saw her. Deceased stated that she had been in the casual ward, but did not say which one. She did not say she had been refused admission. Deceased was a very industrious woman when she was sober. I have seen her often the worse for drink. She could not take much without making her drunk. She had been living a very irregular life during the whole time that I have known her. Since the death of her husband she has seemed to give way altogether. I understood that she had a sister and mother living at Brompton, but I do not think they were on friendly terms. I have never known her to stay with her relatives even for a night. On the Monday she observed: "If my sister will send me the boots, I shall go hopping." She had two children - a boy and a girl. They were at Windsor until her husband's death, and since then they have been in a school. Deceased was a very respectable woman, and never used bad language. She has stayed out in the streets all night.

[Coroner] Do you know of any one that would be likely to have injured her? - No.

The Coroner (having read a communication handed to him by the police): It seems to be very doubtful whether the husband was a veterinary surgeon. He may have been a coachman.

Timothy Donovan, 35, Dorset-street, Spitalfields, said: I am the deputy of a common lodging house. I have seen the body of the deceased, and have identified it as that of a woman who stayed at my house for the last four months. She was not there last week until Friday afternoon, between two and three o'clock. I was coming out of the office after getting up, and she asked me if she could go down in the kitchen, and I said "Yes," and asked her where she had been all the week. She replied that she had been in the infirmary, but did not say which.

A police-officer stated that the deceased had been in the casual ward.

Witness resumed: Deceased went down in the kitchen, and I did not see her again until half-past one or a quarter to two on Saturday morning. At that time I was sitting in the office, which faces the front door. She went into the kitchen. I sent the watchman's wife, who was in the office with me, downstairs to ask her husband about the bed. Deceased came upstairs to the office and said, "I have not sufficient money for my bed. Don't let it. I shan't be long before I am in."

[Coroner] How much was it? - Eightpence for the night. The bed she occupied, No. 29, was the one that she usually occupied. Deceased was then eating potatoes, and went out. She stood in the door two or three minutes, and then repeated, "Never mind, Tim; I shall soon be back. Don't let the bed." It was then about ten minutes to two a.m. She left the house, going in the direction of Brushfield-street. John Evans, the watchman, saw her leave the house. I did not see her again.

[Coroner] Was she the worse for drink when you saw her last? - She had had enough; of that I am certain. She walked straight. Generally on Saturdays she was the worse for drink. She was very sociable in the kitchen. I said to her, "You can find money for your beer, and you can't find money for your bed." She said she had been only to the top of the street - where there is a public-house.

[Coroner] Did you see her with any man that night? - No, sir.

[Coroner] Where did you think she was going to get the money from? - I did not know. She used to come and stay at the lodging-house on Saturdays with a man - a pensioner - of soldierly appearance, whose name I do not know.

[Coroner] Have you seen her with other men? - At other times she has come with other men, and I have refused her.

[Coroner] You only allow the women at your place one husband? - The pensioner told me not to let her a bed if she came with any other man. She did not come with a man that night. I never saw her with any man that week.

In answer to the jury witness said the beds were double at 8d per night, and as a rule deceased occupied one of them by herself.

The Coroner: When was the pensioner last with deceased at the lodging-house? - On Sunday, Sept. 2. I cannot say whether they left together. I have heard the

deceased say, "Tim, wait a minute. I am just going up the street to see if I can see him." She added that he was going to draw his pension. This occurred on Saturday, Aug. 25, at three a.m.

In reply to the Coroner, the police said nothing was known of the pensioner.

Examination continued: I never heard deceased call the man by any name. He was between forty and forty-five years of age, about 5 ft. 6 in. or 5 ft. 8 in. in height. Sometimes he would come dressed as a dock labourer; at other times he had a gentlemanly appearance. His hair was rather dark. I believe she always used to find him at the top of the street. Deceased was on good terms with the lodgers. About Tuesday, Aug. 28, she and another woman had a row in the kitchen. I saw them both outside. As far as I know she was not injured at that time. I heard from the watchman that she had had a clout. I noticed a day or two afterwards, on the Thursday, that she had a slight touch of a black eye. She said, "Tim, this is lovely," but did not explain how she got it. The bruise was to be seen on Friday last. I know the other woman, but not her name. Her husband hawks laces and other things.

John Evans testified: I am night watchman at 35, Dorset-street, and have identified the deceased as having lived at the lodging-house. I last saw her there on Saturday morning, and she left at about a quarter to two o'clock. I was sent down in the kitchen to see her, and she said she had not sufficient money. When she went upstairs I followed her, and as she left the house, I watched her go through a court called Paternoster-street, into Brushfield-street, and then turn towards Spitalfields Church. Deceased was the worse for drink, but not badly so. She came in soon after twelve (midnight), when she said she had been over to her sister's in Vauxhall. She sent one of the lodgers for a pint of beer, and then went out again, returning shortly before a quarter to two. I knew she had been living a rough night life. She associated with a man, a pensioner, every Saturday, and this individual called on Saturday at 2.30 p.m. and inquired for the deceased. He had heard something about her death, and came to see if it was true. I do not know his name or address. When I told him what had occurred he went straight out, without saying a word, towards Spitalfields Church. I did not see deceased and this man leave the house last Sunday week.

[Coroner] Did you see the deceased and another woman have a row in the kitchen? - Yes, on Thursday, Aug. 30. Deceased and a woman known as "Eliza," at 11.30 a.m., quarrelled about a piece of soap, and Chapman received a blow in the chest. I noticed that she had a slight black eye. There are marks on the body in a similar position.

By the Jury: I have never heard any one threaten her, nor express any fear of any one. I have never heard any one of the women in the lodging-house say that they had been threatened.

At this stage the inquiry was adjourned until tomorrow (Wednesday).

Day 2, Wednesday, September 12, 1888

(The Daily Telegraph, Thursday, September 13, 1888, Page 3)

Mr. Wynne Baxter yesterday [12 Sep] resumed the inquiry into the circumstances attending the death of Annie Chapman, whose body was found brutally mutilated in the back yard of 29, Hanbury-street, Spitalfields, at six o'clock on the morning of Saturday last.

The Police were represented by Inspector Abberline, of the Criminal Investigation Department, and Inspector Helson, J Division.

Fontain Smith, printer's warehouseman, stated: I have seen the body in the mortuary, and recognise it as that of my eldest sister, Annie, the widow of John Chapman, who lived at Windsor, a coachman. She had been separated from her husband for about three years. Her age was forty-seven. I last saw her alive a fortnight ago, in Commercial-street, where I met her promiscuously. Her husband died at Christmas, 1886. I gave her 2s; she did not say where she was living nor what she was doing. She said she wanted the money for a lodging.

[Coroner] Did you know anything about her associates? - No.

James Kent, 20, Drew's Blocks, Shadwell, a packing-case maker, said: I work for Mr. Bayley, 23A, Hanbury-street, and go there at six a.m. On Saturday I arrived about ten minutes past that hour. Our employer's gate was open, and there I waited for some other men. Davis, who lives two or three doors away, ran from his house into the road and cried, "Men, come here." James Green and I went together to 29, Hanbury-street, and on going through the passage, standing on the top of the back door steps, I saw a woman lying in the yard between the steps and the partition between the yard and the next. Her head was near the house, but no part of the body was against the wall. The feet were lying towards the back of Bayley's premises. (Witness indicated the precise position upon a plan produced by the police-officers). Deceased's clothes were disarranged, and her apron was thrown over them. I did not go down the steps, but went outside and returned after Inspector Chandler had arrived. I could see that the woman was dead. She had some kind of handkerchief around her throat which seemed soaked in blood. The face and hands were besmeared with blood, as if she had struggled. She appeared to have been on her back and fought with her hands to free herself. The hands were turned toward her throat. The legs were wide apart, and there were marks of blood upon them. The entrails were protruding, and were lying across her left side. I got a piece of canvass from the shop to throw over the body, and by that time a mob had assembled, and Inspector Chandler was in possession of the yard. The foreman gets to the shop at ten minutes to six every morning, and he was there before us.

James Green, of Ackland-street, Burdett-road, a packing-case maker, in the same employ as last witness, said: I arrived in Hanbury-street at ten minutes past six on Saturday morning, and accompanied Kent to the back door of No. 29. I left the premises with him. I saw no one touch the body.

Amelia Richardson, 29, Hanbury-street, deposed: I am a widow, and occupy half of the house - i.e., the first floor, ground floor, and workshops in the cellar. I carry on the business of a packing-case maker there, and the shops are used by my son John, aged thirty-seven, and a man Francis Tyler, who have worked for me eighteen years. The latter ought to have come at six a.m., but he did not arrive until eight o'clock, when I sent for him. He is often late when we are slack. My son lives in John-street, Spitalfields, and he works also in the market on market mornings. At six a.m. my grandson, Thomas Richardson, aged fourteen, who lives with me, got up. I sent him down to see what was the matter, as there was so much noise in the passage. He came back and said, "Oh, grandmother, there is a woman murdered." I went down immediately, and saw the body of the deceased lying in the yard. There was no one there at the time, but there were people in the passage. Soon afterwards a constable came and took possession of the place. As far as I know the officer was the first to enter the yard.

[Coroner] Which room do you occupy? - The first floor front, and my grandson slept in the same room on Friday night. I went to bed about half-past nine, and was very wakeful half the night. I was awake at three a.m., and only dozed after that.

[Coroner] Did you hear any noise during the night? - No.

[Coroner] Who occupies the first floor back? - Mr. Walker, a maker of lawn-tennis boots. He is an old gentleman, and he sleeps there with his son, twenty-seven years of age. The son is weak-minded and inoffensive. On the ground floor there are two rooms. Mrs. Hardman occupies them with her son, aged sixteen. She uses the front room as a cats' meat shop. In the front room on the first floor on Friday night I had a prayer meeting, and before I went to bed I locked the door of this room, and took the key with me. It was still locked in the morning. John Davies and his family tenant the third floor front, and Mrs. Sarah Cox has the back room on the same floor. She is an old lady I keep out of charity. Mr. Thompson and his wife, with an adopted little girl, have the front room on the second floor. On Saturday morning I called to Thompson at ten minutes to four o'clock. I heard him leave the house. He did not go into the back yard. Two unmarried sisters reside in the second floor back. They work at a cigar factory. When I went down all the tenants were in the house except Mr. Thompson and Mr. Davies. I am not the owner of the house.

[Coroner] Were the front and back doors always left open? - Yes, you can open the front and back doors of any of the houses about there. They are all let out in rooms. People are coming in or going out all the night.

[Coroner] Did you ever see anyone in the passage? - Yes, about a month ago I heard a man on the stairs. I called Thompson, and the man said he was waiting for market.

[Coroner] At what time was this? - Between half-past three and four o'clock. I could hear anyone going through the passage. I did not hear any one going through on Saturday morning.

[Coroner] You heard no cries? - None. Supposing a person had gone through at half-past three, would that have attracted your attention? - Yes.

[Coroner] You always hear people going to the back-yard? - Yes; people frequently do go through.

[Coroner] People go there who have no business to do so? - Yes; I daresay they do.

[Coroner] On Saturday morning you feel confident no one did go through? - Yes; I should have heard the sound. They must have walked purposely quietly? - Yes; or I should have heard them.

By the Jury: I should not allow any stranger to go through for an immoral purpose if I knew it.

Harriett Hardiman [Hardyman, Hardman], living at 29, Hanbury-street, catsmeat saleswoman, the occupier of the ground-floor front room, stated: I went to bed on Friday night at half-past ten. My son sleeps in the same room. I did not wake during the night. I was awakened by the trampling through the passage at about six o'clock. My son was asleep, and I told him to go to the back as I thought there was a fire. He returned and said that a woman had been killed in the yard. I did not go out of my room. I have often heard people going through the passage into the yard, but never got up to look who they were.

John Richardson, of John-street, Spitalfields, market porter, said: I assist my mother in her business. I went to 29, Hanbury-street, between 4,45 a.m. and 4.50 a.m. on Saturday last. I went to see if the cellar was all secure, as some while ago there was a robbery there of some tools. I have been accustomed to go on market mornings since the time when the cellar was broken in.

[Coroner] Was the front door open? - No, it was closed. I lifted the latch and went through the passage to the yard door.

[Coroner] Did you go into the yard? - No, the yard door was shut. I opened it and sat on the doorstep, and cut a piece of leather off my boot with an old table-knife, about five inches long. I kept the knife upstairs at John-street. I had been feeding a rabbit with a carrot that I had cut up, and I put the knife in my pocket. I do not usually carry it there. After cutting the leather off my boot I tied my boot up, and went out of the house into the market. I did not close the back door. It closed itself. I shut the front door.

[Coroner] How long were you there? - About two minutes at most.

[Coroner] Was it light? - It was getting light, but I could see all over the place.

[Coroner] Did you notice whether there was any object outside? - I could not have failed to notice the deceased had she been lying there then. I saw the body two or three minutes before the doctor came. I was then in the adjoining yard. Thomas Pierman had told me about the murder in the market. When I was on the doorstep I saw that the padlock on the cellar door was in its proper place.

[Coroner] Did you sit on the top step? - No, on the middle step; my feet were on the flags of the yard.

[Coroner] You must have been quite close to where the deceased was found? - Yes, I must have seen her.

[Coroner] You have been there at all hours of the night? - Yes.

[Coroner] Have you ever seen any strangers there? - Yes, plenty, at all hours - both men and women. I have often turned them out. We have had them on our first floor as well, on the landing.

[Coroner] Do you mean to say that they go there for an immoral purpose? - Yes, they do.

At this stage witness was despatched by the coroner to fetch his knife.


Mrs. Richardson, recalled, said she had never missed anything, and had such confidence in her neighbours that she had left the doors of some rooms unlocked. A saw and a hammer had been taken from the cellar a long time ago. The padlock was broken open.

[Coroner] Had you an idea at any time that a part of the house or yard was used for an immoral purpose? - Witness (emphatically): No, sir.

[Coroner] Did you say anything about a leather apron? - Yes, my son wears one when he works in the cellar.

The Coroner: It is rather a dangerous thing to wear, is it not?

Witness: Yes. On Thursday, Sept. 6, I found my son's leather apron in the cellar mildewed. He had not used it for a month. I took it and put it under the tap in the yard, and left it there. It was found there on Saturday morning by the police, who took charge of it. The apron had remained there from Thursday to Saturday.

[Coroner] Was this tap used? - Yes, by all of us in the house. The apron was on the stones. The police took away an empty box, used for nails, and the steel out of a boy's gaiter. There was a pan of clean water near to the tap when I went in the yard at six o'clock on Saturday. It was there on Friday night at eight o'clock, and it looked as if it had not been disturbed.

[Coroner] Did you ever know of strange women being found on the first-floor landing? - No.

[Coroner] Your son had never spoken to you about it? - No.


John Piser [Pizer] was then called. He said: I live at 22, Mulberry-street, Commercial- road East. I am a shoemaker.

[Coroner] Are you known by the nickname of "Leather Apron?" - Yes, sir.

[Coroner] Where were you on Friday night last? - I was at 22, Mulberry-street. On Thursday, the 6th inst. I arrived there.

[Coroner] From where? - From the west end of town. The Coroner: I am afraid we shall have to have a better address than that presently.

[Coroner] What time did you reach 22, Mulberry-street? - Shortly before eleven p.m.

[Coroner] Who lives at 22, Mulberry-street? - My brother and sister-in-law and my stepmother. I remained indoors there.

[Coroner] Until when? - Until I was arrested by Sergeant Thicke, on Monday last at nine a.m.

[Coroner] You say you never left the house during that time? - I never left the house.

[Coroner] Why were you remaining indoors? - Because my brother advised me.

[Coroner] You were the subject of suspicion? - I was the object of a false suspicion.

[Coroner] You remained on the advice of your friends? - Yes; I am telling you what I did.

The Coroner: It was not the best advice that you could have had. You have been released, and are not now in custody? - I am not.

Piser: I wish to vindicate my character to the world at large.

The Coroner: I have called you in your own interests, partly with the object of giving you an opportunity of doing so.

[Coroner] Can you tell us where you were on Thursday, Aug. 30?

Witness (after considering): In the Holloway-road.

[Coroner] You had better say exactly where you were. It is important to account for your time from that Thursday to the Friday morning.

[Pizer] What time, may I ask?

The Coroner: It was the week before you came to Mulberry-street.

Witness: I was staying at a common lodging-house called the Round House, in the Holloway-road.

[Coroner] Did you sleep the night there? - Yes. At what time did you go in? - On the night of the London Dock fire I went in about two or a quarter-past. It was on the Friday morning.

[Coroner] When did you leave the lodging-house? - At eleven a.m. on the same day. I saw on the placards, "Another Horrible Murder." Where were you before two o'clock on Friday morning? - At eleven p.m. on Thursday I had my supper at the Round House.

[Coroner] Did you go out? - Yes, as far as the Seven Sisters-road, and then returned towards Highgate way, down the Holloway-road. Turning, I saw the reflection of a fire. Coming as far as the church in the Holloway-road I saw two constables and the lodging-housekeeper talking together. There might have been one or two constables, I cannot say which. I asked a constable where the fire was, and he said it was a long way off. I asked him where he thought it was, and he replied: "Down by the Albert Docks." It was then about half-past one, to the best of my recollection. I went as far as Highbury Railway Station on the same side of the way, returned, and then went into the lodging house.

[Coroner] Did any one speak to you about being so late? - No: I paid the night watchman. I asked him if my bed was let, and he said: "They are let by eleven o'clock. You don't think they are to let to this hour." I paid him 4d for another bed. I stayed up smoking on the form of the kitchen, on the right hand side near the fireplace, and then went to bed.

[Coroner] You got up at eleven o'clock? - Yes. The day man came, and told us to get up, as he wanted to make the bed. I got up and dressed, and went down into the kitchen.

[Coroner] Is there anything else you want to say? - Nothing.

[Coroner] When you said the West-end of town did you mean Holloway? - No; another lodging house in Peter-street, Westminster.

The Coroner: It is only fair to say that the witness's statements can be corroborated.

William Thicke [Thick], detective sergeant, deposed: Knowing that "Leather Apron" was suspected of being concerned in the murder, on Monday morning I arrested Piser at 22, Mulberry-street. I have known him by the name of "Leather Apron" for many years.

[Coroner] When people in the neighbourhood speak of the "Leather Apron" do they mean Piser? - They do.

[Coroner] He has been released from custody? - He was released last night at 9.30.


John Richardson (recalled) produced the knife - a much-worn dessert knife - with which he had cut his boot. He added that as it was not sharp enough he had borrowed another one at the market.

By the Jury: My mother has heard me speak of people having been in the house. She has heard them herself.

The Coroner: I think we will detain this knife for the present.


Henry John Holland, a boxmaker, stated: As I was passing 29, Hanbury-street, on my way to work in Chiswell-street, at about eight minutes past six on Saturday. I spoke to two of Bayley's men. An elderly man came out of the house and asked us to have a look in his back yard. I went through the passage and saw the deceased lying in the yard by the back door. I did not touch the body. I then went for a policeman in Spitalfields Market. The officer told me he could not come. I went outside and could find no constable. Going back to the house I saw an inspector run up with a young man, at about twenty minutes past six o'clock. I had told the first policeman that it was a similar case to Buck's-row, and he referred me to two policemen outside the market, but I could not find them. I afterwards complained of the policeman's conduct at the Commercial-street police station the same afternoon.

The Coroner: There does not seem to have been much delay. The inspector says there are certain spots where constables are stationed with instructions not to leave them. Their duty is to send some one else.

The Foreman of the Jury: That is the explanation.

The Coroner: The doctor will be here first thing tomorrow.

This afternoon the inquiry will be resumed.

Day 3, Thursday, September 13, 1888

(The Daily Telegraph, Friday, September 14, 1888, Page 3)

Yesterday [13 Sep] Mr. Wynne Baxter, coroner, resumed, at the Working Lads' Institute, Whitechapel-road, his adjourned inquiry relative to the death of Annie Chapman, who was murdered in the back yard of 29, Hanbury-street, on Saturday morning last.

The police were represented by Inspectors Abberline, Helson, and Chandler.

Joseph Chandler, Inspector H Division Metropolitan Police, deposed: On Saturday morning, at ten minutes past six, I was on duty in Commercial-street. At the corner of Hanbury-street I saw several men running. I beckoned to them. One of them said, "Another woman has been murdered." I at once went with him to 29, Hanbury-street, and through the passage into the yard. There was no one in the yard. I saw the body of a woman lying on the ground on her back. Her head was towards the back wall of the house, nearly two feet from the wall, at the bottom of the steps, but six or nine inches away from them. The face was turned to the right side, and the left arm was resting on the left breast. The right hand was lying down the right side. Deceased's legs were drawn up, and the clothing was above the knees. A portion of the intestines, still connected with the body, were lying above the right shoulder, with some pieces of skin. There were also some pieces of skin on the left shoulder. The body was lying parallel with the fencing dividing the two yards. I remained there and sent for the divisional surgeon, Mr. Phillips, and to the police-station for the ambulance and for further assistance. When the constables arrived I cleared the passage of people, and saw that no one touched the body until the doctor arrived. I obtained some sacking to cover it before the arrival of the surgeon, who came at about half- past six o'clock, and he, having examined the body, directed that it should be removed to the mortuary. After the body had been taken away I examined the yard, and found a piece of coarse muslin, a small tooth comb, and a pocket hair comb in a case. They were lying near the feet of the woman. A portion of an envelope was found near her head, which contained two pills.

[Coroner] What was on the envelope? - On the back there was a seal with the words, embossed in blue, "Sussex Regiment." The other part was torn away. On the other side there was a letter "M" in writing.

[Coroner] A man's handwriting? - I should imagine so.

[Coroner] Any postage stamp? - No. There was a postal stamp "London, Aug. 3, 1888." That was in red. There was another black stamp, which was indistinct.

[Coroner] Any other marks on the envelope? - There were also the letters "Sp" lower down, as if some one had written "Spitalfields." The other part was gone. There were no other marks.

[Coroner] Did you find anything else in the yard? - There was a leather apron, lying in the yard, saturated with water. It was about two feet from the water tap.

[Coroner] Was it shown to the doctor? - Yes. There was also a box, such as is commonly used by casemakers for holding nails. It was empty. There was also a piece of steel, flat, which has since been identified by Mrs. Richardson as the spring of her son's leggings.

[Coroner] Where was that found? - It was close to where the body had been. The apron and nail box have also been identified by her as her property. The yard was paved roughly with stones in parts; in other places it was earth.

[Coroner] Was there any appearance of a struggle there? - No.

[Coroner] Are the palings strongly erected? - No; to the contrary.

[Coroner] Could they support the weight of a man getting over them? - No doubt they might.

[Coroner] Is there any evidence of anybody having got over them? - No. Some of them in the adjoining yard have been broken since. They were not broken then.

[Coroner] You have examined the adjoining yard? - Yes.

[Coroner] Was there any staining as of blood on any of the palings? - Yes, near the body.

[Coroner] Was it on any of the other yards? - No.

[Coroner] Were there no other marks? - There were marks discovered on the wall of No. 25. They were noticed on Tuesday afternoon. They have been seen by Dr. Phillips.

[Coroner] Were there any drops of blood outside the yard of No. 29? - No; every possible examination has been made, but we could find no trace of them. The blood-stains at No. 29 were in the immediate neighbourhood of the body only. There were also a few spots of blood on the back wall, near the head of the deceased, 2ft from the ground. The largest spot was of the size of a sixpence. They were all close together. I assisted in the preparation of the plan produced, which is correct.

[Coroner] Did you search the body? - I searched the clothing at the mortuary. The outside jacket - a long black one, which came down to the knees - had bloodstains round the neck, both upon the inside and out, and two or three spots on the left arm. The jacket was hooked at the top, and buttoned down the front. By the appearance of the garment there did not seem to have been any struggle. A large pocket was worn under the skirt (attached by strings), which I produce. It was torn down the front and also at the side, and it was empty. Deceased wore a black skirt. There was a little blood on the outside. The two petticoats were stained very little; the two bodices were stained with blood round the neck, but they had not been damaged. There was no cut in the clothing at all. The boots were on the feet of deceased. They were old. No part of the clothing was torn. The stockings were not bloodstained.

[Coroner] Did you see John Richardson? - I saw him about a quarter to seven o'clock. He told me he had been to the house that morning about a quarter to five. He said he came to the back door and looked down to the cellar, to see if all was right, and then went away to his work.

[Coroner] Did he say anything about cutting his boot? - No.

[Coroner] Did he say that he was sure the woman was not there at that time? - Yes.

By the Jury: The back door opens outwards into the yard, and swung on the left hand to the palings where the body was. If Richardson were on the top of the steps he might not have seen the body. He told me he did not go down the steps.

The Foreman of the Jury: Reference has been made to the Sussex Regiment and the pensioner. Are you going to produce the man Stanley? Witness: We have not been able to find him as yet.

The Foreman: He is a very important witness. There is evidence that he has associated with the woman week after week. It is important that he should be found. Witness: There is nobody that can give us the least idea where he is. The parties were requested to communicate with the police if he came back. Every inquiry has been made, but nobody seems to know anything about him.

The Coroner: I should think if that pensioner knows his own business he will come forward himself.

Sergeant Baugham [Badham], 31 H, stated that he conveyed the body of the deceased to the mortuary on the ambulance.

[Coroner] Are you sure that you took every portion of the body away with you? - Yes.

[Coroner] Where did you deposit the body? - In the shed, still on the ambulance. I remained with it until Inspector Chandler arrived. Detective-Sergeant Thicke viewed the body, and I took down the description. There were present two women, who came to identify the body, and they described the clothing. They came from 35, Dorset-street.

[Coroner] Who touched the clothing? - Sergeant Thicke. I did not see the women touch the clothing nor the body. I did not see Sergeant Thicke touch the body.

Inspector Chandler, recalled, said he reached the mortuary a few minutes after seven. The body did not appear to have been disturbed. He did not stay until the doctor arrived. Police-constable 376 H was left in charge, with the mortuary keeper. Robert Marne, the mortuary keeper and an inmate of the Whitechapel Union Workhouse, said he received the body at seven o'clock on Saturday morning. He remained at the mortuary until Dr. Phillips came. The door of the mortuary was locked except when two nurses from an infirmary came and undressed the body. No one else touched the corpse. He gave the key into the hands of the police.

The Coroner: The fact is that Whitechapel does not possess a mortuary. The place is not a mortuary at all. We have no right to take a body there. It is simply a shed belonging to the workhouse officials. Juries have over and over again reported the matter to the District Board of Works. The East-end, which requires mortuaries more than anywhere else, is most deficient. Bodies drawn out of the river have to be put in boxes, and very often they are brought to this workhouse arrangement all the way from Wapping. A workhouse inmate is not the proper man to take care of a body in such an important matter as this.

The foreman of the jury called attention to the fact that a fund to provide a reward had been opened by residents in the neighbourhood, and that Mr. Montagu, M.P., had offered a reward of £100. If the Government also offered a reward some information might be forthcoming.

The Coroner: I do not speak with any real knowledge, but I am told that the Government have determined not to give any rewards in future, not with the idea to economise but because the money does not get into right channels.

To Witness: Were you present when the doctor was making his post-mortem? - Yes.

[Coroner] Did you see the doctor find the handkerchief produced? - It was taken off the body. I picked it up from off the clothing, which was in the corner of the room. I gave it to Dr. Phillips, and he asked me to put it in some water, which I did.

[Coroner] Did you see the handkerchief taken off the body? - I did not. The nurses must have taken it off the throat.

[Coroner] How do you know? - I don't know.

[Coroner] Then you are guessing? - I am guessing.

The Coroner: That is all wrong, you know. (To the jury). He is really not the proper man to have been left in charge.


Timothy Donovan, the deputy of the lodging-house, 35, Dorset-street, was recalled.

[Coroner] You have seen that handkerchief? - I recognise it as one which the deceased used to wear. She bought it of a lodger, and she was wearing it when she left the lodging-house. She was wearing it three-corner ways, placed round her neck, with a black woollen scarf underneath. It was tied in front with one knot.

The Foreman of the Jury: Would you recognise Ted Stanley, the pensioner?

A Juryman: Stanley is not the pensioner.

The Coroner (to witness): Do you know the name of Stanley? Witness: No.

The Foreman: He has been mentioned, and also "Harry the Hawker."

Witness: I know "Harry the Hawker."

The Coroner, having referred to the evidence, said: It may be an inference - there is no actual evidence - that the pensioner was called Ted Stanley.

The Foreman said he referred to the man who came to see the deceased regularly. The man ought to be produced.

The Coroner (to witness): Would you recognise the pensioner? - Yes.

[Coroner] When did you see him last? - On Saturday.

[Coroner] Why did you not then send him to the police? - Because he would not stop.

The Foreman: What was he like? - He had a soldierly appearance. He dressed differently at times - sometimes gentlemanly. A Juror: He is not Ted Stanley.


Mr. George Baxter Phillips, divisional-surgeon of police, said: On Saturday last I was called by the police at 6.20 a.m. to 29, Hanbury-street, and arrived at half-past six. I found the body of the deceased lying in the yard on her back, on the left hand of the steps that lead from the passage. The head was about 6in in front of the level of the bottom step, and the feet were towards a shed at the end of the yard. The left arm was across the left breast, and the legs were drawn up, the feet resting on the ground, and the knees turned outwards. The face was swollen and turned on the right side, and the tongue protruded between the front teeth, but not beyond the lips; it was much swollen. The small intestines and other portions were lying on the right side of the body on the ground above the right shoulder, but attached. There was a large quantity of blood, with a part of the stomach above the left shoulder. I searched the yard and found a small piece of coarse muslin, a small-tooth comb, and a pocket-comb, in a paper case, near the railing. They had apparently been arranged there. I also discovered various other articles, which I handed to the police. The body was cold, except that there was a certain remaining heat, under the intestines, in the body. Stiffness of the limbs was not marked, but it was commencing. The throat was dissevered deeply. I noticed that the incision of the skin was jagged, and reached right round the neck. On the back wall of the house, between the steps and the palings, on the left side, about 18in from the ground, there were about six patches of blood, varying in size from a sixpenny piece to a small point, and on the wooden fence there were smears of blood, corresponding to where the head of the deceased laid, and immediately above the part where the blood had mainly flowed from the neck, which was well clotted. Having received instructions soon after two o'clock on Saturday afternoon, I went to the labour- yard of the Whitechapel Union for the purpose of further examining the body and making the usual post-mortem investigation. I was surprised to find that the body had been stripped and was laying ready on the table. It was under great disadvantage I made my examination. As on many occasions I have met with the same difficulty, I now raise my protest, as I have before, that members of my profession should be called upon to perform their duties under these inadequate circumstances.

The Coroner: The mortuary is not fitted for a post-mortem examination. It is only a shed. There is no adequate convenience, and nothing fit, and at certain seasons of the year it is dangerous to the operator.

The Foreman: I think we can all endorse the doctor's view of it.

The Coroner: As a matter of fact there is no public mortuary from the City of London up to Bow. There is one at Mile-end, but it belongs to the workhouse, and is not used for general purposes.

Examination resumed: The body had been attended to since its removal to the mortuary, and probably partially washed. I noticed a bruise over the right temple. There was a bruise under the clavicle, and there were two distinct bruises, each the size of a man's thumb, on the fore part of the chest. The stiffness of the limbs was then well-marked. The finger nails were turgid. There was an old scar of long standing on the left of the frontal bone. On the left side the stiffness was more noticeable, and especially in the fingers, which were partly closed. There was an abrasion over the bend of the first joint of the ring finger, and there were distinct markings of a ring or rings - probably the latter. There were small sores on the fingers. The head being opened showed that the membranes of the brain were opaque and the veins loaded with blood of a dark character. There was a large quantity of fluid between the membranes and the substance of the brain. The brain substance was unusually firm, and its cavities also contained a large amount of fluid. The throat had been severed. The incisions of the skin indicated that they had been made from the left side of the neck on a line with the angle of the jaw, carried entirely round and again in front of the neck, and ending at a point about midway between the jaw and the sternum or breast bone on the right hand. There were two distinct clean cuts on the body of the vertebrae on the left side of the spine. They were parallel to each other, and separated by about half an inch. The muscular structures between the side processes of bone of the vertebrae had an appearance as if an attempt had been made to separate the bones of the neck. There are various other mutilations of the body, but I am of opinion that they occurred subsequently to the death of the woman and to the large escape of blood from the neck. The witness, pausing, said: I am entirely in your hands, sir, but is it necessary that I should describe the further mutilations. From what I have said I can state the cause of death.

The Coroner: The object of the inquiry is not only to ascertain the cause of death, but the means by which it occurred. Any mutilation which took place afterwards may suggest the character of the man who did it. Possibly you can give us the conclusions to which you have come respecting the instrument used.

The Witness: You don't wish for details. I think if it is possible to escape the details it would be advisable. The cause of death is visible from injuries I have described.

The Coroner: You have kept a record of them?

Witness: I have.

The Coroner: Supposing any one is charged with the offence, they would have to come out then, and it might be a matter of comment that the same evidence was not given at the inquest.

Witness: I am entirely in your hands.

The Coroner: We will postpone that for the present. You can give your opinion as to how the death was caused.

Witness: From these appearances I am of opinion that the breathing was interfered with previous to death, and that death arose from syncope, or failure of the heart's action, in consequence of the loss of blood caused by the severance of the throat.

[Coroner] Was the instrument used at the throat the same as that used at the abdomen? - Very probably. It must have been a very sharp knife, probably with a thin, narrow blade, and at least six to eight inches in length, and perhaps longer.

[Coroner] Is it possible that any instrument used by a military man, such as a bayonet, would have done it? - No; it would not be a bayonet.

[Coroner] Would it have been such an instrument as a medical man uses for post-mortem examinations? - The ordinary post-mortem case perhaps does not contain such a weapon.

[Coroner] Would any instrument that slaughterers employ have caused the injuries? - Yes; well ground down.

[Coroner] Would the knife of a cobbler or of any person in the leather trades have done? - I think the knife used in those trades would not be long enough in the blade.

[Coroner] Was there any anatomical knowledge displayed? - I think there was. There were indications of it. My own impression is that that anatomical knowledge was only less displayed or indicated in consequence of haste. The person evidently was hindered from making a more complete dissection in consequence of the haste.

[Coroner] Was the whole of the body there? - No; the absent portions being from the abdomen.

[Coroner] Are those portions such as would require anatomical knowledge to extract? - I think the mode in which they were extracted did show some anatomical knowledge.

[Coroner] You do not think they could have been lost accidentally in the transit of the body to the mortuary? - I was not present at the transit. I carefully closed up the clothes of the woman. Some portions had been excised.

[Coroner] How long had the deceased been dead when you saw her? - I should say at least two hours, and probably more; but it is right to say that it was a fairly cold morning, and that the body would be more apt to cool rapidly from its having lost the greater portion of its blood.

[Coroner] Was there any evidence of any struggle? - No; not about the body of the woman. You do not forget the smearing of blood about the palings.

[Coroner] In your opinion did she enter the yard alive? - I am positive of it. I made a thorough search of the passage, and I saw no trace of blood, which must have been visible had she been taken into the yard.

[Coroner] You were shown the apron? - I saw it myself. There was no blood upon it. It had the appearance of not having been unfolded recently.

[Coroner] You were shown some staining on the wall of No. 25, Hanbury-street? - Yes; that was yesterday morning. To the eye of a novice I have no doubt it looks like blood. I have not been able to trace any signs of it. I have not been able to finish my investigation. I am almost convinced I shall not find any blood. We have not had any result of your examination of the internal organs.

[Coroner] Was there any disease? - Yes. It was not important as regards the cause of death. Disease of the lungs was of long standing, and there was disease of the membranes of the brain. The stomach contained a little food.

[Coroner] Was there any appearance of the deceased having taken much alcohol? - No. There were probably signs of great privation. I am convinced she had not taken any strong alcohol for some hours before her death.

[Coroner] Were any of these injuries self-inflicted? - The injuries which were the immediate cause of death were not self-inflicted.

[Coroner] Was the bruising you mentioned recent? - The marks on the face were recent, especially about the chin and sides of the jaw. The bruise upon the temple and the bruises in front of the chest were of longer standing, probably of days. I am of opinion that the person who cut the deceased's throat took hold of her by the chin, and then commenced the incision from left to right.

[Coroner] Could that be done so instantaneously that a person could not cry out?

Witness: By pressure on the throat no doubt it would be possible.

The Forman: There would probably be suffocation.

The Coroner: The thickening of the tongue would be one of the signs of suffocation? - Yes. My impression is that she was partially strangled. Witness added that the handkerchief produced was, when found amongst the clothing, saturated with blood. A similar article was round the throat of the deceased when he saw her early in the morning at Hanbury-street.

[Coroner] It had not the appearance of having been tied on afterwards? - No. Sarah Simonds, a resident nurse at the Whitechapel Infirmary, stated that, in company of the senior nurse, she went to the mortuary on Saturday, and found the body of the deceased on the ambulance in the yard. It was afterwards taken into the shed, and placed on the table. She was directed by Inspector Chandler to undress it, and she placed the clothes in a corner. She left the handkerchief round the neck. She was sure of this. They washed stains of blood from the body. It seemed to have run down from the throat. She found the pocket tied round the waist. The strings were not torn. There were no tears or cuts in the clothes.

Inspector Chandler: I did not instruct the nurses to undress the body and to wash it.

**Day 4, Wednesday, September 19, 1888**

(The Daily Telegraph, Thursday, September 20, 1888, Page 2)

In the Whitechapel Working Lads' Institute, yesterday [19 Sep] afternoon, Mr. Wynne E. Baxter, Coroner for East Middlesex, resumed his inquiry respecting the death of Mrs. Annie Chapman, who was found dead in the yard of the house 29, Hanbury- street, Whitechapel, her body dreadfully cut and mutilated, early on the morning of Saturday, the 8th inst. The following evidence was called:

Eliza Cooper: I am a hawker, and lodge in Dorset-street, Spitalfields. Have done so for the last five months. I knew the deceased, and had a quarrel with her on the Tuesday before she was murdered. The quarrel arose in this way: On the previous Saturday she brought Mr. Stanley into the house where I lodged in Dorset-street, and coming into the kitchen asked the people to give her some soap. They told her to ask "Liza" - meaning me. She came to me, and I opened the locker and gave her some. She gave it to Stanley, who went outside and washed himself in the lavatory. When she came back I asked for the soap, but she did not return it. She said, "I will see you by and bye." Mr. Stanley gave her two shillings, and paid for her bed for two nights. I saw no more of her that night. On the following Tuesday I saw her in the kitchen of the lodging-house. I said, "Perhaps you will return my soap." She threw a halfpenny on the table, and said, "Go and get a halfpennyworth of soap." We got quarrelling over this piece of soap, and we went out to the Ringers Public-house and continued the quarrel. She slapped my face, and said, "Think yourself lucky I don't do more." I struck her in the left eye, I believe, and then in the chest. I afterwards saw that the blow I gave her had marked her face.

[Coroner] When was the last time you saw her alive? - On the Thursday night, in the Ringers.

[Coroner] Was she wearing rings? - Yes, she was wearing three rings on the middle finger of the left hand. They were all brass.

[Coroner] Had she ever a gold wedding ring to your knowledge? - No, not since I have known her. I have known her about fifteen months. I know she associated with Stanley, "Harry the Hawker," and several others.

The Foreman: Are there any of those with whom she associated missing? - I could not tell.

A Juryman: Was she on the same relations with them as she was with Stanley? - No, sir. She used to bring them casually into the lodging-house.


Dr. Phillips, divisional surgeon of the metropolitan police, was then recalled.

The Coroner, before asking him to give evidence, said: Whatever may be your opinion and objections, it appears to me necessary that all the evidence that you ascertained from the post-mortem examination should be on the records of the Court for various reasons, which I need not enumerate. However painful it may be, it is necessary in the interests of justice.

Dr. Phillips: I have not had any notice of that. I should have been glad if notice had been given me, because I should have been better prepared to give the evidence; however, I will do my best.

The Coroner: Would you like to postpone it?

Dr. Phillips: Oh, no. I will do my best. I still think that it is a very great pity to make this evidence public. Of course, I bow to your decision; but there are matters which have come to light now which show the wisdom of the course pursued on the last occasion, and I cannot help reiterating my regret that you have come to a different conclusion. On the last occasion, just before I left the court, I mentioned to you that there were reasons why I thought the perpetrator of the act upon the woman's throat had caught hold of her chin. These reasons were that just below the lobe of the left ear were three scratches, and there was also a bruise on the right cheek. When I come to speak of the wounds on the lower part of the body I must again repeat my opinion that it is highly injudicious to make the results of my examination public. These details are fit only for yourself, sir, and the jury, but to make them public would simply be disgusting.

The Coroner: We are here in the interests of justice, and must have all the evidence before us. I see, however, that there are several ladies and boys in the room, and I think they might retire. (Two ladies and a number of newspaper messenger boys accordingly left the court.)

Dr. Phillips again raised an objection to the evidence, remarking: In giving these details to the public I believe you are thwarting the ends of justice.

The Coroner: We are bound to take all the evidence in the case, and whether it be made public or not is a matter for the responsibility of the press.

The Foreman: We are of opinion that the evidence the doctor on the last occasion wished to keep back should be heard. (Several Jurymen: Hear, hear.)

The Coroner: I have carefully considered the matter and have never before heard of any evidence requested being kept back.

Dr. Phillips: I have not kept it back; I have only suggested whether it should be given or not.

The Coroner: We have delayed taking this evidence as long as possible, because you said the interests of justice might be served by keeping it back; but it is now a fortnight since this occurred, and I do not see why it should be kept back from the jury any longer.

Dr. Phillips: I am of opinion that what I am about to describe took place after death, so that it could not affect the cause of death, which you are inquiring into.

The Coroner: That is only your opinion, and might be repudiated by other medical opinion.

Dr. Phillips: Very well. I will give you the results of my post-mortem examination. Witness then detailed the terrible wounds which had been inflicted upon the woman, and described the parts of the body which the perpetrator of the murder had carried away with him. He added: I am of opinion that the length of the weapon with which the incisions were inflicted was at least five to six inches in length - probably more - and must have been very sharp. The manner in which they had been done indicated a certain amount of anatomical knowledge.

The Coroner: Can you give any idea how long it would take to perform the incisions found on the body?

Dr. Phillips: I think I can guide you by saying that I myself could not have performed all the injuries I saw on that woman, and effect them, even without a struggle, under a quarter of an hour. If I had done it in a deliberate way, such as would fall to the duties of a surgeon, it would probably have taken me the best part of an hour. The whole inference seems to me that the operation was performed to enable the perpetrator to obtain possession of these parts of the body.

The Coroner: Have you anything further to add with reference to the stains on the wall?

Dr. Phillips: I have not been able to obtain any further traces of blood on the wall.

The Foreman: Is there anything to indicate that the crime in the case of the woman Nicholls was perpetrated with the same object as this?

The Coroner: There is a difference in this respect, at all events, that the medical expert is of opinion that, in the case of Nicholls, the mutilations were made first.

The Foreman: Was any photograph of the eyes of the deceased taken, in case they should retain any impression of the murderer.

Dr. Phillips: I have no particular opinion upon that point myself. I was asked about it very early in the inquiry, and I gave my opinion that the operation would be useless, especially in this case. The use of a blood-hound was also suggested. It may be my ignorance, but the blood around was that of the murdered woman, and it would be more likely to be traced than the murderer. These questions were submitted to me by the police very early. I think within twenty- four hours of the murder of the woman.

The Coroner: Were the injuries to the face and neck such as might have produced insensibility?

The witness: Yes; they were consistent with partial suffocation.


Mrs. Elizabeth Long said: I live in Church-row, Whitechapel, and my husband, James Long, is a cart minder. On Saturday, Sept. 8, about half past five o'clock in the morning, I was passing down Hanbury-street, from home, on my way to Spitalfields Market. I knew the time, because I heard the brewer's clock strike half-past five just before I got to the street. I passed 29, Hanbury-street. On the right-hand side, the same side as the house, I saw a man and a woman standing on the pavement talking. The man's back was turned towards Brick-lane, and the woman's was towards the market. They were standing only a few yards nearer Brick-lane from 29, Hanbury-street. I saw the woman's face. Have seen the deceased in the mortuary, and I am sure the woman that I saw in Hanbury-street was the deceased. I did not see the man's face, but I noticed that he was dark. He was wearing a brown low-crowned felt hat. I think he had on a dark coat, though I am not certain. By the look of him he seemed to me a man over forty years of age. He appeared to me to be a little taller than the deceased.

[Coroner] Did he look like a working man, or what? - He looked like a foreigner.

[Coroner] Did he look like a dock labourer, or a workman, or what? - I should say he looked like what I should call shabby-genteel.

[Coroner] Were they talking loudly? - They were talking pretty loudly. I overheard him say to her "Will you?" and she replied, "Yes." That is all I heard, and I heard this as I passed. I left them standing there, and I did not look back, so I cannot say where they went to.

[Coroner] Did they appear to be sober? - I saw nothing to indicate that either of them was the worse for drink.

Was it not an unusual thing to see a man and a woman standing there talking? - Oh no. I see lots of them standing there in the morning.

[Coroner] At that hour of the day? - Yes; that is why I did not take much notice of them.

[Coroner] You are certain about the time? - Quite.

[Coroner] What time did you leave home? - I got out about five o'clock, and I reached the Spitalfields Market a few minutes after half-past five.

The Foreman of the jury: What brewer's clock did you hear strike half-past five? - The brewer's in Brick-lane.

Edward Stanley, Osborn-place, Osborn-street, Spitalfields, deposed: I am a bricklayer's labourer.

The Coroner: Are you known by the name of the Pensioner? - Yes.

[Coroner] Did you know the deceased? - I did.

[Coroner] And you sometimes visited her? - Yes.

[Coroner] At 35, Dorset-street? - About once there, or twice, something like that. Other times I have met her elsewhere.

[Coroner] When did you last see her alive? - On Sunday, Sept. 2, between one and three o'clock in the afternoon.

[Coroner] Was she wearing rings when you saw her? - Yes, I believe two. I could not say on which finger, but they were on one of her fingers.

[Coroner] What sort of rings were they - what was the metal? - Brass, I should think by the look of them.

[Coroner] Do you know any one she was on bad terms with? - No one, so far as I know. The last time I saw her she had some bruises on her face - a slight black eye, which some other woman had given her. I did not take much notice of it. She told me something about having had a quarrel. It is possible that I may have seen deceased after Sept. 2, as I was doing nothing all that week. If I did see her I only casually met her, and we might have had a glass of beer together. My memory is rather confused about it.

The Coroner: The deputy of the lodging-house said he was told not to let the bed to the deceased with any other man but you? - It was not from me he received those orders. I have seen it described that the man used to come on the Saturday night, and remain until the Monday morning. I have never done so.

The Foreman: You were supposed to be the pensioner.

The Coroner: It must be some other man?

Witness: I cannot say; I am only speaking for myself.

[Coroner] Are you a pensioner? - Can I object to answer that question, sir? It does not touch on anything here.

Coroner: It was said the man was with her on one occasion when going to receive his pension?

Witness: Then it could not have been me. It has been stated all over Europe that it was me, but it was not.

The Coroner: It will affect your financial position all over Europe when it is known that you are not a pensioner? - It will affect my financial position in this way, sir, in that I am a loser by having to come here for nothing, and may get discharged for not being at my work.

[Coroner] Were you ever in the Royal Sussex Regiment? - Never, sir. I am a law-abiding man, sir, and interfere with no person who does not interfere with me.

The Coroner: Call the deputy.


Timothy Donovan, deputy of the lodging-house, who gave evidence on a previous occasion, was then recalled.

The Coroner: Did ever you see that man (pointing to Stanley) before? - Yes.

[Coroner] Is he the man you call "the pensioner"? - Yes.

[Coroner] Was it he who used to come with the deceased on Saturday and stay till Monday? - Yes.

[Coroner] Was it he who told you not to let the bed to the deceased with any other man? - Yes; on the second Saturday he told me.

[Coroner] How many times have you seen him there? - I should think five or six Saturdays.

[Coroner] When was he last there? - On the Saturday before the woman's death. He stayed until Monday. He paid for one night, and the woman afterwards came down and paid for the other.

The Coroner: What have you got to say to that, Mr. Stanley?

Stanley: You can cross it all out, sir.

[Coroner] Cross your evidence out, you mean? - Oh, no; not mine, but his. It is all wrong. I went to Gosport on Aug. 6 and remained there until Sept. 1.

The Coroner: Probably the deputy has made a mistake.

A Juror (to Stanley): Had you known deceased at Windsor at all? - No; she told me she knew some one about Windsor, and that she once lived there.

[Juror?]You did not know her there? - No; I have only known her about two years. I have never been to Windsor.

[Juror?] Did you call at Dorset-street on Saturday, the 8th, after the murder? - Yes; I was told by a shoeblack it was she who was murdered, and I went to the lodging- house to ask if it was the fact. I was surprised, and went away.

[Juror?] Did you not give any information to the police that you knew her? You might have volunteered evidence, you know? - I did volunteer evidence. I went voluntarily to Commercial-street Police-station, and told them what I knew.

The Coroner: They did not tell you that the police wanted you? - Not on the 8th, but afterwards. They told me the police wanted to see me after I had been to the police.

Albert Cadosch [Cadoche] deposed: I live at 27, Hanbury-street, and am a carpenter. 27 is next door to 29, Hanbury-street. On Saturday, Sept. 8, I got up about a quarter past five in the morning, and went into the yard. It was then about twenty minutes past five, I should think. As I returned towards the back door I heard a voice say "No" just as I was going through the door. It was not in our yard, but I should think it came from the yard of No. 29. I, however, cannot say on which side it came from. I went indoors, but returned to the yard about three or four minutes afterwards. While coming back I heard a sort of a fall against the fence which divides my yard from that of 29. It seemed as if something touched the fence suddenly.

The Coroner: Did you look to see what it was? - No.

[Coroner] Had you heard any noise while you were at the end of your yard? - No.

[Coroner] Any rustling of clothes? - No. I then went into the house, and from there into the street to go to my work. It was about two minutes after half-past five as I passed Spitalfields Church.

[Coroner] Do you ever hear people in these yards? - Now and then, but not often.

By a Juryman: I informed the police the same night after I returned from my work.

The Foreman: What height are the palings? - About 5 ft. 6 in. to 6 ft. high.

[Coroner] And you had not the curiosity to look over? - No, I had not.

[Coroner] It is not usual to hear thumps against the palings? - They are packing-case makers, and now and then there is a great case goes up against the palings. I was thinking about my work, and not that there was anything the matter, otherwise most likely I would have been curious enough to look over.

The Foreman of the Jury: It's a pity you did not.

By the Coroner. - I did not see any man and woman in the street when I went out.

William Stevens, 35, Dorset-street, stated: I am a painter. I knew the deceased. I last saw her alive at twenty minutes past twelve on the morning of Saturday, Sept. 8. She was in the kitchen. She was not the worse for drink.

[Coroner] Had she got any rings on her fingers? - Yes.

[Witness was] Shown a piece of an envelope, witness said he believed it was the same as she picked up near the fireplace. Did not notice a crest, but it was about that size, and it had a red postmark on it. She left the kitchen, and witness thought she was going to bed. Never saw her again. Did not know any one that she was on bad terms with. This was all the evidence obtainable.

A Juryman: Is there any chance of a reward being offered by the Home Secretary?

The Foreman: There is already a reward of £100 offered by Mr. Samuel Montagu, M.P. There is a committee getting up subscriptions, and they expect to get about £200. The coroner has already said that the Government are not prepared to offer a reward.

A Juror: There is more dignity about a Government reward, and I think one ought to be offered.

The Foreman of the Jury: There are several ideas of rewards, and it is supposed that about £300 will be got up. It will all be done by private individuals.

The Coroner: As far as we know, the case is complete.

The Foreman of the Jury: It seems to be a case of murder against some person or persons unknown.

It was then agreed to adjourn the inquiry until next Wednesday before deciding upon the terms of the verdict.

Day 5, Wednesday, September 26, 1888

(The Daily Telegraph, Thursday, September 27, 1888, Page 2)

Yesterday [26 Sep] afternoon Mr. Wynne Baxter, coroner for East Middlesex, concluded his inquiry, at the Whitechapel Working Lads' Institute, relative to the death of Mrs. Annie Chapman, whose body was found dreadfully cut and mutilated in the yard of 29, Hanbury-street, Whitechapel, early on the morning of Saturday, the 8th inst.

The Coroner inquired if there was any further evidence to be adduced.

Inspector Chandler replied in the negative.

The Coroner then addressed the jury. He said: I congratulate you that your labours are now nearly completed. Although up to the present they have not resulted in the detection of any criminal, I have no doubt that if the perpetrator of this foul murder is eventually discovered, our efforts will not have been useless. The evidence is now on the records of this court, and could be used even if the witnesses were not forthcoming; while the publicity given has already elicited further information, which I shall presently have to mention, and which, I hope I am not sanguine in believing, may perhaps be of the utmost importance. We shall do well to recall the important facts. The deceased was a widow, forty-seven years of age, named Annie Chapman. Her husband was a coachman living at Windsor. For three or four years before his death she had lived apart from her husband, who allowed her 10s a week until his death at Christmas, 1886. Evidently she had lived an immoral life for some time, and her habits and surroundings had become worse since her means had failed. Her relations were no longer visited by her, and her brother had not seen her for five months, when she borrowed a small sum from him. She lived principally in the common lodging houses in the neighbourhood of Spitalfields, where such as she herd like cattle, and she showed signs of great deprivation, as if she had been badly fed. The glimpses of life in these dens which the evidence in this case discloses is sufficient to make us feel that there is much in the nineteenth century civilisation of which we have small reason to be proud; but you who are constantly called together to hear the sad tale of starvation, or semi-starvation, of misery, immorality, and wickedness which some of the occupants of the 5,000 beds in this district have every week to relate to coroner's inquests, do not require to be reminded of what life in a Spitalfields lodging-house means. It was in one of these that the older bruises found on the temple and in front of the chest of the deceased were received, in a trumpery quarrel, a week before her death. It was in one of these that she was seen a few hours before her mangled remains were discovered. On the afternoon and evening of Friday, Sept. 7, she divided her time partly in such a place at 35, Dorset- street, and partly in the Ringers public-house, where she spent whatever money she had; so that between one and two on the morning of Saturday, when the money for her bed is demanded, she is obliged to admit that she is without means, and at once turns out into the street to find it. She leaves there at 1.45 a.m., is seen off the premises by the night watchman, and is observed to turn down Little Paternoster-row into Brushfield-street, and not in the more direct route to Hanbury-street. On her wedding finger she was wearing two or three rings, which appear to have been palpably of base metal, as the witnesses are all clear about their material and value. We now lose sight of her for about four hours, but at half-past five, Mrs. Long is in Hanbury-street on her way from home in Church- street, Whitechapel, to Spitalfields Market. She walked on the northern side of the road going westward, and remembers having seen a man and woman standing a few yards from the place where the deceased is afterwards found. And, although she did not know Annie Chapman, she is positive that that woman was deceased. The two were talking loudly, but not sufficiently so to arouse her suspicions that there was anything wrong. Such words as she overheard were not calculated to do so. The laconic inquiry of the man, "Will you?" and the simple assent of the woman, viewed in the light of subsequent events, can be easily translated and explained. Mrs. Long passed on her way, and neither saw nor heard anything more of her, and this is the last time she is known to have been alive. There is some conflict in the evidence about the time at which the deceased was despatched. It is not unusual to find inaccuracy in such details, but this variation is not very great or very important. She was found dead about six o'clock. She was not in the yard when Richardson was there at 4.50 a.m. She was talking outside the house at half-past five when Mrs. Long passed them. Cadosh says it was about 5.20 when he was in the backyard of the adjoining house, and heard a voice say "No," and three or four minutes afterwards a fall against the fence; but if he is out of his reckoning but a quarter of an hour, the discrepancy in the evidence of fact vanishes, and he may be mistaken, for he admits that he did not get up till a quarter past five, and that it was after the half-hour when he passed Spitalfields clock. It is true that Dr. Phillips thinks that when he saw the body at 6.30 the deceased had been dead at least two hours, but he admits that the coldness of the morning and the great loss of blood may affect his opinion; and if the evidence of the other witnesses be correct, Dr. Phillips has miscalculated the effect of those forces. But many minutes after Mrs. Long passed the man and woman cannot have elapsed before the deceased became a mutilated corpse in the yard of 29, Hanbury-street, close by where she was last seen by any witness. This place is a fair sample of a large number of houses in the neighbourhood. It was built, like hundreds of others, for the Spitalfields weavers, and when hand-looms were driven out by steam and power, these were converted into dwellings for the poor. Its size is about such as a superior artisan would occupy in the country, but its condition is such as would to a certainty leave it without a tenant. In this place seventeen persons were living, from a woman and her son sleeping in a cat's-meat shop on the ground floor to Davis and his wife and their three grown-up sons, all sleeping together in an attic. The street door and the yard door were never locked, and the passage and yard appear to have been constantly used by people who had no legitimate business there. There is little doubt that the deceased knew the place, for it was only 300 or 400 yards from where she lodged. If so, it is quite unnecessary to assume that her companion had any knowledge - in fact, it is easier to believe that he was ignorant both of the nest of living beings by whom he was surrounded, and of their occupations and habits. Some were on the move late at night, some were up long before the sun. A carman, named Thompson, left the house for his work as early as 3.50 a.m.; an hour later John Richardson was paying the house a visit of inspection; shortly after 5.15 Cadosh, who lived in the next house, was in the adjoining yard twice. Davis, the carman, who occupied the third floor front, heard the church clock strike a quarter to six, got up, had a cup of tea, and went into the back yard, and was horrified to find the mangled body of deceased. It was then a little after six a.m. - a very little, for at ten minutes past the hour Inspector Chandler had been informed of the discovery while on duty in Commercial-street. There is nothing to suggest that the deceased was not fully conscious of what she was doing. It is true that she had passed through some stages of intoxication, for although she appeared perfectly sober to her friend who met her in Dorset-street at five o'clock the previous evening, she had been drinking afterwards; and when she left the lodging-house shortly before two o'clock the night watchman noticed that she was the worse for drink, but not badly so, while the deputy asserts that, though she had evidently been drinking, she could walk straight, and it was probably only malt liquor that she had taken, and its effects would pass off quicker than if she had taken spirits. Consequently it is not surprising to find that Mrs. Long saw nothing to make her think that the deceased was the worse for drink. Moreover, it is unlikely that she could have had the opportunity of getting intoxicants. Again the post-mortem examination shows that while the stomach contained a meal of food there was no sign of fluid and no appearance of her having taken alcohol, and Dr. Phillips is convinced that she had not taken any alcohol for some time. The deceased, therefore, entered the yard in full possession of her faculties; although with a very different object from her companion. From the evidence which the condition of the yard affords and the medical examination discloses, it appears that after the two had passed through the passage and opened the swing-door at the end, they descended the three steps into the yard. On their left hand side there was a recess between those steps and the palings. Here a few feet from the house and a less distance from the paling they must have stood. The wretch must have then seized the deceased, perhaps with Judas-like approaches. He seized her by the chin. He pressed her throat, and while thus preventing the slightest cry, he at the same time produced insensibility and suffocation. There is no evidence of any struggle. The clothes are not torn. Even in these preliminaries, the wretch seems to have known how to carry out efficiently his nefarious work. The deceased was then lowered to the ground, and laid on her back; and although in doing so she may have fallen slightly against the fence, this movement was probably effected with care. Her throat was then cut in two places with savage determination, and the injuries to the abdomen commenced. All was done with cool impudence and reckless daring; but, perhaps, nothing is more noticeable than the emptying of her pockets, and the arrangement of their contents with business-like precision in order near her feet. The murder seems, like the Buck's-row case, to have been carried out without any cry. Sixteen people were in the house. The partitions of the different rooms are of wood. Davis was not asleep after three a.m., except for three-quarters of an hour, or less, between five and 5.45. Mrs. Richardson only dosed after three a.m., and heard no noise during the night. Mrs. Hardman, who occupies the front ground-floor room, did not awake until the noise succeeding the finding of the body had commenced, and none of the occupants of the houses by which the yard is surrounded heard anything suspicious. The brute who committed the offence did not even take the trouble to cover up his ghastly work, but left the body exposed to the view of the first comer. This accords but little with the trouble taken with the rings, and suggests either that he had at length been disturbed, or that as the daylight broke a sudden fear suggested the danger of detection that he was running. There are two things missing. Her rings had been wrenched from her fingers and have not been found, and the uterus has been removed. The body has not been dissected, but the injuries have been made by some one who had considerable anatomical skill and knowledge. There are no meaningless cuts. It was done by one who knew where to find what he wanted, what difficulties he would have to contend against, and how he should use his knife, so as to abstract the organ without injury to it. No unskilled person could have known where to find it, or have recognised it when it was found. For instance, no mere slaughterer of animals could have carried out these operations. It must have been some one accustomed to the post-mortem room. The conclusion that the desire was to possess the missing part seems overwhelming. If the object were robbery, these injuries were meaningless, for death had previously resulted from the loss of blood at the neck. Moreover, when we find an easily accomplished theft of some paltry brass rings and such an operation, after, at least, a quarter of an hour's work, and by a skilled person, we are driven to the deduction that the mutilation was the object, and the theft of the rings was only a thin-veiled blind, an attempt to prevent the real intention being discovered. Had not the medical examination been of a thorough and searching character, it might easily have been left unnoticed. The difficulty in believing that this was the real purport of the murderer is natural. It is abhorrent to our feelings to conclude that a life should be taken for so slight an object; but, when rightly considered, the reasons for most murders are altogether out of proportion to the guilt. It has been suggested that the criminal is a lunatic with morbid feelings. This may or may not be the case; but the object of the murderer appears palpably shown by the facts, and it is not necessary to assume lunacy, for it is clear that there is a market for the object of the murder. To show you this, I must mention a fact which at the same time proves the assistance which publicity and the newspaper press afford in the detection of crime. Within a few hours of the issue of the morning papers containing a report of the medical evidence given at the last sitting of the Court, I received a communication from an officer of one of our great medical schools, that they had information which might or might not have a distinct bearing on our inquiry. I attended at the first opportunity, and was told by the sub-curator of the Pathological Museum that some months ago an American had called on him, and asked him to procure a number of specimens of the organ that was missing in the deceased. He stated his willingness to give œ20 for each, and explained that his object was to issue an actual specimen with each copy of a publication on which he was then engaged. Although he was told that his wish was impossible to be complied with, he still urged his request. He desired them preserved, not in spirits of wine, the usual medium, but in glycerine, in order to preserve them in a flaccid condition, and he wished them sent to America direct. It is known that this request was repeated to another institution of a similar character. Now, is it not possible that the knowledge of this demand may have incited some abandoned wretch to possess himself of a specimen. It seems beyond belief that such inhuman wickedness could enter into the mind of any man, but unfortunately our criminal annals prove that every crime is possible. I need hardly say that I at once communicated my information to the Detective Department at Scotland- yard. Of course I do not know what use has been made of it, but I believe that publicity may possibly further elucidate this fact, and, therefore, I have not withheld from you my knowledge. By means of the press some further explanation may be forthcoming from America if not from here. I have endeavoured to suggest to you the object with which this offence was committed, and the class of person who must have perpetrated it. The greatest deterrent from crime is the conviction that detection and punishment will follow with rapidity and certainty, and it may be that the impunity with which Mary Ann Smith and Anne Tabram were murdered suggested the possibility of such horrid crimes as those which you and another jury have been recently considering. It is, therefore, a great misfortune that nearly three weeks have elapsed without the chief actor in this awful tragedy having been discovered. Surely, it is not too much even yet to hope that the ingenuity of our detective force will succeed in unearthing this monster. It is not as if there were no clue to the character of the criminal or the cause of his crime. His object is clearly divulged. His anatomical skill carries him out of the category of a common criminal, for his knowledge could only have been obtained by assisting at post-mortems, or by frequenting the post-mortem room. Thus the class in which search must be made, although a large one, is limited. Moreover it must have been a man who was from home, if not all night, at least during the early hours of Sept. 8. His hands were undoubtedly blood-stained, for he did not stop to use the tap in the yard as the pan of clean water under it shows. If the theory of lunacy be correct - which I very much doubt - the class is still further limited; while, if Mrs. Long's memory does not fail, and the assumption be correct that the man who was talking to the deceased at half-past five was the culprit, he is even more clearly defined. In addition to his former description, we should know that he was a foreigner of dark complexion, over forty years of age, a little taller than the deceased, of shabby-genteel appearance, with a brown dear-stalker hat on his head, and a dark coat on his back. If your views accord with mine, you will be of opinion that we are confronted with a murder of no ordinary character, committed not from jealousy, revenge, or robbery, but from motives less adequate than the many which still disgrace our civilization, mar our progress, and blot the pages of our Christianity. I cannot conclude my remarks without thanking you for the attention you have given to the case, and the assistance you have rendered me in our efforts to elucidate the truth of this horrible tragedy. The Foreman: We can only find one verdict - that of willful murder against some person or persons unknown. We were about to add a rider with respect to the condition of the mortuary, but that having been done by a previous jury it is unnecessary.

A verdict of willful murder against a person or persons unknown was then entered.

## Elizabeth Stride

**Elizabeth Stride aka 'Long Liz' Elizabeth Stride was born Elisabeth Gustafsdotter on November 27, 1843 on a farm called Stora Tumlehed in Torslanda parish, north**

of Gothenburg, Sweden. She was baptized on December 5 of that year and confirmed in a church in Torslanda. At the time of her death she was 45 years old. She had a pale complexion, light gray eyes and had curly dark brown hair. All the teeth in her lower left jaw were missing and she stood five foot five inches tall. On a Certificate of Change notice filed in Sweden at the time that Liz moved to London it is stated that she could read tolerably well but had little understanding of the Bible or catechism. Lodgers described her as a quiet woman who would do a "good turn for anyone." However she had frequently appeared before the Thames Magistrate Court on charges of being drunk and disorderly, sometimes with obscene language. She made money by sewing and charring, received money from Michael Kidney and was an occasional prostitute.

History: Her father was Gustaf Ericsson and her mother Beatta Carlsdotter. On October 14, 1860 she moved to the parish of Carl Johan in Gothenburg. While there she worked as a domestic for Lars Frederick Olofsson, a workman with 4 children. February 2nd of 1862 finds her moving to Cathedral parish in Gothenburg. In March 1865 she is registered by police as a prostitute and on April 21 of that year she gives birth to a stillborn baby girl. According to the official ledger wherein she is entry number 97, she is living in Philgaten in Ostra

Haga, a suburb of Gothenburg in October 1865. During October and November she is treated at the special hospital Kurhuset for venereal disease. The October 17 entry states that she is treated for a venereal chancre. She is reported as healthy in the November 3, 7, 10, 14 entries and after the last entry she is told she will no longer have to report to the police.

On February 7th of 1866 she applies to move to the Swedish parish in London, England. She enters the London register as an unmarried woman on July 10, 1866. According to testimony by Charles Preston, who lived at the same lodging house, she came to London in the service of a "foreign gentleman." Michael Kidney, with whom she lived on and off prior to her death, says she told him that she worked for a family in Hyde Park and that she "came to see the country." He also believes that she had family in London. July 10, 1886 -- she is registered as an unmarried woman at the Swedish Church in Prince's Square, St. George in the East. On March 7, 1869 she marries John Stride at the parish church, St. Giles in the Fields. The Service is conducted by Rev. Will Powell and witnessed by Daniel H. Wyatt and N. Taylor. Stride gives her address as 67 Gower Street. Soon after the marriage John and Liz are living in East India Dock road in Poplar. They keep a coffee shop at Chrisp Street, Poplar and in 1870 in Upper North Street, Poplar. They move themselves and the business to 178 Poplar High Street and remain there until the business is taken over by John Dale in 1875. In 1878 the Princess Alice, a saloon steam ship collides with the steamer Bywell Castle in the Thames. There is a loss of 600-700 lives. Liz will claim that her husband and children were killed in this disaster and that her palate was injured by being kicked in the mouth while climbing the mast to escape. No corroborative evidence exists for this statement and we know that her husband actually died in 1884. The post mortem report on her specifically states that there was no damage to either her hard or soft palate. This story may have been told by her to elicit sympathy when asking for financial aid from the Swedish Church. On December 28, 1881 through January 4, 1882 she is treated at the Whitechapel Infirmary for bronchitis. From the Infirmary she moves directly into the Whitechapel Workhouse. From 1882 onwards she lodges on and off at the common lodging house at 32 Flower and Dean Street. As her husband is still alive at this time it is reasonable to assume that the marriage has irrevocably fallen apart. On October 24, 1884, John Stride dies of heart disease.

In 1885 she is living with Michael Kidney. They live together for three years although she often leaves him for periods of time to go off on the town. Michael Kidney is a waterside laborer. He is born in 1852 and is 7 years younger than Liz. they live at 35 Devonshire Street, moving to 36 Devonshire Street five months prior to her murder. At the time of the murder Kidney is living at 33 Dorset Street. Their relationship is best described as stormy. He says that she was frequently absent when she was drinking and he even tried, unsuccessfully, to padlock her in. On May 20 and again on the 23rd of 1886 She receives alms from the Swedish Church. Sven Olsson, Clerk of the Church remembers her as "very poor." She gives her address as Devonshire Street off Commercial Road. On March 21, 1887 she is registered as an inmate at the Poplar Workhouse. In April of 1887 she charges Kidney with assault but then fails to appear at Thames Magistrate Court. In July of 1888 Kidney is sent down for three days charges with being drunk and disorderly and using obscene language. On September 15 and 20 of 1888 she again receives financial assistance from the Swedish Church. Charles Preston, a barber, had lived at 32 Flower and Dean Street for 18 months says that Liz Stride had been arrested one Saturday night for being drunk and disorderly at the Queen's Head Public House on Commercial Street. She was released on bail the following day. During the 20 months prior to her death she appeared 8 times before the Magistrate on similar charges. On Tuesday, September 25, 1888, Michael Kidney sees her for the last time. He expects her to be home when he arrives from work but she is not. Kidney is unconcerned as she has done this often. "It was drink that made her go away," he said. "She always returned without me going after her. I think she liked me better than any other man." Wednesday, September 26 finds her at the lodging house at 32 Flower and Dean Street. She had not been there in the last three months. She tells Catherine Lane that she had words with the man she was living with.

Thursday-Friday, September 27-28. Liz continues to lodge at 32 Flower and Dean Street. According to Elizabeth Tanner, the lodging house deputy, she arrived at the house after a quarrel with Kidney. Kidney will deny this.

Saturday-Sunday, September 29-30, 1888. The weather this evening is showery and windy. Elizabeth spends the afternoon cleaning two rooms at the lodging house. For her services she is paid 6d by Elizabeth Tanner.

September 30th, 1888 6:30 PM: Tanner sees her again at the Queen's Head Public House. They drank together and then walked back to the lodging house.

7:00-8:00 PM: She is seen leaving the lodging house by Charles Preston and Catherine Lane. She gives Lane a large piece of green velvet and asks her to hold it for her until she returns. She ask Preston to borrow his clothes brush but he has mislaid it. She then leaves passing by Thomas Bates, watchman at the lodging house who says she looked quite cheerful. Lane will later state that "I know the deceased had 6d when she left, she showed it to me, stating that the deputy had given it to her."

11:00 PM: Two laborers, J. Best and John Gardner were going into the Bricklayer's Arms Public House on Settles street, north of Commercial Road and almost opposite Berner Street. As they went in Stride was leaving with a short man with a dark mustache and sandy eyelashes. The man was wearing a billycock hat, mourning suit and coat. Best says "They had been served in the public house and went out when me and my friends came in. It was raining very fast and they did not appear willing to go out. He was hugging and kissing her, and as he seemed a respectably dressed man, we were rather astonished at the way he was going on at the woman." Stride and her man stood in the doorway for some time hugging and kissing. The workmen tried to get the man to come in for a drink but he refused. They then called to Stride. "That's Leather Apron getting 'round you." The man and Stride moved off towards Commercial Road and Berner Street. "He and the woman went off like a shot soon after eleven."

11:45 PM: William Marshall, a laborer, sees her on Berner Street. He is standing in the doorway of 64 Berner Street on the west side of the street between Fairclough and Boyd Streets. He notices her talking to a man in a short black cutaway coat and sailor's hat outside number 63. They are kissing and carrying on. He hears the man say "You would say anything but your prayers."

12:00 AM: Matthew Packer claims to sell Stride and a man grapes. This is a very dubious piece of evidence. See Sugden's The Complete History of Jack the Ripper for the pros and cons of this story.

12:35 AM: Police Constable William Smith sees Stride with a young man on Berner Street opposite the International Working Men's Educational Club. The man is described as 28 years old, dark coat and hard deerstalker hat. He is carrying a parcel approximately 6 inches high and 18 inches in length. the package is wrapped in newspaper.

12:45 AM (approximately): Quoting Home Office File:

"Israel Schwartz of 22 Helen Street, Backchurch Lane, stated that at this hour, turning into Berner Street from Commercial Road, and having gotten as far as the gateway where the murder was committed, he saw a man stop and speak to a woman, who was standing in the gateway. He tried to pull the woman into the street, but he turned her round and threw her down on the footway and the woman screamed three times, but not very loudly. On crossing to the opposite side of the street, he saw a second man lighting his pipe. The man who threw the woman down called out, apparently to the man on the opposite side of the road, "Lipski", and then Schwartz walked away, but finding that he was followed by the second man, he ran as far as the railway arch, but the man did not follow so far.

Schwartz cannot say whether the two men were together or known to each other. Upon being taken to the mortuary Schwartz identified the body as that of the woman he had seen."

The discovery of Elizabeth Stride's body in Dutfield's Yard, from The Pictorial News, 6th October 1888.

Later in the deposition: "It will be observed that allowing for differences of opinion between PC Smith and Schwartz as to the apparent age and height of the man each saw with the woman whose body they both identified, there are serious differences in the description of the dress...so at least it is rendered doubtful that they are describing the same man.

If Schwartz is to be believed, and the police report of his statement casts no doubt upon it, it follows that if they are describing different men that the man Schwartz saw is the more probable of the two to be the murderer..."

Schwartz describes the man as about 30 years old, 5' 5" tall with a fresh complexion, dark hair and small brown mustache. He is dressed in an overcoat and an old black felt hat with a wide brim. At the same time, James Brown says he sees Stride with a man as he was going home with his supper down Fairclough Street. She was leaning against the wall talking to a stoutish man about 5' 7" tall in a long black coat that reached to his heels. He has his arm against the wall. Stride is saying "No, not tonight, some other night." 1:00 AM: Louis Diemschutz, a salesman of jewelry, entered Dutfield's Yard driving his cart and pony. Immediately at the entrace, his pony shied and refused to proceed --

Diemschutz suspected something was in the way but could not see since the yard was utterly pitch black. He probed forward with his whip and came into contact with a body, whom he initially believed to be either drunk or asleep. He entered the International Working Men's Educational Club to get some help in rousing the woman, and upon returning to the yard with Isaac Kozebrodsky and Morris Eagle, the three discover that she was dead, her throat cut. It was believed that Diemschutz's arrival frightened the Ripper, causing him to flee before he performed the mutilations. Diemschutz himself stated that he believed the Ripper was still in the yard when he had entered, due to the warm temperature of the body and the continuingly odd behavior of his pony. Dr. Frederick Blackwell of 100 Commercial Road was called; he arrived at 1.16am and pronounced Stride dead at the scene. International Worker's Educational Club: A two story wooden building, barn like. The club was spacious with a capacity of over two hundred people and contained a stage. Here amateurs performed, mostly in the Russian language, plays by well-known Russian revolutionists. On Saturday and Sunday evenings there would be an international gathering of Russian, Jewish, British, French, Italian, Czech, and Polish radicals. Members thought of the club as the "cradle of Liberty' for the worker's manumission.

At the time of her death Elizabeth Stride was wearing: Long black cloth jacket, fur trimmed around the bottom with a red rose and white maiden hair fern pinned to it. (She was not wearing the flowers when she left the lodging house.)

Black skirt Black crepe bonnet Checked neck scarf knotted on left side Dark brown velveteen bodice 2 light serge petticoats 1 white chemise White stockings Spring sided boots 2 handkerchiefs (one, the larger, is noticed at the post-mortem to have fruit stains on it.) A thimble A piece of wool wound around a card In the pocket in her underskirt: A key (as of a padlock) A small piece of lead pencil Six large and one small button A comb A broken piece of comb A metal spoon A hook (as from a dress) A piece of muslin One or two small pieces of paper She is found clutching a packet of Cachous in her hand. Cachous is a pill used by smokers to sweeten their breath.

Post-mortem Dr. George Bagster Phillips (who also handled the Chapman and Kelly murders) performed the post mortem on Stride. He was also present at the scene and, after examining the body, asserts the deceased had not eaten any grapes. His report is as follows: "The body was lying on the near side, with the face turned toward the wall, the head up the yard and the feet toward the street. The left arm was extended and there was a packet of cachous in the left hand. The right arm was over the belly, the back of the hand and wrist had on it clotted blood. The legs were drawn up with the feet close to the wall. The body and face were warm and the hand cold. The legs were quite warm. Deceased had a silk handkerchief round her neck, and it appeared to be slightly torn. I have since ascertained it was cut. This corresponded with the right angle of the jaw. The throat was deeply gashed and there was an abrasion of the skin about one and a half inches in diameter, apparently stained with blood, under her right arm. At three o'clock p.m. on Monday at St. George's Mortuary, Dr. Blackwell and I made a post mortem examination. Rigor mortis was still thoroughly marked. There was mud on the left side of the face and it was matted in the head.; The Body was fairly nourished. Over both shoulders, especially the right, and under the collarbone and in front of the chest there was a bluish discoloration, which I have watched and have seen on two occasions since. There was a clear-cut incision on the neck. It was six inches in length and commenced two and a half inches in a straight line below the angle of the jaw, one half inch in over an undivided muscle, and then becoming deeper, dividing the sheath. The cut was very clean and deviated a little downwards. The arteries and other vessels contained in the sheath were all cut through. The cut through the tissues on the right side was more superficial, and tailed off to about two inches below the right angle of the jaw. The deep vessels on that side were uninjured. From this is was evident that the hemorrhage was caused through the partial severance of the left carotid artery. Decomposition had commenced in the skin. Dark brown spots were on the anterior surface of the left chin. There was a deformity in the bones of the right leg, which was not straight, but bowed forwards. There was no recent external injury save to the neck. The body being washed more thoroughly I could see some healing sores. The lobe of the left ear was torn as if from the removal or wearing through of an earring, but it was thoroughly healed. On removing the scalp there was no sign of extravasation of blood. The heart was small, the left ventricle firmly contracted, and the right slightly so. There was no clot in the pulmonary artery, but the right ventricle was full of dark clot. The left was firmly contracted as to be absolutely empty. The stomach was large and the mucous membrane only congested. It contained partly digested food, apparently consisting of cheese, potato, and farinaceous powder. All the teeth on the lower left jaw were absent." The day after the murder, a citizen mob formed outside of Berner Street protesting the continuation of the murders and the seemingly slipshod work of the police to catch the Ripper. From

**here on in, the Ripper is public enemy number one, and Home Office begins to consider offering awards for his capture and arrest.**

## Inquest: Elizabeth Stride

Day 1, Monday, October 1, 1888

(The Daily telegraph, Tuesday, October 2, 1888, Page 3)

Yesterday [1 Oct], at the Vestry Hall in Cable-street, St. George-in-the-East, Mr. Wynne E. Baxter, coroner for East Middlesex, opened an inquest on the body of the woman who was found dead, with her throat cut, at one o'clock on Sunday morning, in Berner-street, Commercial-road East. At the outset of the inquiry the deceased was described as Elizabeth Stride, but it subsequently transpired that she had not yet been really identified. A jury of twenty-four having been empanelled, they proceeded to view the body at the St. George's Mortuary.

Detective-Inspector Reid, H Division, watched the case on behalf of the police.

William Wess [West], who affirmed instead of being sworn, was the first witness examined, and, in reply to the coroner, he said: I reside at No. 2, William-street, Cannon-street-road, and am overseer in the printing office attached to No. 40, Berner-street, Commercial-road, which premises are in the occupation of the International Working Men's Education Society, whose club is carried on there. On the ground floor of the club is a room, the door and window of which face the street. At the rear of this is the kitchen, whilst the first floor consists of a large room which is used for our meetings and entertainments, I being a member of the club. At the south side of the premises is a courtyard, to which entrance can be obtained through a double door, in one section of which is a smaller one, which is used when the larger barriers are closed. The large doors are generally closed at night, but sometimes remain open. On the left side of the yard is a house, which is divided into three tenements, and occupied, I believe, by that number of families. At the end is a store or workshop belonging to Messrs. Hindley and Co., sack manufacturers. I do not know that a way out exists there. The club premises and the printing-office occupy the entire length of the yard on the right side. Returning to the club-house, the front room on the ground floor is used for meals. In the kitchen is a window which faces the door opening into the yard. The intervening passage is illuminated by means of a fanlight over the door. The printing-office, which does not communicate with the club, consists of two rooms, one for compositors and the other for the editor. On Saturday the compositors finished their labours at two o'clock in the afternoon. The editor concluded earlier, but remained at the place until the discovery of the murder.

[Coroner] How many members are there in the club? - From seventy-five to eighty. Working men of any nationality can join.

[Coroner] Is any political qualification required of members? - It is a political - a Socialist - club.

[Coroner] Do the members have to agree with any particular principles? - A candidate is proposed by one member and seconded by another, and a member would not nominate a candidate unless he knew that he was a supporter of Socialist principles. On Saturday last I was in the printing-office during the day and in the club during the evening. From nine to half-past ten at night I was away seeing an English friend home, but I was in the club again till a quarter-past midnight. A discussion was proceeding in the lecture-room, which has three windows overlooking the courtyard. From ninety to 100 persons attended the discussion, which terminated soon after half-past eleven, when the bulk of the members left, using the street door, the most convenient exit. From twenty to thirty members remained, some staying in the lecture-room and the others going downstairs. Of those upstairs a few continued the discussion, while the rest were singing. The windows of the lecture-room were partly open.

[Coroner] How do you know that you finally left at a quarter-past twelve o'clock? - Because of the time when I reached my lodgings. Before leaving I went into the yard, and thence to the printing-office, in order to leave some literature there, and on returning to the yard I observed that the double door at the entrance was open. There is no lamp in the yard, and none of the street lamps light it, so that the yard is only lit by the lights through the windows at the side of the club and of the tenements opposite. As to the tenements, I only observed lights in two first-floor windows. There was also a light in the printing- office, the editor being in his room reading.

[Coroner] Was there much noise in the club? - Not exactly much noise; but I could hear the singing when I was in the yard.

[Coroner] Did you look towards the yard gates? - Not so much to the gates as to the ground, but nothing unusual attracted my attention.

[Coroner] Can you say that there was no object on the ground? - I could not say that.

[Coroner] Do you think it possible that anything can have been there without your observing it? - It was dark, and I am a little shortsighted, so that it is possible. The distance from the gates to the kitchen door is 18 ft.

[Coroner] What made you look towards the gates at all? - Simply because they were open. I went into the club, and called my brother, and we left together by the front door.

[Coroner] On leaving did you see anybody as you passed the yard? - No.

[Coroner] Or did you meet any one in the street? - Not that I recollect. I generally go home between twelve and one o'clock.

[Coroner] Do low women frequent Berner-street? - I have seen men and women standing about and talking to each other in Fairclough-street.

[Coroner] But have you observed them nearer the club? - No.

[Coroner] Or in the club yard? - I did once, at eleven o'clock at night, about a year ago. They were chatting near the gates. That is the only time I have noticed such a thing, nor have I heard of it.


Morris Eagle, who also affirmed, said: I live at No. 4, New-road, Commercial-road, and travel in jewellery. I am a member of the International Workmen's Club, which meets at 40, Berner-street. I was there on Saturday, several times during the day, and was in the chair during the discussion in the evening. After the discussion, between half-past eleven and a quarter to twelve o'clock, I left the club to take my young lady home, going out through the front door. I returned about twenty minutes to one. I tried the front door, but, finding it closed, I went through the gateway into the yard, reaching the club in that way.

[Coroner] Did you notice anything lying on the ground near the gates? - I did not.

[Coroner] Did you pass in the middle of the gateway? - I think so. The gateway is 9 ft. 2 in. wide. I naturally walked on the right side, that being the side on which the club door was.

[Coroner] Do you think you are able to say that the deceased was not lying there then? - I do not know, I am sure, because it was rather dark. There was a light from the upper part of the club, but that would not throw any illumination upon the ground. It was dark near the gates.

[Coroner] You have formed no opinion, I take it, then, as to whether there was anything there? - No.

[Coroner] Did you see anyone about in Berner-street? - I dare say I did, but I do not remember them.

[Coroner] Did you observe any one in the yard? - I do not remember that I did.

[Coroner] If there had been a man and woman there you would have remembered the circumstance? - Yes; I am sure of that.

[Coroner] Did you notice whether there were any lights in the tenements opposite the club? - I do not recollect.

[Coroner] Are you often at the club late at night? - Yes, very often.

[Coroner] In the yard, too? - No, not in the yard.

[Coroner] And you have never seen a man and woman there? - No, not in the yard; but I have close by, outside the beershop, at the corner of Fairclough-street. As soon as I entered the gateway on Saturday night I could hear a friend of mine singing in the upstair room of the club. I went up to him. He was singing in the Russian language, and we sang together. I had been there twenty minutes when a member named Gidleman came upstairs, and said "there is a woman dead in the yard." I went down in a second and struck a match, when I saw a woman lying on the ground in a pool of blood, near the gates. Her feet were towards the gates, about six or seven feet from them. She was lying by the side of and facing the club wall. When I reached the body and struck the match another member was present.

[Coroner] Did you touch the body? - No. As soon as I struck the match I perceived a lot of blood, and I ran away and called the police.

[Coroner] Were the clothes of the deceased disturbed? - I cannot say. I ran towards the Commercial-road, Dienishitz, the club steward, and another member going in the opposite direction down Fairclough-street. In Commercial-road I found two constables at the corner of

Grove-street. I told them that a woman had been murdered in Berner-street, and they returned with me.

[Coroner] Was any one in the yard then? - Yes, a few persons - some members of the club and some strangers. One of the policemen turned his lamp on the deceased and sent me to the station for the inspector, at the same time telling his comrade to fetch a doctor. The onlookers seemed afraid to go near and touch the body. The constable, however, felt it.

[Coroner] Can you fix the time when the discovery was first made? - It must have been about one o'clock. On Saturday nights there is free discussion at the club, and among those present last Saturday were about half a dozen women, but they were those we knew - not strangers. It was not a dancing night, but a few members may have danced after the discussion.

[Coroner] If there was dancing and singing in the club you would not hear the cry of a woman in the yard? - It would depend upon the cry.

[Coroner] The cry of a woman in great distress - a cry of "Murder"? - Yes, I should have heard that.


Lewis Dienishitz [Diemschutz], having affirmed, deposed: I reside at No. 40 Berner-street, and am steward of the International Workmen's Club. I am married, and my wife lives at the club too, and assists in the management. On Saturday I left home about half-past eleven in the morning, and returned exactly at one o'clock on Sunday morning. I noticed the time at the baker's shop at the corner of Berner-street. I had been to the market near the Crystal Palace, and had a barrow like a costermonger's, drawn by a pony, which I keep in George-yard Cable-street. I drove home to leave my goods. I drove into the yard, both gates being wide open. It was rather dark there. All at once my pony shied at some object on the right. I looked to see what the object was, and observed that there was something unusual, but could not tell what. It was a dark object. I put my whip handle to it, and tried to lift it up, but as I did not succeed I jumped down from my barrow and struck a match. It was rather windy, and I could only get sufficient light to see that there was some figure there. I could tell from the dress that it was the figure of a woman.

[Coroner] You did not disturb it? - No. I went into the club and asked where my wife was. I found her in the front room on the ground floor.

[Coroner] What did you do with the pony? - I left it in the yard by itself, just outside the club door. There were several members in the front room of the club, and I told them all that there was a woman lying in the yard, though I could not say whether she was drunk or dead. I then got a candle and went into the yard, where I could see blood before I reached the body.

[Coroner] Did you touch the body? - No, I ran off at once for the police. I could not find a constable in the direction which I took, so I shouted out "Police!" as loudly as I could. A man whom I met in Grove- street returned with me, and when we reached the yard he took hold of the head of the deceased. As he lifted it up I saw the wound in the throat.

[Coroner] Had the constables arrived then? - At the very same moment Eagle and the constables arrived.

[Coroner] Did you notice anything unusual when you were approaching the club? - No.

[Coroner] You saw nothing suspicious? - Not at all.

[Coroner] How soon afterwards did a doctor arrive? - About twenty minutes after the constables came up. No one was allowed by the police to leave the club until they were searched, and then they had to give their names and addresses.

[Coroner] Did you notice whether the clothes of the deceased were in order? - They were in perfect order.

[Coroner] How was she lying? - On her left side, with her face towards the club wall.

[Coroner] Was the whole of the body resting on the side? - No, I should say only her face. I cannot say how much of the body was sideways. I did not notice what position her hands were in, but when the police came I observed that her bodice was unbuttoned near the neck. The doctor said the body was quite warm.

[Coroner] What quantity of blood should you think had flowed from the body? - I should say quite two quarts.

[Coroner] In what direction had it run? - Up the yard from the street. The body was about one foot from the club wall. The gutter of the yard is paved with large stones, and the centre with smaller irregular stones.

[Coroner] Have you ever seen men and women together in the yard? - Never.

[Coroner] Nor heard of such a thing? - No.

A Juror: Could you in going up the yard have passed the body without touching it? - Oh, yes.

[Coroner] Any person going up the centre of the yard might have passed without noticing it? - I, perhaps, should not have noticed it if my pony had not shied. I had passed it when I got down from my barrow.

[Coroner] How far did the blood run? - As far as the kitchen door of the club.

[Coroner] Was any person left with the body while you ran for the police? - Some members of the club remained; at all events, when I came back they were there. I cannot say whether any of them touched the body.

Inspector Reid (interposing): When the murder was discovered the members of the club were detained on the premises, and I searched them, whilst Dr. Phillips examined them.

A Juror; Was it possible for anybody to leave the yard between the discovery of the body and the arrival of the police?

Witness: Oh, yes - or, rather, it would have been possible before I informed the members of the club, not afterwards.

[Coroner] When you entered the yard, if any person had run out you would have seen them in the dark? - Oh, yes, it was light enough for that. It was dark in the gateway, but not so dark further in the yard.

The Coroner: The body has not yet been identified? - Not yet.

The Foreman: I do not quite understand that. I thought the inquest had been opened on the body of one Elizabeth Stride.

The Coroner: That was a mistake. Something is known of the deceased, but she has not been fully identified. It would be better at present to describe her as a woman unknown. She has been partially identified. It is known where she lived. It was thought at the beginning of the inquest that she had been identified by a relative, but that turns out to have been a mistake.

The inquiry was then adjourned till this (Tuesday) afternoon, at two o'clock.

Day 2, Tuesday, October 2, 1888

(The Daily Telegraph, Wednesday, October 3, 1888, Page 3)

Yesterday afternoon [2 oct], in the Vestry Hall of St. George-in-the-East, Cable-street, Mr. Wynne E. Baxter, coroner for East Middlesex, resumed the inquiry into the circumstances attending the death of the woman who was found with her throat cut in a yard adjoining the clubhouse of the International Working Men's Education Society, No. 40, Berner-street, Commercial-road East, at one o'clock on Sunday morning last.

Constable Henry Lamb, 252 H division, examined by the coroner, said: Last Sunday morning, shortly before one o'clock, I was on duty in Commercial-road, between Christian-street and Batty-street, when two men came running towards me and shouting. I went to meet them, and they called out, "Come on, there has been another murder." I asked where, and as they got to the corner of Berner-street they pointed down and said, "There." I saw people moving some distance down the street. I ran, followed by another constable - 426 H. Arriving at the gateway of No. 40 I observed something dark lying on the ground on the right-hand side. I turned my light on, when I found that the object was a woman, with her throat cut and apparently dead. I sent the other constable for the nearest doctor, and a young man who was standing by I despatched to the police station to inform the inspector what had occurred. On my arrival there were about thirty people in the yard, and others followed me in. No one was nearer than a yard to the body. As I was examining the deceased the crowd gathered round, but I begged them to keep back, otherwise they might have their clothes soiled with blood, and thus get into trouble.

[Coroner] Up to this time had you touched the body? - I had put my hand on the face.

[Coroner] Was it warm? - Slightly. I felt the wrist, but could not discern any movement of the pulse. I then blew my whistle for assistance.

[Coroner] Did you observe how the deceased was lying? - She was lying on her left side, with her left hand on the ground.

[Coroner] Was there anything in that hand? - I did not notice anything. The right arm was across the breast. Her face was not more than five or six inches away from the club wall.

[Coroner] Were her clothes disturbed? - No.

[Coroner] Only her boots visible? - Yes, and only the soles of them. There were no signs of a struggle. Some of the blood was in a liquid state, and had run towards the kitchen door of the club. A little - that nearest to her on the ground - was slightly congealed. I can hardly say whether any was still flowing from the throat. Dr. Blackwell was the first doctor to arrive; he came ten or twelve minutes after myself, but I had no watch with me.

[Coroner] Did any one of the crowd say whether the body had been touched before your arrival? - No. Dr. Blackwell examined the body and its surroundings. Dr. Phillips came ten minutes later. Inspector Pinhorn arrived directly after Dr. Blackwell. When I blew my whistle other constables came, and I had the entrance of the yard closed. This was while Dr. Blackwell was looking at the body. Before that the doors were wide open. The feet of the deceased extended just to the swing of the gate, so that the barrier could be closed without disturbing the body. I entered the club and left a constable at the gate to prevent any one passing in or out. I examined the hands and clothes of all the members of the club. There were from fifteen to twenty present, and they were on the ground floor.

[Coroner] Did you discover traces of blood anywhere in the club? - No.

[Coroner] Was the steward present? - Yes.

[Coroner] Did you ask him to lock the front door? - I did not. There was a great deal of commotion. That was done afterwards.

The Coroner: But time is the essence of the thing.

Witness: I did not see any person leave. I did not try the front door of the club to see if it was locked. I afterwards went over the cottages, the occupants of which were in bed. I was admitted by men, who came down partly dressed; all the other people were undressed. As to the watercloses in the yard, one was locked and the other unlocked, but no one was there. There is a recess near the dust-bin.

[Coroner] Did you go there? - Yes, afterwards, with Dr. Phillips.

The Coroner: But I am speaking of at the time.

Witness: I did it subsequently. I do not recollect looking over the wooden partition. I, however, examined the store belonging to Messrs. Hindley, sack manufacturers, but I saw nothing there.

[Coroner] How long were the cottagers in opening their doors? - Only a few minutes, and they seemed frightened. When I returned Dr. Phillips and Chief Inspector West had arrived.

[Coroner] Was there anything to prevent a man escaping while you were examining the body? - Several people were inside and outside the gates, and I should think that they would be sure to observe a man who had marks of blood.

[Coroner] But supposing he had no marks of blood? - It was quite possible, of course, for a person to escape while I was examining the corpse. Every one was more or less looking towards the body. There was much confusion.

[Coroner] Do you think that a person might have got away before you arrived? - I think he is more likely to have escaped before than after.

Detective-Inspector Reid: How long before had you passed this place?

Witness: I am not on the Berner-street beat, but I passed the end of the street in Commercial-road six or seven minutes before.

[Coroner] When you were found what direction were you going in? - I was coming towards Berner-street. A constable named Smith was on the Berner-street beat. He did not accompany me, but the constable who was on fixed-point duty between Grove-street and Christian-street in Commercial-road. Constables at fixed-points leave duty at one in the morning. I believe that is the practice nearly all over London.

The Coroner: I think this is important. The Hanbury-street murder was discovered just as the night police were going off duty. (To witness): Did you see anything suspicious? - I did not at any time. There were squabbles and rows in the streets, but nothing more.

The Foreman: Was there light sufficient to enable you to see, as you were going down Berner-street, whether any person was running away from No. 40? - It was rather dark, but I think there was light enough for that, though the person would be somewhat indistinct from Commercial-road.

The Foreman: Some of the papers state that Berner-street is badly lighted; but there are six lamps within 700 feet, and I do not think that is very bad.

The Coroner: The parish plan shows that there are four lamps within 350 feet, from Commercial-road to Fairclough-street.

Witness: There are three, if not four, lamps in Berner-street between Commercial- road and Fairclough-street. Berner-street is about as well lighted as other side streets. Most of them are rather dark, but more lamps have been erected lately.

The Coroner: I do not think that London altogether is as well lighted as some capitals are.

Witness: There are no public-house lights in Berner-street. I was engaged in the yard and at the mortuary all the night afterwards.

Edward Spooner, in reply to the coroner, said: I live at No. 26, Fairclough-street, and am a horse-keeper with Messrs. Meredith, biscuit bakers. On Sunday morning, between half-past twelve and one o'clock, I was standing outside the Beehive Public- house, at the corner of Christian-street, with my young woman. We had left a public- house in Commercial-road at closing time, midnight, and walked quietly to the point named. We stood outside the Beehive about twenty-five minutes, when two Jews came running along, calling out "Murder" and "Police." They ran as far as Grove- street, and then turned back. I stopped them and asked what was the matter, and they replied that a woman had been murdered. I thereupon proceeded down Berner-street and into Dutfield's-yard, adjoining the International Workmen's Club-house, and there saw a woman lying just inside the gate.

[Coroner] Was any one with her? - There were about fifteen people in the yard.

[Coroner] Was any one near her? - They were all standing round.

[Coroner] Were they touching her? - No. One man struck a match, but I could see the woman before the match was struck. I put my hand under her chin when the match was alight.

[Coroner] Was the chin warm? - Slightly.

[Coroner] Was any blood coming from the throat? - Yes; it was still flowing. I noticed that she had a piece of paper doubled up in her right hand, and some red and white flowers pinned on her breast. I did not feel the body, nor did I alter the position of the head. I am sure of that. Her face was turned towards the club wall.

[Coroner] Did you notice whether the blood was still moving on the ground? - It was running down the gutter. I stood by the side of the body for four or five minutes, until the last witness arrived.

[Coroner] Did you notice any one leave the yard while you were there? - No.

[Coroner] Could any one have left without your observing it? - I cannot say, but I think there were too many people about. I believe it was twenty-five minutes to one o'clock when I arrived in the yard.

[Coroner] Have you formed any opinion as to whether the people had moved the body before you came? - No.

The Foreman: As a rule, Jews do not care to touch dead bodies.

Witness: The legs of the deceased were drawn up, but her clothes were not disturbed. When Police-constable Lamb came I helped him to close the gates of the yard, and I left through the club.

Inspector Reid: I believe that was after you had given your name and address to the police? - Yes. And had been searched? - Yes. And examined by Dr. Phillips? - Yes.

The Coroner: Was there no blood on your hands? - No.

[Coroner] Then there was no blood on the chin of the deceased? - No.

By the Jury: I did not meet any one as I was hastening through Berner-street.


Mary Malcolm was the next witness, and she was deeply affected while giving her evidence. In answer to the coroner she said: I live at No. 50, Eagle-street, Red Lion- square, Holborn, and am married. My husband, Andrew Malcolm, is a tailor. I have seen the body at the mortuary. I saw it once on Sunday and twice yesterday.

[Coroner] Who is it? - It is the body of my sister, Elizabeth Watts.

[Coroner] You have no doubt about that? - Not the slightest.

[Coroner] You did have some doubts about it at one time? - I had at first.

[Coroner] When did you last see your sister alive? - Last Thursday, about a quarter to seven in the evening.

[Coroner] Where? - She came to see me at No. 59, Red Lion-street, where I work as a trousermaker.

[Coroner] What did she come to you for? - To ask me for a little assistance. I have been in the habit of assisting her for five years.

[Coroner] Did you give her anything? - I gave her a shilling and a short jacket - not the jacket which is now on the body.

[Coroner] How long was she with you? - Only a few moments.

[Coroner] Did she say where she was going? - No.

[Coroner] Where was she living? - I do not know. I know it was somewhere in the neighbourhood of the tailoring Jews - Commercial-road or Commercial-street, or somewhere at the East-end.

[Coroner] Did you understand that she was living in lodging-houses? - Yes.

[Coroner] Did you know what she was doing for a livelihood? - I had my doubts.

[Coroner] Was she the worse for drink when she came to you on Thursday? - No, sober.

[Coroner] But she was sometimes the worse for drink, was she not? - That was, unfortunately, a failing with her. She was thirty-seven years of age last March.

[Coroner] Had she ever been married? - Yes.

[Coroner] Is her husband alive? - Yes, so far as I know. She married the son of Mr. Watts, wine and spirit merchant, of Walcot-street, Bath. I think her husband's Christian name was Edward. I believe he is now in America.

[Coroner] Did he get into trouble? - No.

[Coroner] Why did he go away? - Because my sister brought trouble upon him.

[Coroner] When did she leave him? - About eight years ago, but I cannot be quite certain as to the time. She had two children. Her husband caught her with a porter, and there was a quarrel.

[Coroner] Did the husband turn her out of doors? - No, he sent her to my poor mother, with the two children.

[Coroner] Where does your mother live? - She is dead. She died in the year 1883.

[Coroner] Where are the children now? - The girl is dead, but the boy is at a boarding school kept by his aunt.

[Coroner] Was the deceased subject to epileptic fits? - Witness (sobbing bitterly): No, she only had drunken fits.

[Coroner] Was she ever before the Thames police magistrate? - I believe so.

[Coroner] Charged with drunkenness? - Yes.

[Coroner] Are you aware that she has been let off on the supposition that she was subject to epileptic fits? - I believe that is so, but she was not subject to epileptic fits.

[Coroner] Has she ever told you of troubles she was in with any man? - Oh yes; she lived with a man.

[Coroner] Do you know his name? - I do not remember now, but I shall be able to tell you to- morrow. I believe she lived with a man who kept a coffee-house at Poplar.

Inspector Reid: Was his name Stride? - No; I think it was Dent, but I can find out for certain by to-morrow.

The Coroner: How long had she ceased to live with that man? - Oh, some time. He went away to sea, and was wrecked on the Isle of St. Paul, I believe.

[Coroner] How long ago should you think that was? - It must be three years and a half; but I could tell you all about it by to-morrow, even the name of the vessel that was wrecked.

[Coroner] Had the deceased lived with any man since then? - Not to my knowledge, but there is some man who says that he has lived with her.

[Coroner] Have you ever heard of her getting into trouble with this man? - No, but at times she got locked up for drunkenness. She always brought her trouble to me.

[Coroner] You never heard of any one threatening her? - No; she was too good for that.

[Coroner] Did you ever hear her say that she was afraid of any one? - No.

[Coroner] Did you know of no man with whom she had relations? - No.

Inspector Reid: Did you ever visit her in Flower and Dean-street? - No.

[Coroner] Did you ever hear her called "Long Liz"? - That was generally her nickname, I believe.

[Coroner] Have you ever heard of the name of Stride? - She never mentioned such a name to me. I think that if she had lived with any one of that name she would have told me. I have heard what the man Stride has said, but I think he is mistaken.

The Coroner: How often did your sister come to you? - Every Saturday, and I always gave her 2s. That was for her lodgings.

[Coroner] Did she come to you at all last Saturday? - No, I did not see her on that day.

[Coroner] The Thursday visit was an unusual one, I suppose? - Yes.

[Coroner] Did you think it strange that she did not come on the Saturday? - I did.

[Coroner] Had she ever missed a Saturday before? - Not for nearly three years.

[Coroner] What time in the day did she usually come to you? - At four o'clock in the afternoon.

[Coroner] Where? - At the corner of Chancery-lane. I was there last Saturday afternoon from half-past three till five, but she did not turn up.

[Coroner] Did you think there was something the matter with her? - On the Sunday morning when I read the accounts in the newspapers I thought it might be my sister who had been murdered. I had a presentiment that that was so. I came down to Whitechapel and was directed to the mortuary; but when I saw the body I did not recognise it as that of my sister.

[Coroner] How was that? Why did you not recognise it in the first instance? - I do not know, except that I saw it in the gaslight, between nine and ten at night. But I recognised her the next day.

[Coroner] Did you not have some special presentiment that this was your sister? - Yes.

[Coroner] Tell the jury what it was? - I was in bed, and about twenty minutes past one on Sunday morning I felt a pressure on my breast and heard three distinct kisses. It was that which made me afterwards suspect that the woman who had been murdered was my sister.

The Coroner (to the jury): The only reason why I allow this evidence is that the witness has been doubtful about her identification. (To witness) Did your sister ever break a limb? - No. Never? - Not to my knowledge.

The Foreman: Had she any special marks upon her? - Yes, on her right leg there was a small black mark.

The Coroner: Have you seen that mark on the deceased? - Yes.

[Coroner] When did you see it? - Yesterday morning.

[Coroner] But when, before death, did you see it on your sister? - Oh not for years. It was the size of a pea. I have not seen it for 20 years.

[Coroner] Did you mention the mark before you saw the body? - I said that I could recognise my sister by this particular mark.

[Coroner] What was the mark? - It was from the bite of an adder. One day, when children, we were rolling down a hill together, and we came across an adder. The thing bit me first and my sister afterwards. I have still the mark of the bite on my left hand.

The Coroner (examining the mark): Oh, that is only a scar. Are you sure that your sister, in her youth, never broke a limb? - Not to my knowledge.

[Coroner] Has your husband seen your sister? - Yes.

[Coroner] Has he been to the mortuary? - No; he will not go.

[Coroner] Have you any brothers and sisters alive? - Yes, a brother and a sister, but they have not seen her for years. My brother might recognise her. He lives near Bath. My sister resides at Folkestone. My sister (the deceased) had a hollowness in her right foot, caused by some sort of accident. It was the absence of this hollowness that made me doubt whether the deceased was really my sister. Perhaps it passed away in death. But the adder mark removed all doubt.

[Coroner] Did you recognise the clothes of the deceased at all? - No. (Bursting into tears). Indeed, I have had trouble with her. On one occasion she left a naked baby outside my door.

[Coroner] One of her babies? - One of her own.

[Coroner] One of the two children by her husband? - No, another one; one she had by a policeman, I believe. She left it with me, and I had to keep it until she fetched it away.

Inspector Reid: Is that child alive, do you know? - I believe it died in Bath.

The Coroner: It is important that the evidence of identification should be unmistakable, and I think that the witness should go to the same spot in Chancery- lane on Saturday next, in order to see if her sister comes. Witness: I have no doubt.

The Coroner: Still, it is better that the matter should be tested.

Witness (in reply to the jury): I did not think it strange that my sister came to me last Thursday instead of the Saturday, because she has done it before. But on previous occasions she has come on the Saturday as well. When she came last Thursday she asked me for money, stating that she had not enough to pay for her lodgings, and I said, "Elizabeth, you are a pest to me."

The Coroner: Has your sister been in prison? - Witness: Yes.

[Coroner] Has she never been in prison on a Saturday? - No; she has only been locked up for the night.

[Coroner] Never more? - No; she has been fined.

A Juror: You say that before when she has come on the Thursday she has also come on the Saturday as well? - Always.

The Coroner: So that the Thursday was an extra. You are quite confident now about the identity? - I have not a shadow of doubt.

Mr. Frederick William Blackwell deposed: I reside at No. 100, Commercial-road, and am a physician and surgeon. On Sunday morning last, at ten minutes past one o'clock, I was called to Berner-street by a policeman. My assistant, Mr. Johnston, went back with the constable, and I followed immediately I was dressed. I consulted my watch on my arrival, and it was 1.16 a.m. The deceased was lying on her left side obliquely across the passage, her face looking towards the right wall. Her legs were drawn up, her feet close against the wall of the right side of the passage. Her head was resting beyond the carriage-wheel rut, the neck lying over the rut. Her feet were three yards from the gateway. Her dress was unfastened at the neck. The neck and chest were quite warm, as were also the legs, and the face was slightly warm. The hands were cold. The right hand was open and on the chest, and was smeared with blood. The left hand, lying on the ground, was partially closed, and contained a small packet of cachous wrapped in tissue paper. There were no rings, nor marks of rings, on her hands. The appearance of the face was quite placid. The mouth was slightly open. The deceased had round her neck a check silk scarf, the bow of which was turned to the left and pulled very tight. In the neck there was a long incision which exactly corresponded with the lower border of the scarf. The border was slightly frayed, as if by a sharp knife. The incision in the neck commenced on the left side, 2 inches below the angle of the jaw, and almost in a direct line with it, nearly severing the vessels on that side, cutting the windpipe completely in two, and terminating on the opposite side 1 inch below the angle of the right jaw, but without severing the vessels on that side. I could not ascertain whether the bloody hand had been moved. The blood was running down the gutter into the drain in the opposite direction from the feet. There was about 1lb of clotted blood close by the body, and a stream all the way from there to the back door of the club.

[Coroner] Were there no spots of blood about? - No; only some marks of blood which had been trodden in.

[Coroner] Was there any blood on the soles of the deceased's boots? - No.

[Coroner] No splashing of blood on the wall? - No, it was very dark, and what I saw was by the aid of a policeman's lantern. I have not examined the place since. I examined the clothes, but found no blood on any part of them. The bonnet of the deceased was lying on the ground a few inches from the head. Her dress was unbuttoned at the top.

[Coroner] Can you say whether the injuries could have been self-inflicted? - It is impossible that they could have been.

[Coroner] Did you form any opinion as to how long the deceased had been dead? - From twenty minutes to half an hour when I arrived. The clothes were not wet with rain. She would have bled to death comparatively slowly on account of vessels on one side only of the neck being cut and the artery not completely severed.

[Coroner] After the infliction of the injuries was there any possibility of any cry being uttered by the deceased? - None whatever. Dr. Phillips came about twenty minutes to half an hour after my arrival. The double doors of the yard were closed when I arrived, so that the previous witness must have made a mistake on that point.

A Juror: Can you say whether the throat was cut before or after the deceased fell to the ground? - I formed the opinion that the murderer probably caught hold of the silk scarf, which was tight and knotted, and pulled the deceased backwards, cutting her throat in that way. The throat might have been cut as she was falling, or when she was on the ground. The blood would have spurted about if the act had been committed while she was standing up.

The Coroner: Was the silk scarf tight enough to prevent her calling out? - I could not say that.

[Coroner] A hand might have been put on her nose and mouth? - Yes, and the cut on the throat was probably instantaneous.

The inquest was then adjourned till one o'clock today.


Day 3, Monday, October 3, 1888

(The Daily Telegraph, Thursday, October 4, 1888, page 5)


Yesterday [3 Oct], at St. George's Vestry Hall, Cable-street, Mr. Wynne E. Baxter, coroner for East Middlesex, again resumed the inquiry into the circumstances attending the death of the woman who was found with her throat cut at one o'clock on Sunday morning last in a yard adjoining the International Working Men's Club, Berner-street, Commercial-road East.


Elizabeth Tanner, examined by the Coroner, said: I am deputy of the common lodging-house, No. 32, Flower and Dean-street, and am a widow. I have seen the body of the deceased at St. George's Mortuary, and recognise it as that of a woman who has lodged in our house, on and off, for the last six years.

[Coroner] Who is she? - She was known by the nick-name of "Long Liz."

[Coroner] Do you know her right name? - No.

[Coroner] Was she an English woman? - She used to say that she was a Swedish woman. She never told me where she was born. She said that she was married, and that her husband and children were drowned in the Princess Alice.

[Coroner] When did you last see her alive? - Last Saturday evening, at half-past six o'clock.

[Coroner] Where was she then? - With me in a public-house, called the Queen's Head, in Commercial-street.

[Coroner] Did she leave you there? - She went back with me to the lodging-house. At that time she had no bonnet or cloak on. She never told me what her husband was.

[Coroner] Where did you actually leave her? - She went into the kitchen, and I went to another part of the building.

[Coroner] Did you see her again? - No, until I saw the body in the mortuary to-day.

[Coroner] You are quite certain it is the body of the same woman? - Quite sure. I recognise, beside the features, that the roof of her mouth is missing. Deceased accounted for this by stating that she was in the Princess Alice when it went down, and that her mouth was injured.

[Coroner] How long had she been staying at the lodging-house? - She was there last week only on Thursday and Friday nights.

[Coroner] Had she paid for her bed on Saturday night? - No.

[Coroner] Do you know any of her male acquaintances? - Only of one.

[Coroner] Who is he? - She was living with him. She left him on Thursday to come and stay at our house, so she told me.

[Coroner] Have you seen this man? - I saw him last Sunday.

Detective-Inspector Reid: He is present to-day.

Witness: I do not know that she was ever up at the Thames Police-court, or that she suffered from epileptic fits. I am aware that she lived in Fashion-street, but not that she has ever resided at Poplar. I never heard of a sister at Red Lion-square. I never heard of any relative except her late husband and children.

[Coroner] What sort of a woman was she? - Very quiet.

[Coroner] A sober woman? - Yes.

[Coroner] Did she use to stop out late at night? - Sometimes.

[Coroner] Do you know if she had any money? - She cleaned two rooms for me on Saturday, and I paid her 6d for doing it. I do not know whether she had any other money.

[Coroner] Are you able to say whether the two handkerchiefs now at the mortuary belonged to the deceased? - No.

[Coroner] Do you recognise her clothes? - Yes. I recognise the long cloak which is hanging up in the mortuary. The other clothes she had on last Saturday.

[Coroner] Did she ever tell you that she was afraid of any one? - No.

[Coroner] Or that any one had ever threatened to injure her? - No.

[Coroner] The fact of her not coming back on Saturday did not surprise you, I suppose? - We took no notice of it.

[Coroner] What made you go to the mortuary, then? - Because I was sent for. I do not recollect at what hour she came to the lodging-house last Thursday. She was wearing the long cloak then. She did not bring any parcel with her.

By the jury: I do not know of any one else of the name of Long Liz. I never heard of her sister allowing her any money, nor have I heard the name of Stride mentioned in connection with her. Before last Thursday she had been away from my house about three months.

The Coroner: Did you see her during that three months? - Yes, frequently; sometimes once a week, and at other times almost every other day.

[Coroner] Did you understand what she was doing? - She told me that she was at work among the Jews, and was living with a man in Fashion-street.

[Coroner] Could she speak English well? - Yes, but she spoke Swedish also.

[Coroner] When she spoke English could you detect that she was a foreigner? - She spoke English as well as an English woman. She did not associate much with Swedish people. I never heard of her having hurt her foot, nor of her having broken a limb in childhood. I had no doubt that she was what she represented herself to be - a Swede.

Catherine Lane: I live in Flower and Dean-street, and am a charwoman and married. My husband is a dock labourer, and is living with me at the lodging house of which the last witness is deputy. I have been there since last February. I have seen the body of the deceased at the mortuary.

The Coroner: Did you recognise it? - Yes, as the body of Long Liz, who lived occasionally in the lodging-house. She came there last Thursday.

[Coroner] Had you ever seen her before? - I have known her for six or seven months. I used to see her frequently in Fashion-street, where she lived, and I have seen her at our lodging-house.

[Coroner] Did you speak to her last week? - On Thursday and Saturday.

[Coroner] At what time did you see her first on Thursday? - Between ten and eleven o'clock.

[Coroner] Did she explain why she was coming back? - She said she had had a few words with the man she was living with.

[Coroner] When did you see her on Saturday? - When she was cleaning the deputy's room.

[Coroner] And after that? - I last saw her in the kitchen, between six and seven in the evening. She then had on a long cloak and a black bonnet.

[Coroner] Did she say where she was going? - No. I first saw the body in the mortuary on Sunday afternoon, and I recognised it then.

[Coroner] Did you see her leave the lodging-house? - Yes; she gave me a piece of velvet as she left, and asked me to mind it until she came back. (The velvet was produced, and proved to be a large piece, green in colour.)

[Coroner] Had she no place to leave it? - I do not know why she asked me, as the deputy would take charge of anything. I know deceased had sixpence when she left; she showed it to me, stating that the deputy had given it to her.

[Coroner] Had she been drinking then? - Not that I am aware of.

[Coroner] Do you know of any one who was likely to have injured her? - No one.

[Coroner] Have you heard her mention any person but this man she was living with? - No. I have heard her say she was a Swede, and that at one time she lived in Devonshire-street, Commercial-road - never in Poplar.

[Coroner] Did you ever hear her speak of her husband? - She said he was dead. She never said that she was afraid, or that any one had threatened her life. I am satisfied the deceased is the same woman.

By the jury: I could tell by her accent that she was a foreigner. She did not bring all her words out plainly.

[Coroner] Have you ever heard of her speaking to any one in her own language? - Yes; with women for whom she worked. I never heard of her having a sister, or of her having left a child at her sister's door.

Charles Preston deposed: I live at No. 32, Flower and Dean-street, and I am a barber. I have been lodging at my present address for eighteen months, and have seen the deceased there. I saw the body on Sunday last, and am quite sure it is that of Long Liz.

The Coroner: When did you last see her alive? - On Saturday morning between six and seven o'clock.

[Coroner] Where was she then? - In the kitchen of the lodging-house.

[Coroner] Was she dressed to go out? - Yes, and asked me for a brush to brush her clothes with, but I did not let her have one.

[Coroner] What was she wearing? - The jacket I have seen at the mortuary, but no flowers in the breast. She had the striped silk handkerchief round her neck.

[Coroner] Do you happen to have seen her pocket-handkerchiefs? - No.

[Coroner] You cannot say whether she had two? - No.

[Coroner] Do you know anything about her? - I always understood that she was born at Stockholm, and came to England in the service of a gentleman.

[Coroner] Did she ever tell you her age? - She said once that she was thirty-five.

[Coroner] Did she ever tell you that she was married? - Yes; and that her husband and children went down in the Princess Alice - that she had been saved while they were lost.

[Coroner] Did she ever state what her husband was? - I have some recollection that she said he was a seafaring man, and that he had kept a coffee-house in Chrisp-street, Poplar.

[Coroner] Did she ever tell you that she was taken to the Thames Police-court? - I only remember her having been taken into custody for being drunk and disorderly at the Ten Bells public-house, Commercial- street, one Sunday morning from four to five months ago.

[Coroner] Do you know of any one who was likely to have injured her? - No.

[Coroner] Did she ever state that she was afraid of any one? - Never.

[Coroner] Did she say where she was going on Saturday? - No.

[Coroner] Or when she was coming back? - No.

[Coroner] Did she say whether she was coming back? - She never said anything about it. She always gave me to understand that her name was Elizabeth Stride. She never mentioned any sister. She stated that her mother was still alive in Sweden. She apparently spoke Swedish fluently to people who came into the lodging-house.


Michael Kidney said: I live at No. 38, Dorset-street, Spitalfields, and am a waterside labourer. I have seen the body of the deceased at the mortuary.

The Coroner: Is it the woman you have been living with? - Yes.

[Coroner] You have no doubt about it? - No doubt whatever.

[Coroner] What was her name? - Elizabeth Stride.

[Coroner] How long have you known her? - About three years.

[Coroner] How long has she been living with you? - Nearly all that time.

[Coroner] What was her age? - Between thirty-six and thirty-eight years.

[Coroner] Was she a Swede? - She told me that she was a Swede, and I have no doubt she was. She said she was born three miles from Stockholm, that her father was a farmer, and that she first came to England for the purpose of seeing the country; but I have grave doubts about that. She afterwards told me that she came to England in a situation with a family.

[Coroner] Had she got any relatives in England? - When I met her she told me she was a widow, and that her husband had been a ship's carpenter at Sheerness.

[Coroner] Did he ever keep a coffee-house? - She told me that he had.

[Coroner] Where? - In Chrisp-street, Poplar.

[Coroner] Did she say when he died? - She informed me that he was drowned in the Princess Alice disaster.

[Coroner] Was the roof of her mouth defective? - Yes.

[Coroner] You had a quarrel with her on Thursday? - I did not see her on Thursday.

[Coroner] When did you last see her? - On the Tuesday, and I then left her on friendly terms in Commercial- street. That was between nine and ten o'clock at night, as I was coming from work.

[Coroner] Did you expect her home? - I expected her home half an hour afterwards. I subsequently ascertained that she had been in and had gone out again, and I did not see her again alive.

[Coroner] Can you account for her sudden disappearance? Was she the worse for drink when you last saw her? - She was perfectly sober.

[Coroner] You can assign no reason whatever for her going away so suddenly? - She would occasionally go away.

[Coroner] Oh, she has left you before? - During the three years I have known her she has been away from me about five months altogether.

[Coroner] Without any reason? - Not to my knowledge. I treated her the same as I would a wife.

[Coroner] Do you know whether she had picked up with any one? - I have seen the address of the brother of the gentleman with whom she lived as a servant, somewhere near Hyde Park, but I cannot find it now.

[Coroner] Did she have any reason for going away? - It was drink that made her go on previous occasions. She always came back again. I think she liked me better than any other man. I do not believe she left me on Tuesday to take up with any other man.

[Coroner] Had she any money? - I do not think she was without a shilling when she left me. From what I used to give her I fancy she must either have had money or spent it in drink.

[Coroner] You know of nobody whom she was likely to have complications with or fall foul of? - No, but I think the police authorities are very much to blame, or they would have got the man who murdered her. At Leman-street Police-station, on Monday night, I asked for a detective to give information to get the man.

[Coroner] What information had you? - I could give information that would enable the detectives to discover the man at any time.

[Coroner] Then will you give us your information now? - I told the inspector on duty at the police-station that I could give information provided he would let me have a young, strange detective to act on it, and he would not give me one.

[Coroner] What do you think should be inquired into? - I might have given information that would have led to a great deal if I had been provided with a strange young detective.

Inspector Reid: When you went to Leman-street and saw the inspector on duty, were you intoxicated? - Yes; I asked for a young detective, and he would not let me have one, and I told him that he was uncivil. (Laughter.)

[Coroner] You have been in the army, and I believe have a good pension? - Only the reserve.

A Juror: Have you got any information for a detective? - I am a great lover of discipline, sir. (Laughter.)

The Coroner: Had you any information that required the service of a detective? - Yes. I thought that if I had one, privately, he could get more information than I could myself. The parties I obtained my information from knew me, and I thought someone else would be able to derive more from them.

Inspector Reid: Will you give me the information directly, if you will not give it to the coroner? - I believe I could catch the man if I had a detective under my command.

The Coroner: You cannot expect that. I have had over a hundred letters making suggestions, and I dare say all the writers would like to have a detective at their service. (Laughter.)

Witness: I have information which I think might be of use to the police.

The Coroner: You had better give it, then.

Witness: I believe that, if I could place the policeman myself, the man would be captured.

The Coroner: You must know that the police would not be placed at the disposal of a man the worse for drink.

Witness: If I were at liberty to place 100 men about this city the murderer would be caught in the act.

Inspector Reid: But you have no information to give to the police?

Witness: No, I will keep it to myself.

A Juror: Do you know of any sister who gave money to the deceased? - No. On Monday I saw Mrs. Malcolm, who said the deceased was her sister. She is very like the deceased.

[Coroner] Did the deceased have a child by you? - No.

[Coroner] Or by a policeman? - She told me that a policeman used to court her when she was at Hyde Park, before she was married to Stride.

Stride and the policeman courted her at the same time, but I never heard of her having a child by the policeman. She said she was the mother of nine children, two of whom were drowned with her husband in the Princess Alice, and the remainder were either in a school belonging to the Swedish Church on the other side of London Bridge, or with the husband's friends. I thought she was telling the truth when she spoke of Swedish people. I understood that the deceased and her husband were employed on the Princess Alice.

Mr. Edward Johnson: I live at 100, Commercial-road, and am assistant to Drs. Kaye and Blackwell. On Sunday morning last, at a few minutes past one o'clock, I received a call from Constable 436 H. After informing Dr. Blackwell, who was in bed, of the case, I accompanied the officer to Berner-street, and in a courtyard adjoining No. 40 I was shown the figure of a woman lying on her left side.

The Coroner: Were there many people about? - There was a crowd in the yard.

[Coroner] And police? - Yes.

[Coroner] Was any one touching the deceased? - No.

[Coroner] Was there much light? - Very little.

[Coroner] What light there was, where did it come from? - From the policeman's lantern. I examined the woman and found an incision in the throat.

[Coroner] Was blood coming from the wound? - No, it had stopped bleeding. I felt the body and found all warm except the hands, which were quite cold.

[Coroner] Did you undo the dress? - The dress was not undone when I came. I undid it to see if the chest was warm.

[Coroner] Did you move the head at all? - I left the body precisely as I found it. There was a stream of blood down to the gutter; it was all clotted. There was very little blood near the neck; it had all run away. I did not notice at the time that one of the hands was smeared with blood. The left arm was bent, away from the body. The right arm was also bent, and across the body.

[Coroner] Can you say whether any one had stepped into the stream of blood? - There was no mark of it.

[Coroner] Did you look for any? - Yes. I had no watch with me, but Dr. Blackwell looked at his when he arrived, and the time was 1.16 a.m. I preceded him by three or four minutes. The bonnet of the deceased was lying three or four inches beyond the head on the ground. The outer gates were closed shortly after I came.

Thomas Coram: I live at No. 67, Plummer's-road, and work for a cocoanut dealer. On Monday shortly after midnight I left a friend's house in Bath-gardens, Brady-street. I walked straight down Brady-street and into Whitechapel-road towards Aldgate. I first walked on the right side of Whitechapel-road, and afterwards crossed over to the left, and when opposite No. 253 I saw a knife lying on the doorstep.

[Coroner] What is No. 253? - A laundry. There were two steps to the front door, and the knife was on the bottom step. The production of the knife created some sensation, its discovery not having been generally known. It was a knife such as would be used by a baker in his trade, it being flat at the top instead of pointed, as a butcher's knife would be. The blade, which was discoloured with something resembling blood, was quite a foot long and an inch broad, whilst the black handle was six inches in length, and strongly rivetted in three places. Witness (continuing): There was a handkerchief round the handle of the knife, the handkerchief having been first folded and then twisted round the blade. A policeman coming towards me, I called his attention to the knife, which I did not touch.

[Coroner] Did the policeman take the knife away? - Yes, to the Leman-street station, I accompanying him.

[Coroner] Were there many people passing at the time? - Very few. I do not think I passed more than a dozen from Brady-street to where I found the knife. The weapon could easily be seen; it was light there.

[Coroner] Did you pass any policeman between Brady-street and where the knife was? - I passed three policemen.

Constable Joseph Drage, 282 H Division: On Monday morning at half-past twelve o'clock I was on fixed point duty opposite Brady-street, Whitechapel-road, when I saw the last witness stooping down to pick up something about twenty yards from me. As I went towards him he beckoned with his finger, and said, "Policeman, there is a knife lying here." I then saw a long-bladed knife on the doorstep. I picked up the knife, and found it was smothered with blood.

[Coroner] Was it wet? - Dry. A handkerchief, which was also blood-stained, was bound round the handle and tied with a string. I asked the lad how he came to see it, and he said, "I was just looking around, and I saw something white." I asked him what he did out so late, and he replied, "I have been to a friend's in Bath-gardens." I took down his name and address, and he went to the police-station with me. The knife and handkerchief are those produced. The boy was sober, and his manner natural. He said that the knife made his blood run cold, adding, "We hear of such funny things nowadays." I had passed the step a quarter of an hour before. I could not be positive, but I do not think the knife was there then. About an hour earlier I stood near the door, and saw the landlady let out a woman. The knife was not there then. I handed the knife and handkerchief to Dr. Phillips on Monday afternoon.

Mr. George Baxter Phillips: I live at No. 2, Spital-square, and am surgeon of the H Division of police. I was called on Sunday morning last at twenty past one to Leman-street Police-station, and was sent on to Berner-street, to a yard at the side of what proved to be a club-house. I found Inspector Pinhorn and Acting-Superintendent West in possession of a body, which had already been seen by Dr. Blackwell, who had arrived some time before me. The body was lying on its left side, the face being turned towards the wall, the head towards the yard, and the feet toward the street. The left arm was extended from elbow, and a packet of cachous was in the hand. Similar ones were in the gutter. I took them from the hand and gave them to Dr. Blackwell. The right arm was lying over the body, and the back of the hand and wrist had on them clotted blood. The legs were drawn up, feet close to wall, body still warm, face warm, hands cold, legs quite warm, silk handkerchief round throat, slightly torn (so is my note, but I since find it is cut). I produce the handkerchief. This corresponded to the right angle of the jaw. The throat was deeply gashed, and there was an abrasion of the skin, about an inch and a quarter in diameter, under the right clavicle. On Oct. 1, at three p.m., at St. George's Mortuary, present Dr. Blackwell and for part of the time Dr. Reigate and Dr. Blackwell's assistant; temperature being about 55 degrees, Dr. Blackwell and I made a post-mortem examination, Dr. Blackwell kindly consenting to make the dissection, and I took the following note: "Rigor mortis still firmly marked. Mud on face and left side of the head. Matted on the hair and left side. We removed the clothes. We found the body fairly nourished. Over both shoulders, especially the right, from the front aspect under colar bones and in front of chest there is a bluish discolouration which I have watched and seen on two occasions since. On neck, from left to right, there is a clean cut incision six inches in length; incision commencing two and a half inches in a straight line below the angle of the jaw. Three-quarters of an inch over undivided muscle, then becoming deeper, about an inch dividing sheath and the vessels, ascending a little, and then grazing the muscle outside the cartilages on the left side of the neck. The carotid artery on the left side and the other vessels contained in the sheath were all cut through, save the posterior portion of the carotid, to a line about 1-12th of an inch in extent, which prevented the separation of the upper and lower portion of the artery. The cut through the tissues on the right side of the cartilages is more superficial, and tails off to about two inches below the right angle of the jaw. It is evident that the haemorrhage which produced death was caused through the partial severance of the left carotid artery. There is a deformity in the lower fifth of the bones of the right leg, which are not straight, but bow forward; there is a thickening above the left ankle. The bones are here straighter. No recent external injury save to neck. The lower lobe of the ear was torn, as if by the forcible removing or wearing through of an earring, but it was thoroughly healed. The right ear was pierced for an earring, but had not been so injured, and the earring was wanting. On removing the scalp there was no sign of bruising or extravasation of blood between it and the skull-cap. The skull was about one-sixth of an inch in thickness, and dense in texture. The brain was fairly normal. Both lungs were unusually pale. The heart was small; left ventricle firmly contracted, right less so. Right ventricle full of dark clot; left absolutely empty. Partly digested food, apparently consisting of cheese, potato, and farinaceous edibles. Teeth on left lower jaw absent." On Tuesday, at the mortuary, I found the total circumference of the neck 12« inches. I found in the pocket of the underskirt of the deceased a key, as of a padlock, a small piece of lead pencil, a comb, a broken piece of comb, a metal spoon, half a dozen large and one small button, a hook, as if off a dress, a piece of muslin, and one or two small pieces of paper. Examining her jacket I found that although there was a slight amount of mud on the right side, the left was well plastered with mud.

A Juror: You have not mentioned anything about the roof of the mouth. One witness said part of the roof of the mouth was gone. - Witness: That was not noticed.

The Coroner: What was the cause of death? - Undoubtedly the loss of blood from the left carotid artery and the division of the windpipe.

[Coroner] Did you examine the blood at Berner-street carefully, as to its direction and so forth? - Yes.

[Coroner] The blood near to the neck and a few inches to the left side was well clotted, and it had run down the waterway to within a few inches of the side entrance to the club-house.

[Coroner] Were there any spots of blood anywhere else? - I could trace none except that which I considered had been transplanted - if I may use the term - from the original flow from the neck. Roughly estimating it, I should say there was an unusual flow of blood, considering the stature and the nourishment of the body.

By a Juror: I did notice a black mark on one of the legs of the deceased, but could not say that it was due to an adder bite.

Before the witness had concluded his evidence the inquiry was adjourned until Friday, at two o'clock.

Day 4, Monday, October 5, 1888

(The Daily Telegraph, Saturday, October 6, 1888, Page 3)

Yesterday [5 Oct] afternoon at the Vestry Hall of St. George-in-the-East, Cable-street, Mr. Wynne E. Baxter, coroner for East Middlesex, resumed the inquiry concerning the death of the woman who was found early on Sunday last with her throat cut, in a yard adjoining the International Working Men's Club, Berner-street, Commercial-road East.

Dr. Phillips, surgeon of the H Division of police, being recalled, said: On the last occasion I was requested to make a re-examination of the body of the deceased, especially with regard to the palate, and I have since done so at the mortuary, along with Dr. Blackwell and Dr. Gordon

Brown. I did not find any injury to, or absence of, any part of either the hard or the soft palate. The Coroner also desired me to examine the two handkerchiefs which were found on the deceased. I did not discover any blood on them, and I believe that the stains on the larger handkerchief are those of fruit. Neither on the hands nor about the body of the deceased did I find grapes, or connection with them. I am convinced that the deceased had not swallowed either the skin or seed of a grape within many hours of her death. I have stated that the neckerchief which she had on was not torn, but cut. The abrasion which I spoke of on the right side of the neck was only apparently an abrasion, for on washing it it was removed, and the skin found to be uninjured. The knife produced on the last occasion was delivered to me, properly secured, by a constable, and on examination I found it to be such a knife as is used in a chandler's shop, and is called a slicing knife. It has blood upon it, which has characteristics similar to the blood of a human being. It has been recently blunted, and its edge apparently turned by rubbing on a stone such as a kerbstone. It evidently was before a very sharp knife.

The Coroner: Is it such as knife as could have caused the injuries which were inflicted upon the deceased? - Such a knife could have produced the incision and injuries to the neck, but it is not such a weapon as I should have fixed upon as having caused the injuries in this case; and if my opinion as regards the position of the body is correct, the knife in question would become an improbable instrument as having caused the incision.

[Coroner] What is your idea as to the position the body was in when the crime was committed? - I have come to a conclusion as to the position of both the murderer and the victim, and I opine that the latter was seized by the shoulders and placed on the ground, and that the murderer was on her right side when he inflicted the cut. I am of opinion that the cut was made from the left to the right side of the deceased, and taking into account the position of the incision it is unlikely that such a long knife inflicted the wound in the neck.

[Coroner] The knife produced on the last occasion was not sharp pointed, was it? - No, it was rounded at the tip, which was about an inch across. The blade was wider at the base.

[Coroner] Was there anything to indicate that the cut on the neck of the deceased was made with a pointed knife? - Nothing.

[Coroner] Have you formed any opinion as to the manner in which the deceased's right hand became stained with blood? - It is a mystery. There were small oblong clots on the back of the hand. I may say that I am taking it as a fact that after death the hand always remained in the position in which I found it - across the body.

[Coroner] How long had the woman been dead when you arrived at the scene of the murder, do you think? - Within an hour she had been alive.

[Coroner] Would the injury take long to inflict? - Only a few seconds - it might be done in two seconds.

[Coroner] Does the presence of the cachous in the left hand indicate that the murder was committed very suddenly and without any struggle? - Some of the cachous were scattered about the yard.

The Foreman: Do you not think that the woman would have dropped the packet of cachous altogether if she had been thrown to the ground before the injuries were inflicted? - That is an inference which the jury would be perfectly entitled to draw.

The Coroner: I assume that the injuries were not self-inflicted? - I have seen several self-inflicted wounds more extensive than this one, but then they have not usually involved the carotid artery. In this case, as in some others, there seems to have been some knowledge where to cut the throat to cause a fatal result.

[Coroner] Is there any similarity between this case and Annie Chapman's case? - There is very great dissimilarity between the two. In Chapman's case the neck was severed all round down to the vertebral column, the vertebral bones being marked with two sharp cuts, and there had been an evident attempt to separate the bones.

[Coroner] From the position you assume the perpetrator to have been in, would he have been likely to get bloodstained? - Not necessarily, for the commencement of the wound and the injury to the vessels would be away from him, and the stream of blood - for stream it was - would be directed away from him, and towards the gutter in the yard.

[Coroner] Was there any appearance of an opiate or any smell of chloroform? - There was no perceptible trace of any anaesthetic or narcotic. The absence of noise is a difficult question under the circumstances of this case to account for, but it must not be taken for granted that there was not any noise. If there was an absence of noise I cannot account for it.

The Foreman: That means that the woman might cry out after the cut? - Not after the cut.

[Coroner] But why did she not cry out while she was being put on the ground? - She was in a yard, and in a locality where she might cry out very loudly and no notice be taken of her. It was possible for the woman to draw up her legs after the wound, but she could not have turned over. The wound was inflicted by drawing the knife across the throat. A short knife, such as a shoemaker's well-ground knife, would do the same thing. My reason for believing that deceased was injured when on the ground was partly on account of the absence of blood anywhere on the left side of the body and between it and the wall.

A Juror: Was there any trace of malt liquor in the stomach? - There was no trace.

Dr. Blackwell [recalled] (who assisted in making the post-mortem examination) said: I can confirm Dr. Phillips as to the appearances at the mortuary. I may add that I removed the cachous from the left hand of the deceased, which was nearly open. The packet was lodged between the thumb and the first finger, and was partially hidden from view. It was I who spilt them in removing them from the hand. My impression is that the hand gradually relaxed while the woman was dying, she dying in a fainting condition from the loss of blood. I do not think that I made myself quite clear as to whether it was possible for this to have been a case of suicide. What I meant to say was that, taking all the facts into consideration, more especially the absence of any instrument in the hand, it was impossible to have been a suicide. I have myself seen many equally severe wounds self-inflicted. With respect to the knife which was found, I should like to say that I concur with Dr. Phillips in his opinion that, although it might possibly have inflicted the injury, it is an extremely unlikely instrument to have been used. It appears to me that a murderer, in using a round-pointed instrument, would seriously handicap himself, as he would be only able to use it in one particular way. I am told that slaughterers always use a sharp- pointed instrument.

The Coroner: No one has suggested that this crime was committed by a slaughterer. - Witness: I simply intended to point out the inconvenience that might arise from using a blunt-pointed weapon.

The Foreman: Did you notice any marks or bruises about the shoulders? - They were what we call pressure marks. At first they were very obscure, but subsequently they became very evident. They were not what are ordinarily called bruises; neither is there any abrasion. Each shoulder was about equally marked.

A Juror: How recently might the marks have been caused? - That is rather difficult to say.

[Coroner] Did you perceive any grapes near the body in the yard? - No.

[Coroner] Did you hear any person say that they had seen grapes there? - I did not.

Mr. Sven Ollsen deposed: I live at No. 23, Prince's-square, St. George's-in-the-East, and am clerk of the Swedish Church there. I have examined the body of the deceased at the mortuary. I have seen her before.

The Coroner: Often? - Yes. For how many years? - Seventeen.

[Coroner] Was she a Swede? - Yes.

[Coroner] What was her name? - Her name was Elizabeth Stride, and she was the wife of John Thomas Stride, carpenter. Her maiden name was Elizabeth Gustafdotter. She was born at Torlands, near Gothenburg, on Nov. 27, 1843.

How do you get these facts? - From the register at our church. Do you keep a register of all the members of your church? - [Coroner] Of course. We register those who come into this country bringing a certificate and desiring to be registered.

[Coroner] When was she registered? - Her registry is dated July 10, 1866, and she was then registered as an unmarried woman.

[Coroner] Was she married at your church? - No.

[Coroner] Then how do you know she was the wife of John Thomas Stride? - In the registry I find a memorandum, undated, in the handwriting of the Rev. Mr, Palmayer, in Swedish, that she was married to an Englishman named John Thos. Stride. This registry is a new one, and copied from an older book. I have seen the original, and it was written by Mr. Frost, our pastor, until two years ago. I know the Swedish hymn book produced, dated 1821. I gave it to the deceased.

[Coroner] When? - Last winter, I think. Do you know when she was married to Stride? - I think it was in 1869.

[Coroner] Do you know when he died? - No. She told me about the time the Princess Alice went down that her husband was drowned in that vessel.

[Coroner] Was she in good circumstances then? - She was very poor.

[Coroner] Then she would have been glad of any assistance? - Yes.

[Coroner] Did you give her some? - I did about that time.

[Coroner] Do you remember that there was a subscription raised for the relatives of the sufferers by the Princess Alice? - No.

[Coroner] I can tell you that there was, and I can tell you another thing - that no person of the name of Stride made any application. If her story had been true, don't you think she would have applied? - I do not know.

[Coroner] Have you any schools connected with the Swedish Church? - No, not in London.

[Coroner] Did not ever hear that this woman had any children? - I do not remember.

[Coroner] Did you ever see her husband? - No.

[Coroner] Did your church ever assist her before her husband died? - Yes, I think so; just before he died.

[Coroner] Where has she been living lately? - I have nothing to show. Two years ago she gave her address as Devonshire-street, Commercial-road.

[Coroner] Did she then explain what she was doing? - She stated that she was doing a little work in sewing.

[Coroner] Could she speak English well? - Pretty well.

[Coroner] Do you know when she came to England? - I believe a little before the register was made, in 1866.

William Marshall, examined by the Coroner, said: I reside at No. 64, Berner-street, and am a labourer at an indigo warehouse. I have seen the body at the mortuary. I saw the deceased on Saturday night last.

[Coroner] Where? - In our street, three doors from my house, about a quarter to twelve o'clock. She was on the pavement, opposite No. 58, between Fairclough-street and Boyd-street.

[Coroner] What was she doing? - She was standing talking to a man.

[Coroner] How do you know this was the same woman? - I recognise her both by her face and dress. She did not then have a flower in her breast.

[Coroner] Were the man and woman whom you saw talking quietly? - They were talking together.

[Coroner] Can you describe the man at all? - There was no gas-lamp near. The nearest was at the corner, about twenty feet off. I did not see the face of the man distinctly.

[Coroner] Did you notice how he was dressed? - In a black cut-away coat and dark trousers.

[Coroner] Was he young or old? - Middle-aged he seemed to be.

[Coroner] Was he wearing a hat? - No, a cap.

[Coroner] What sort of a cap? - A round cap, with a small peak. It was something like what a sailor would wear.

[Coroner] What height was he? - About 5ft. 6in.

[Coroner] Was he thin or stout? - Rather stout.

[Coroner] Did he look well dressed? - Decently dressed.

[Coroner] What class of man did he appear to be? - I should say he was in business, and did nothing like hard work.

[Coroner] Not like a dock labourer? - No.

[Coroner] Nor a sailor? - No.

[Coroner] Nor a butcher? - No.

[Coroner] A clerk? - He had more the appearance of a clerk.

[Coroner] Is that the best suggestion you can make? - It is.

[Coroner] You did not see his face. Had he any whiskers? - I cannot say. I do not think he had.

[Coroner] Was he wearing gloves? - No.

[Coroner] Was he carrying a stick or umbrella in his hands? - He had nothing in his hands that I am aware of.

[Coroner] You are quite sure that the deceased is the woman you saw? - Quite. I did not take much notice whether she was carrying anything in her hands.

[Coroner] What first attracted your attention to the couple? - By their standing there for some time, and he was kissing her.

[Coroner] Did you overhear anything they said? - I heard him say, "You would say anything but your prayers."

[Coroner] Different people talk in a different tone and in a different way. Did his voice give you the idea of a clerk? - Yes, he was mild speaking.

[Coroner] Did he speak like an educated man? - I thought so. I did not hear them say anything more. They went away after that. I did not hear the woman say anything, but after the man made that observation she laughed. They went away down the street, towards Ellen-street. They would not then pass No. 40 (the club).

[Coroner] How was the woman dressed? - In a black jacket and skirt.

[Coroner] Was either the worse for drink? - No, I thought not.

[Coroner] When did you go indoors? - About twelve o'clock.

[Coroner] Did you hear anything more that night? - Not till I heard that the murder had taken place, just after one o'clock. While I was standing at my door, from half-past eleven to twelve, there was no rain at all. The deceased had on a small black bonnet. The couple were standing between my house and the club for about ten minutes.

Detective-Inspector Reid: Then they passed you? - Yes.

A Juror: Did you not see the man's face as he passed? - No; he was looking towards the woman, and had his arm round her neck. There is a gas lamp at the corner of Boyd-street. It was not closing time when they passed me.

James Brown: I live in Fairclough-street, and am a dock labourer. I have seen the body in the mortuary. I did not know deceased, but I saw her about a quarter to one on Sunday morning last.

The Coroner: Where were you? - I was going from my house to the chandler's shop at the corner of the Berner-street and Fairclough-street, to get some supper. I stayed there three or four minutes, and then went back home, when I saw a man and woman standing at the corner of the Board School. I was in the road just by the kerb, and they were near the wall.

[Coroner] Did you see enough to make you certain that the deceased was the woman? - I am almost certain.

[Coroner] Did you notice any flower in her dress? - No.

[Coroner] What were they doing? - He was standing with his arm against the wall; she was inclined towards his arm, facing him, and with her back to the wall.

[Coroner] Did you notice the man? - I saw that he had a long dark coat on.

[Coroner] An overcoat? - Yes; it seemed so.

[Coroner] Had he a hat or a cap on? - I cannot say.

[Coroner] You are sure it was not her dress that you chiefly noticed? - Yes. I saw nothing light in colour about either of them.

[Coroner] Was it raining at the time? - No. I went on.

[Coroner] Did you hear anything more? - When I had nearly finished my supper I heard screams of "Murder" and "Police." This was a quarter of an hour after I had got home. I did not look at any clock at the chandler's shop. I arrived home first at ten minutes past twelve o'clock, and I believe it was not raining then.

[Coroner] Did you notice the height of the man? - I should think he was 5ft. 7in.

[Coroner] Was he thin or stout? - He was of average build.

[Coroner] Did either of them seem the worse for drink? - No.

[Coroner] Did you notice whether either spoke with a foreign accent? - I did not notice any. When I heard screams I opened my window, but could not see anybody. The cries were of moving people going in the direction of Grove-street. Shortly afterwards I saw a policeman standing at the corner of Christian- street, and a man called him to Berner-street.

William Smith, 452 H Division: On Saturday last I went on duty at ten p.m. My beat was past Berner- street, and would take me twenty-five minutes or half an hour to go round. I was in Berner-street about half-past twelve or twenty-five minutes to one o'clock, and having gone round my beat, was at the Commercial-road corner of Berner-street again at one o'clock. I was not called. I saw a crowd outside the gates of No. 40, Berner-street. I heard no cries of "Police." When I came to the spot two constables had already arrived. The gates at the side of the club were not then closed. I do not remember that I passed any person on my way down. I saw that the woman was dead, and I went to the police-station for the ambulance, leaving the other constables in charge of the body. Dr. Blackwell's assistant arrived just as I was going away.

The Coroner: Had you noticed any man or woman in Berner-street when you were there before? - Yes, talking together.

[Coroner] Was the woman anything like the deceased? - Yes. I saw her face, and I think the body at the mortuary is that of the same woman.

[Coroner] Are you certain? - I feel certain. She stood on the pavement a few yards from where the body was found, but on the opposite side of the street.

[Coroner] Did you look at the man at all? - Yes.

[Coroner] What did you notice about him? - He had a parcel wrapped in a newspaper in his hand. The parcel was about 18in. long and 6in. to 8in. broad.

[Coroner] Did you notice his height? - He was about 5ft. 7in.

[Coroner] His hat? - He wore a dark felt deerstalker's hat.

[Coroner] Clothes? - His clothes were dark. The coat was a cutaway coat.

[Coroner] Did you overhear any conversation? - No.

[Coroner] Did they seem to be sober? - Yes, both.

[Coroner] Did you see the man's face? - He had no whiskers, but I did not notice him much. I should say he was twenty-eight years of age. He was of respectable appearance, but I could not state what he was. The woman had a flower in her breast. It rained very little after eleven o'clock. There were but few about in the bye streets. When I saw the body at the mortuary I recognised it at once.

Michael Kidney, the man with whom the deceased last lived, being recalled, stated: I recognise the Swedish hymn-book produced as one belonging to the deceased. She used to have it at my place. I found it in the next room to the one I occupy - in Mrs. Smith's room. Mrs Smith said deceased gave it to her when she left last Tuesday - not as a gift, but to take care of. When deceased and I lived together I put a padlock on the door when we left the house. I had the key, but deceased has got in and out when I have been away. I found she had been there during my absence on Wednesday of last week - the day after she left - and taken some things.

[Coroner] The Coroner: What made you think there was anything the matter with the roof of her mouth? - She told me so.

[Coroner] Have you ever examined it? - No.

[Coroner] Well, the doctors say there is nothing the matter with it? - Well, I only know what she told me.

Philip Krantz (who affirmed) deposed: I live at 40, Berner-street, and am editor of the Hebrew paper called "The Worker's Friend." I work in a room forming part of the printing office at the back of the International Working Men's Club. Last Saturday night I was in my room from nine o'clock until one of the members of the club came and told me that there was a woman lying in the yard.

[Coroner] Had you heard any sound up to that time? - No.

[Coroner] Any cry? - No. Or scream? - No.

[Coroner] Or anything unusual? - No.

[Coroner] Was your window or door open? - No.

[Coroner] Supposing a woman had screamed, would you have heard it? - They were singing in the club, so I might not have heard. When I heard the alarm I went out and saw the deceased, but did not observe any stranger there.

[Coroner] Did you look to see if anybody was about - anybody who might have committed the murder? - I did look. I went out to the gates, and found that some members of the club had gone for the police.

[Coroner] Do you think it possible that any stranger escaped from the yard while you were there? - No, but he might have done so before I came. I was afterwards searched and examined at the club.

Constable Albert Collins, 12 H. R., stated that by order of the doctors, he, at half-past five o'clock on Sunday morning, washed away the blood caused by the murder.

Detective-Inspector Reid said: I received a telegram at 1.25 on Sunday morning last at Commercial- street Police-office. I at once proceeded to No. 40, Berner-street, where I saw several police officers, Drs. Phillips and Blackwell, and a number of residents in the yard and persons who had come there and been shut in by the police. At that time Drs. Phillips and Blackwell were examining the throat of the deceased. A thorough search was made by the police of the yard and the houses in it, but no trace could be found of any person who might have committed the murder. As soon as the search was over the whole of the persons who had come into the yard and the members of the club were interrogated, their names and addresses taken, their pockets searched by the police, and their clothes and hands examined by the doctors. The people were twenty-eight in number. Each was dealt with separately, and they properly accounted for themselves. The houses were inspected a second time and the occupants examined and their rooms searched. A loft close by was searched, but no trace could be found of the murderer. A description was taken of the body, and circulated by wire around the stations. Inquiries were made at the different houses in the street, but no person could be found who had heard screams or disturbance during the night. I examined the wall near where the body was found, but could detect no spots of blood. About half-past four the body was removed to the mortuary. Having given information of the murder to the coroner I returned to the yard and made another examination and found that the blood had been removed. It being daylight I searched the walls thoroughly, but could discover no marks of their having been scaled. I then went to the mortuary and took a description of the deceased and her clothing as follows: Aged forty-two; length 5ft. 2in; complexion pale; hair dark brown and curly; eyes light grey; front upper teeth gone. The deceased had on an old black skirt, dark-brown velvet body, a long black jacket trimmed with black fur, fastened on the right side, with a red rose backed by a maidenhair fern. She had two light serge petticoats, white stockings, white chemise with insertion, side-spring boots, and black crape bonnet. In her jacket pocket were two handkerchiefs, a thimble, and a piece of wool on a card. That description was circulated. Since then the police have made a house-to-house inquiry in the immediate neighbourhood, with the result that we have been able to produce the witnesses who have appeared before the Court. The investigation is still going on. Every endeavour is being made to arrest the assassin, but up to the present without success.

**Day 5, Tuesday, October 23, 1888**

(The Times, October 24, 1888)

Detective-Inspector Edmund Reid, recalled, said, - I have examined the books of the Poplar and Stepney Sick Asylum, and find therein the entry of the death of John Thomas William Stride, a carpenter, of Poplar. His death took place on the 24th day of October, 1884. Witness then said that he had found Mrs. Watts, who would give evidence.

Constable Walter Stride stated that he recognised the deceased by the photograph as the person who married his uncle, John Thomas Stride, in 1872 or 1873. His uncle was a carpenter, and the last time witness saw him he was living in the East India Dock-road, Poplar.

Elizabeth Stokes, 5, Charles-street, Tottenham, said, - My husband's name is Joseph Stokes, and he is a brickmaker. My first husband's name was Watts, a wine merchant of Bath. Mrs. Mary Malcolm, of 15, Eagle-street, Red Lion-square, Holborn, is my sister. I have received an anonymous letter from Shepton Mallet, saying my first husband is alive.

I want to clear my character. My sister I have not seen for years. She has given me a dreadful character. Her evidence is all false. I have five brothers and sisters.

A juryman. - Perhaps she refers to another sister.

Inspector Reid. - She identified the deceased person as her sister, and said she had a crippled foot. This witness has a crippled foot.

Witness. - This has put me to a dreadful trouble and trial. I have only a poor crippled husband, who is now outside. It is a shame my sister should say what she has said about me, and that the innocent should suffer for the guilty.

The Coroner. - Is Mrs. Malcolm here?

Inspector Reid. - No, Sir.

The Coroner, in summing up, said the jury would probably agree with him that it would be unreasonable to adjourn this inquiry again on the chance of something further being ascertained to elucidate the mysterious case on which they had devoted so much time. The first difficulty which presented itself was the identification of the deceased. That was not an unimportant matter. Their trouble was principally occasioned by Mrs. Malcolm, who, after some hesitation, and after having had two further opportunities of viewing again the body, positively swore that the deceased was her sister - Mrs. Elizabeth Watts, of Bath. It had since been clearly proved that she was mistaken, notwithstanding the visions which were simultaneously vouchsafed at the hour of the death to her and her husband. If her evidence was correct, there were points of resemblance between the deceased and Elizabeth Watts which almost reminded one of the Comedy of Errors. Both had been courted by policemen; they both bore the same Christian name, and were of the same age; both lived with sailors; both at one time kept coffee-houses at Poplar; both were nick-named "Long Liz;" both were said to have had children in charge of their husbands' friends; both were given to drink; both lived in East-end common lodging-houses; both had been charged at the Thames Police-court; both had escaped punishment on the ground that they were subject to epileptic fits, although the friends of both were certain that this was a fraud; both had lost their front teeth, and both had been leading very questionable lives. Whatever might be the true explanation of this marvellous similarity, it appeared to be pretty satisfactorily proved that the deceased was Elizabeth Stride, and that about the year 1869 she was married to a carpenter named John Thomas Stride. Unlike the other victims in the series of crimes in this neighborhood - a district teeming with representatives of all nations - she was not an Englishwoman. She was born in Sweden in the year 1843, but, having resided in this country for upwards of 22 years, she could speak English fluently and without much foreign accent. At one time the deceased and her husband kept a coffee-house in Poplar. At another time she was staying in Devonshire-street, Commercial-road, supporting herself, it was said, by sewing and charring. On and off for the last six years she lived in a common lodging-house in the notorious lane called Flower and Dean-street. She was there known only by the nick-name of "Long Liz," and often told a tale, which might have been apocryphal, of her husband and children having gone down with the Princess Alice. The deputy of the lodging-house stated that while with her she was a quiet and sober woman, although she used at times to stay out late at night - an offence very venial, he suspected, among those who frequented the establishment. For the last two years the deceased had been living at a common lodging-house in Dorset-street, Spitalfields, with Michael Kidney, a waterside labourer, belonging to the Army Reserve. But at intervals during that period, amounting altogether to about five months, she left him without any apparent reason, except a desire to be free from the restraint even of that connexion, and to obtain greater opportunity of indulging her drinking habits. She was last seen alive by Kidney in Commercial- street on the evening of Tuesday, September 25. She was sober, but never returned home that night. She alleged that she had some words with her paramour, but this he denied. The next day she called during his absence, and took away some things, but, with this exception, they did not know what became of her until the following Thursday, when she made her appearance at her old quarters in Flower and Dean-street. Here she remained until Saturday, September 29. On that day she cleaned the deputy's rooms, and received a small remuneration for her trouble. Between 6 and 7 o'clock on that evening she was in the kitchen wearing the jacket, bonnet, and striped silk neckerchief which were afterwards found on her. She had at least 6d. in her possession, which was possibly spent during the evening. Before leaving she gave a piece of velvet to a friend to take care of until her return, but she said neither where she was going nor when she would return. She had not paid for her lodgings, although she was in a position to do so. They knew nothing of her movements during the next four or five hours at least - possibly not till the finding of her lifeless body. But three witnesses spoke to having seen a woman that they identified as the deceased with more or less certainty, and at times within an hour and a-quarter of the period when, and at places within 100 yards of the spot where she was ultimately found. William Marshall, who lived at 64, Berner-street, was standing at his doorway from half-past 11 till midnight. About a quarter to 12 o'clock he saw the deceased talking to a man between Fairclough-street and Boyd-street. There was every demonstration of affection by the man during the ten minutes they stood together, and when last seen, strolling down the road towards Ellen- street, his arms were round her neck. At 12 30 p.m. the constable on the beat (William Smith) saw the deceased in Berner-street standing on the pavement a few yards from Commercial-street, and he observed she was wearing a flower in her dress. A quarter of an hour afterwards James Brown, of Fairclough-street, passed the deceased close to the Board school. A man was at her side leaning against the wall, and the deceased was heard to say, "Not to-night, but some other night." Now, if this evidence was to be relied on, it would appear that the deceased was in the company of a man for upwards of an hour immediately before her death, and that within a quarter of an hour of her being found a corpse she was refusing her companion something in the immediate neighbourhood of where she met her death. But was this the deceased? And even if it were, was it one and the same man who was seen in her company on three different occasions? With regard to the identity of the woman, Marshall had the opportunity of watching her for ten minutes while standing talking in the street at a short distance from him, and she afterwards passed close to him. The constable feels certain that the woman he observed was the deceased, and when he afterwards was called to the scene of the crime he at once recognized her and made a statement; while Brown was almost certain that the deceased was the woman to whom his attention was attracted. It might be thought that the frequency of the occurrence of men and women being seen together under similar circumstances might have led to mistaken identity; but the police stated, and several of the witnesses corroborated the statement, that although many couples are to be seen at night in the Commercial-road, it was exceptional to meet them in Berner-street. With regard to the man seen, there were many points of similarity, but some of dissimilarity, in the descriptions of the three witnesses; but these discrepancies did not conclusively prove that there was more than one man in the company of the deceased, for every day's experience showed how facts were differently observed and differently described by honest and intelligent witnesses. Brown, who saw least in consequence of the darkness of the spot at which the two were standing, agreed with Smith that his clothes were dark and that his height was about 5ft. 7in., but he appeared to him to be wearing an overcoat nearly down to his heels; while the description of Marshall accorded with that of Smith in every respect but two. They agreed that he was respectably dressed in a black cut away coat and dark trousers, and that he was of middle age and without whiskers. On the other hand, they differed with regard to what he was wearing on his head. Smith stated he wore a hard felt deer stalker of dark colour; Marshall that he was wearing a round cap with a small peak, like a sailor's. They also differed as to whether he had anything in his hand. Marshall stated that he observed nothing. Smith was very precise, and stated that he was carrying a parcel, done up in a newspaper, about 18in. in length and 6in. to 8in. in width. These differences suggested either that the woman was, during the evening, in the company of more than one man - a not very improbable supposition - or that the witness had been mistaken in detail. If they were correct in assuming that the man seen in the company of deceased by the three was one and the same person it followed that he must have spent much time and trouble to induce her to place herself in his diabolical clutches. They last saw her alive at the corner of Fairclough-street and Berner-street, saying "Not to-night, but some other night." Within a quarter of an hour her lifeless body was found at a spot only a few yards from where she was last seen alive. It was late, and there were few people about, but the place to which the two repaired could not have been selected on account of its being quiet or unfrequented. It had only the merit of darkness. It was the passage-way leading into a court in which several families resided. Adjoining the passage and court there was a club of Socialists, who, having finished their debate, were singing and making merry. The deceased and her companion must have seen the lights of the clubroom, and the kitchen, and of the printing office. They must have heard the music and dancing, for the windows were open. There were persons in the yard but a short time previous to their arrival. At 40 minutes past 12, one of the members of the club, named Morris Eagle, passed the spot where the deceased drew her last breath, passing through the gateway to the back door, which opened into the yard. At 1 o'clock the body was found by the manager of the club. He had been out all day, and returned at the time. He was in a two-wheeled barrow drawn by a pony, and as he entered the gateway his pony shied at some object on his right. There was no lamp in the yard, and having just come out of the street it was too dark to see what the object was and he passed on further down the yard. He returned on foot, and on searching found the body of deceased with her throat cut. If he had not actually disturbed the wretch in the very act, at least he must have been close on his heels; possibly the man was alarmed by the sound of the approaching cart, for the death had only just taken place. He did not inspect the body himself with any care, but blood was flowing from the throat, even when Spooner reached the spot some few minutes afterwards, and although the bleeding had stopped when Dr. Blackwell's assistant arrived, the whole of her body and the limbs, except her hands, were warm, and even at 16 minutes past 1 a.m. Dr. Blackwell found her face slightly warm, and her chest and legs quite warm. In this case, as in other similar cases which had occurred in this neighbourhood, no call for assistance was noticed. Although there might have been some noise in the club, it seemed very unlikely that any cry could have been raised without its being heard by some one of those near. The editor of a Socialist paper was quietly at work in a shed down the yard, which was used as a printing office. There were several families in the cottages in the court only a few yards distant, and there were 20 persons in the different rooms of the club. But if there was no cry, how did the deceased meet with her death? The appearance of the injury to her throat was not in itself inconsistent with that of a self-inflicted wound. Both Dr. Phillips and Dr. Blackwell have seen self-inflicted wounds more extensive and severe, but those have not usually involved the carotid artery. Had some sharp instrument been found near the right hand of the deceased this case might have had very much the appearance of a determined suicide. But no such instrument was found, and its absence made suicide an impossibility. The death was, therefore, one by homicide, and it seemed impossible to imagine circumstances which would fit in with the known facts of the case, and which would reduce the crime to manslaughter. There were no signs of any struggle; the clothes were neither torn nor disturbed. It was true that there were marks over both shoulders, produced by pressure of two hands, but the position of the body suggested either that she was willingly placed or placed herself where she was found. Only the soles of her boots were visible. She was still holding in her left hand a packet of cachous, and there was a bunch of flowers still pinned to her dress front. If she had been forcibly placed on the ground, as Dr. Phillips opines, it was difficult to understand how she failed to attract attention, as it was clear from the appearance of the blood on the ground that the throat was not cut until after she was actually on her back. There were no marks of gagging, no bruises on the face, and no trace of any anaesthetic or narcotic in the stomach; while the presence of the cachous in her hand showed that she did not make use of it in self-defence. Possibly the pressure marks may have had a less tragical origin, as Dr. Blackwell says it was difficult to say how recently they were produced. There was one particular which was not easy to explain. When seen by Dr. Blackwell her right hand was lying on the chest, smeared inside and out with blood. Dr. Phillips was unable to make any suggestion how the hand became soiled. There was no injury to the hand, such as they would expect if it had been raised in self-defence while her throat was being cut. Was it done intentionally by her assassin, or accidentally by those who were early on the spot? The evidence afforded no clue. Unfortunately the murderer had disappeared without leaving the slightest trace. Even the cachous were wrapped up in unmarked paper, so that there was nothing to show where they were bought. The cut in the throat might have been effected in such a manner that bloodstains on the hands and clothes of the operator were avoided, while the domestic history of the deed suggested the strong probability that her destroyer was a stranger to her. There was no one among her associates to whom any suspicion had attached. They had not heard that she had had a quarrel with any one - unless they magnified the fact that she had recently left the man with whom she generally cohabited; but this diversion was of so frequent an occurrence that neither a breach of the peace ensued, nor, so far as they knew, even hard words. There was therefore in the evidence no clue to the murderer and no suggested motive for the murder. The deceased was not in possession of any valuables. She was only known to have had a few pence in her pocket at the beginning of the evening. Those who knew her best were unaware of any one likely to injure her. She never accused any one of having threatened her. She never expressed any fear of anyone, and, although she had outbursts of drunkenness, she was generally a quiet woman. The ordinary motives of murder - revenge, jealousy, theft, and passion - appeared, therefore, to be absent from this case; while it was clear from the accounts of all who saw her that night, as well as from the post-mortem examination, that she was not otherwise than sober at the time of her death. In the absence of motive, the age and class of woman selected as victim, and the place and time of the crime, there was a similarity between this case and those mysteries which had recently occurred in that neighborhoods. There had been no skilful mutilation as in the cases of Nichols and Chapman, and no unskillful injuries as in the case in Mitre-square - possibly the work of an imitator; but there had been the same skill exhibited in the way in which the victim had been entrapped, and the injuries inflicted, so as to cause instant death and prevent blood from soiling the operator, and the same daring defiance of immediate detection, which, unfortunately for the peace of the inhabitants and trade of the neighborhood, had hitherto been only too successful. He himself was sorry that the time and attention which the jury had given to the case had not produced a result that would be a perceptible relief to the metropolis - the detection of the criminal; but he was sure that all had used their utmost effort to accomplish this object, and while he desired to thank the gentlemen of the jury for their kind assistance, he was bound to acknowledge the great attention which Inspector Reid and the police had given to the case. He left it to the jury to say, how, when, and by what means the deceased came by her death.

The jury, after a short deliberation, returned a verdict of "Willful murder against some person or persons unknown."

# Catherine Eddowes

Catherine Eddowes a.k.a. Kate Kelly Catherine Eddowes is born on April 14, 1842 in Graisley Green, Wolverhampton. At the time of her death she is 5 feet tall, has hazel eyes and dark auburn hair. She has a tattoo in blue ink on her left forearm "TC." At the time of her death, Catherine Eddowes is suffering from Bright's Disease, a form of Uremia. Friends spoke of Catherine as an intelligent, scholarly woman but one who was possessed of a fierce temper.

Wearing at the time of her murder: Black straw bonnet trimmed in green and black velvet with black beads. Black strings, worn tied to the head. Black cloth jacket trimmed around the collar and cuffs with imitation fur and around the pockets in black silk braid and fur. Large metal buttons.

Dark green chintz skirt, 3 flounces, brown button on waistband. The skirt is patterned with Michaelmas daisies and golden lilies. Man's white vest, matching buttons down front.

Brown linsey bodice, black velvet collar with brown buttons down front Grey stuff petticoat with white waistband Very old green alpaca skirt (worn as undergarment) Very old ragged blue skirt with red flounces, light twill lining (worn as undergarment) White calico chemise No drawers or stays

Pair of men's lace up boots, mohair laces. Right boot repaired with red thread 1 piece of red gauze silk worn as a neckerchief 1 large white pocket handkerchief 1 large white cotton handkerchief with red and white bird's eye border 2 unbleached calico pockets, tape strings 1 blue stripe bed ticking pocket Brown ribbed knee stockings, darned at the feet with white cotton Possessions

2 small blue bags made of bed ticking 2 short black clay pipes 1 tin box containing tea 1 tin box containing sugar 1 tin matchbox, empty 12 pieces white rag, some slightly bloodstained 1 piece coarse linen, white1 piece of blue and white shirting, 3 cornered1 piece red flannel with pins and needles 6 pieces soap 1 small tooth comb 1 white handle table knife 1 metal teaspoon 1 red leather cigarette case with white metal fittings 1 ball hemp 1 piece of old white apron with repair Several buttons and a thimble Mustard tin containing two pawn tickets, One in the name of Emily Birrell, 52 White's Row, dated August 31, 9d for a man's flannel shirt. The other is in the name of Jane Kelly of 6 Dorset Street and dated September 28, 2S for a pair of men's boots. Both addresses are false.

Printed handbill and according to a press report- a printed card for 'Frank Carter,305,Bethnal Green Road Portion of a pair of spectacles 1 red mitten

History: Her father was George Eddowes, a tin plate worker working or apprenticed at the Old Hall Works in Wolverhampton. Her mother is

Catherine (nee Evans). She has two sisters, Elizabeth Fisher and Eliza Gold (their married names). She also has an uncle named William Eddowes.

One contemporary newspaper report gives her history as follows: "Her father and his brother William left their jobs as tinplate workers in Wolverhampton during the tinmen's strike, about 1848. They and their families walked to London. In London they eventually found employment. George and his family stayed, while William took his family back to Wolverhampton and resumed work at Old Hall Works. In the early 1860s Catherine returned to Wolverhampton to visit her family. Her relatives recalled the visit and described her "as very good looking and jolly sort of girl." Catherine is educated at St. John's Charity School, Potter's Field, Tooley Street until her mother dies in 1855, when most of her siblings entered Bermondsey Workhouse and Industrial School. Her education continues when she returns to the care of her aunt in Bison Street, Wolverhampton. She attends Dowgate Charity School. By 1861-1863 she leaves home with Thomas Conway. The Wolverhampton paper summarizes her history somewhat differently: George Eddowes completes his apprenticeship at Old Hall Works and marries Catherine Evans, a cook at the local hostelry. The two go to London in search of their fortunes. While there, George fathers 12 children. His wife, Catherine, dies in 1851 and George a few months later. Catherine is returned to Wolverhampton into the care of an aunt who lived in Bison Street. This may be the aunt who, according to an article in the January 1995 Black Country Bugle, made a gift of a miniature portrait to Catherine which became the basis for the portrait which appears in the Penny Illustrated Paper at the time of her death. At the age of 21, Catherine is still living with her aunt but becomes involved with Thomas Conway, a pensioner from the 18th Royal Irish (though he was not old). Conway enlisted and drew his pension under the name Thomas Quinn. The couple went to Birmingham and other towns making a living selling cheap books of lives written by the pensioner. Again, according to the article in the January 1995 Black Country Bugle, they also specialized in the production of gallows ballads. On one occasion she hawked such a ballad at the execution of her cousin, Christopher Robinson, hanged at Strafford in January 1866. In the course of their travels they returned to Wolverhampton where Catherine gave birth to a child. They return to London but Kate tries to return to her aunt's house after "running away from the pensioner." Her aunt refused her admittance and Kate took refuge in a lodging house on Bison Street. There is no evidence to suggest that she and Conway were ever married. As a couple they had three children. Annie, born 1865 (later Annie Phillips), George, born around 1868 and another son born around 1873. Conway and Eddowes split in 1881 with Kate taking Annie and Conway the boy. In 1881 Catherine moved to Cooney's Lodging House, 55 Flower and Dean Street and met John Kelly. Kelly jobbed around the markets but had been more or less regularly employed by a fruit salesman named Lander. Somewhere in this period Catherine's daughter Annie marries Louis Phillips and begins to move around Bermondsey and Southwark to avoid her mother's scrounging. Frederick Wilkinson, deputy at Cooney's, says Catherine "was not often in drink and was a very jolly woman, often singing." She was generally in the lodging house for the night between 9 and 10 PM. He says she wasn't in the habit of walking the streets and he had never heard of or seen her being intimate with anyone other than Kelly. Kelly himself claimed no knowledge of her ever walking the streets. He says that she sometimes drank to excess but wasn't in the habit. Another sister, Eliza Gold, said that Catherine was of sober habits. Every year, during the season, Kelly and Eddowes went hop picking. In 1888 they went to Hunton near Maidstone in Kent. "We didn't get along too well and started to hoof it home," Kelly says, "We came along in company with another man and woman who had worked in the same fields, but who parted from us to go to Cheltenham when we turned off towards London. The woman, more than likely Emily Birrell, said to Kate, 'I've got a pawn ticket for a flannel shirt. I wish you'd take it since you're going up to town. It is only for 2d, and it may fit your old man.' Kate took it and we trudged along... We did not have money enough to keep us going till we got to town, but we did get there, and came straight to this house (55 Flower and Dean Street). Luck was dead against us... we were both done up for cash." They reached London on Friday, September 28. John managed to earn 6d. Kate took 2d and told Kelly to take the 4d and get a bed at Cooney's. She said she would get a bed at the casual ward in Shoe Lane. The superintendent of the casual ward said that Kate was well known there, but that this was the first time she had been there for a long time. Eddowes explained that she had been hopping in the country but "I have come back to earn the reward offered for the apprehension of the Whitechapel murderer. I think I know him." The superintendent warned her to be careful he didn't murder her. "Oh, no fear of that." she replied. (There is no corroborative evidence for this story and it should be treated with a great deal of scepticism.)

Saturday and Sunday, September 29-30: At 8:00 AM on September 29 she returns to Cooney's Lodging House and sees Kelly. She has been turned out of the Casual Ward for some unspecified trouble. Kelly decided to pawn a pair of boots he had. He does this with a pawnbroker named Jones in Church Street. It was Kate who took them into the shop and pledged them under the name of Jane Kelly. She receives 2/6 for the boots and she and Kelly take the money and buy some food, tea and sugar. Between 10 and 11 AM they were seen by Frederick Wilkinson eating breakfast in the lodging house kitchen.

By afternoon they were again without money. Eddowes says she is going to see if she can get some money from her daughter in Bermondsey. She parts with Kelly in Houndsditch at 2:00 PM, promising to be back no later than 4:00 PM. "I never knew if she went to her daughter's at all," Kelly says at the inquest. "I only wish she had, for we had lived together for some time and never had a quarrel." Kate could not have seen her daughter who had moved since the last time Kate saw her.

8:00 PM: City PC Louis Robinson comes across Eddowes surrounded by a crowd outside 29 Aldgate High Street. She is very drunk and laying in a heap on the pavement. Robinson asks those in the crowd if anyone knew her, no one replied. He pulled her up to her feet and leaned her against the building's shutters but she slipped sideways. With the aid of City PC 959 George Simmons they brought her to Bishopsgate Police Station.Louis Robinson City Police Constable 931 said at Kate's inquest 'On the 29th at 8.30 I was on duty in Aldgate Hight Street, I saw a crowd of persons outside No. 29 - I saw there a woman whom I have since recognised as the Deceased lying on the footway drunk. I asked if there was one that knew her or knew where she lived but I got no answer.'

8:45 PM: Bishopsgate Police Station Sergeant James Byfield notes Eddowes arrival at the station. Supported by PCs Robinson and Simmons, Eddowes was asked her name and she replied "Nothing." At 8:50 PM PC Robinson looked in on her in her cell. She was asleep and smelled of drink. At 9:45 PM The Gaoler, City PC 968 George Hutt, took charge of the prisoners. He visited the cell every half hour during the night upon the directive of Sergeant Byfield.

9:45 PM: City PCs on night beat leave Bishopsgate Station. They are marched behind their Beat Sergeants from Bishopsgate Station to their respective beats. In amongst these men were City PCs Edward Watkins and James Harvey.


Approx 10:00 PM: City PC 881 Edward Watkins commenced his first full round of his beat. This consisted of Duke Street through Heneage Lane, through a portion of Bury Street, then through Creechurch Lane, into Leadenhall Street, along Leadenhall Street into Mitre Street, then into Mitre Square, around the square, back into Mitre Street, then into King Street, along King Street, into St James Place, around St James Place, thence into Duke Street to continue another patrol.

Approx 10:00 PM: City PC 964 James Harvey commenced his beat. From Bevis Marks he moved to Duke Street, into Little Duke Street, to Houndsditch, from Houndsditch back to Duke Street, along Duke Street to Church Passage, back again into Duke Street, to Aldgate, from there to Mitre Street, back again to Houndsditch, up Houndsditch, to Little Duke Street, again back to Houndsditch, to Goring Street, up Goring Street and back to Bevis Marks.

12:15 AM: Kate is heard singing softly to herself in the cell. 12:30 AM: She calls out to ask when she will be released. "When you are capable of taking care of yourself." Hutt replies. "I can do that now." Kate informs him.

12:55 AM: Sergeant Byfield instructs PC Hutt to see if any prisoners were fit to be released. Kate was found to be sober. She gives her name as Mary Ann Kelly, and her address as 6 Fashion Street. Kate is released.

She leaves the station at 1:00 AM.

"What time is it?" she asks Hutt.

"Too late for you to get anything to drink." he replies.

"I shall get a damn fine hiding when I get home." She tells him.

Hutt replies, " And serve you right, you had no right to get drunk."

Hutt pushes open the swinging door of that station.

"This way missus," he says, "please pull it to."

"All right'" Kate replies, "Goodnight, old cock."

She turned left out the doorway which took her in the opposite direction of what would have been the fastest way back to Flower and Dean Street. She appears to be heading back toward Aldgate High Street where she had become drunk. On going down Houndsditch she would have passed the entrance to Duke Street, at the end of which was Church Passage which led into Mitre Square.

It is estimated that it would have taken less than ten minutes to reach Mitre Square. This leaves a thirty minute gap from the time she leaves the police station to the time she is seen outside of Mitre Square.

1:35 AM: Joseph Lawende, a commercial traveler in the cigarette trade, Joseph Hyam Levy, a butcher and Harry Harris, a furniture dealer leave the Imperial Club at 16-17 Duke Street. At the corner of Duke Street and Church Passage they see Eddowes and a man talking. She is standing facing the man with her hand on his chest, but not in a manner to suggest that she is resisting him. Lawende describes the man as 30 years old, 5 foot 7 inches tall, fair complexion and mustache with a medium build. He is wearing a pepper and salt colored jacket which fits loosely, a grey cloth cap with a peak of the same color. He has a reddish handkerchief knotted around his neck. Over all he gives the appearance of being a sailor. Lawende will later identify Catherine Eddowes clothes as the same as those worn by the woman he saw that night.

Approx 1:45 PM: PC Edward Watkins discovers Eddowes' body in Mitre Square.

Dr. Frederick Gordon Brown, London police surgeon called in at the murder, arrived at Mitre Square around 2:00 AM. His report is as follows. "The body was on its back, the head turned to left shoulder. The arms by the side of the body as if they had fallen there. Both palms upwards, the fingers slightly bent. The left leg extended in a line with the body. The abdomen was exposed. Right leg bent at the thigh and knee. The throat cut across. The intestines were drawn out to a large extent and placed over the right shoulder -- they were smeared over with some feculent matter. A piece of about two feet was quite detached from the body and placed between the body and the left arm, apparently by design. The lobe and auricle of the right ear were cut obliquely through. There was a quantity of clotted blood on the pavement on the left side of the neck round the shoulder and upper part of arm, and fluid blood-coloured serum which had flowed under the neck to the right shoulder, the pavement sloping in that direction. Body was quite warm. No death stiffening had taken place. She must have been dead most likely within the half hour. We looked for superficial bruises and saw none. No blood on the skin of the abdomen or secretion of any kind on the thighs. No spurting of blood on the bricks or pavement around. No marks of blood below the middle of the body. Several buttons were found in the clotted blood after the body was removed. There was no blood on the front of the clothes. There were no traces of recent connexion. When the body arrived at Golden Lane, some of the blood was dispersed through the removal of the body to the mortuary. The clothes were taken off carefully from the body. A piece of deceased's ear dropped from the clothing. I made a post mortem examination at half past two on Sunday afternoon. Rigor mortis was well marked; body not quite cold. Green discoloration over the abdomen. After washing the left hand carefully, a bruise the size of a sixpence, recent and red, was discovered on the back of the left hand between the thumb and first finger. A few small bruises on right shin of older date. The hands and arms were bronzed. No bruises on the scalp, the back of the body, or the elbows. The face was very much mutilated. There was a cut about a quarter of an inch through the lower left eyelid, dividing the structures completely through. The upper eyelid on that side, there was a scratch through the skin on the left upper eyelid, near to the angle of the nose. The right eyelid was cut through to about half an inch. There was a deep cut over the bridge of the nose, extending from the left border of the nasal bone down near the angle of the jaw on the right side of the cheek. This cut went into the bone and divided all the structures of the cheek except the mucous membrane of the mouth. The tip of the nose was quite detached by an oblique cut from the bottom of the nasal bone to where the wings of the nose join on to the face. A cut from this divided the upper lip and extended through the substance of the gum over the right upper lateral incisor tooth. About half an inch from the top of the nose was another oblique cut. There was a cut on the right angle of the mouth as if the cut of a point of a knife. The cut extended an inch and a half, parallel with the lower lip.

There was on each side of cheek a cut which peeled up the skin, forming a triangular flap about an inch and a half. On the left cheek there were two abrasions of the epithelium under the left ear. The throat was cut across to the extent of about six or seven inches. A superficial cut commenced about an inch and a half below the lobe below, and about two and a half inches behind the left ear, and extended across the throat to about three inches below the lobe of the right ear. The big muscle across the throat was divided through on the left side. The large vessels on the left side of the neck were severed. The larynx was severed below the vocal chord. All the deep structures were severed to the bone, the knife marking intervertebral cartilages. The sheath of the vessels on the right side was just opened. The carotid artery had a fine hole opening, the internal jugular vein was opened about an inch and a half -- not divided. The blood vessels contained clot. All these injuries were performed by a sharp instrument like a knife, and pointed. The cause of death was haemorrhage from the left common carotid artery. The death was immediate and the mutilations were inflicted after death. We examined the abdomen. The front walls were laid open from the breast bones to the pubes. The cut commenced opposite the enciform cartilage. The incision went upwards, not penetrating the skin that was over the sternum. It then divided the enciform cartilage. The knife must have cut obliquely at the expense of that cartilage. Behind this, the liver was stabbed as if by the point of a sharp instrument. Below this was another incision into the liver of about two and a half inches, and below this the left lobe of the liver was slit through by a vertical cut. Two cuts were shewn by a jagging of the skin on the left side. The abdominal walls were divided in the middle line to within a quarter of an inch of the navel. The cut then took a horizontal course for two inches and a half towards the right side. It then divided round the navel on the left side, and made a parallel incision to the former horizontal incision, leaving the navel on a tongue of skin. Attached to the navel was two and a half inches of the lower part of the rectus muscle on the left side of the abdomen. The incision then took an oblique direction to the right and was shelving. The incision went down the right side of the vagina and rectum for half an inch behind the rectum. There was a stab of about an inch on the left groin. This was done by a pointed instrument. Below this was a cut of three inches going through all tissues making a wound of the peritoneum about the same extent. An inch below the crease of the thigh was a cut extending from the anterior spine of the ilium obliquely down the inner side of the left thigh and separating the left labium, forming a flap of skin up to the groin. The left rectus muscle was not detached. There was a flap of skin formed by the right thigh, attaching the right labium, and extending up to the spine of the ilium. The muscles on the right side inserted into the frontal ligaments were cut through. The skin was retracted through the whole of the cut through the abdomen, but the vessels were not clotted. Nor had there been any appreciable bleeding from the vessels. I draw the conclusion that the act was made after death, and there would not have been much blood on the murderer. The cut was made by someone on the right side of the body, kneeling below the middle of the body. I removed the content of the stomach and placed it in a jar for further examination. There seemed very little in it in the way of food or fluid, but from the cut end partly digested farinaceous food escaped. The intestines had been detached to a large extent from the mesentery. About two feet of the colon was cut away. The sigmoid flexure was invaginated into the rectum very tightly. Right kidney was pale, bloodless with slight congestion of the base of the pyramids.

There was a cut from the upper part of the slit on the under surface of the liver to the left side, and another cut at right angles to this, which were about an inch and a half deep and two and a half inches long. Liver itself was healthy. The gall bladder contained bile. The pancreas was cut, but not through, on the left side of the spinal column. Three and a half inches of the lower border of the spleen by half an inch was attached only to the peritoneum. The peritoneal lining was cut through on the left side and the left kidney carefully taken out and removed. The left renal artery was cut through. I would say that someone who knew the position of the kidney must have done it. The lining membrane over the uterus was cut through. The womb was cut through horizontally, leaving a stump of three quarters of an inch. The rest of the womb had been taken away with some of the ligaments. The vagina and cervix of the womb was uninjured. The bladder was healthy and uninjured, and contained three or four ounces of water. There was a tongue-like cut through the anterior wall of the abdominal aorta. The other organs were healthy. There were no indications of connexion. I believe the wound in the throat was first inflicted. I believe she must have been lying on the ground. The wounds on the face and abdomen prove that they were inflicted by a sharp, pointed knife, and that in the abdomen by one six inches or longer. I believe the perpetrator of the act must have had considerable knowledge of the position of the organs in the abdominal cavity and the way of removing them. It required a great deal of medical knowledge to have removed the kidney and to know where it was placed. The parts removed would be of no use for any professional purpose.

I think the perpetrator of this act had sufficient time, or he would not have nicked the lower eyelids. It would take at least five minutes. I cannot assign any reason for the parts being taken away. I feel sure that there was no struggle, and believe it was the act of one person. The throat had been so instantly severed that no noise could have been emitted. I should not expect much blood to have been found on the person who had inflicted these wounds. The wounds could not have been self-inflicted. My attention was called to the apron, particularly the corner of the apron with a string attached. The blood spots were of recent origin. I have seen the portion of an apron produced by Dr. Phillips and stated to have been found in Goulston Street. It is impossible to say that it is human blood on the apron. I fitted the piece of apron, which had a new piece of material on it (which had evidently been sewn on to the piece I have), the seams of the borders of the two actually corresponding. Some blood and apparently faecal matter was found on the portion that was found in Goulston Street.

# Inquest: Catherine Eddowes

Day 1, Thursday, October 4, 1888

(The Daily Telegraph, Friday, October 5, 1888, Page 3)

At the Coroner's Court, Golden-lane, yesterday [4 Oct], Mr. S. F. Langham, coroner for the City of London, opened the inquest into the death of Catherine Eddowes, or Conway, or Kelly, who was murdered in Mitre-court, Aldgate, about half-past one o'clock on Sunday morning last. The court was crowded, and much interest was taken in the proceedings, many people standing outside the building during the whole of the day.

Mr. Crawford, City solicitor, appeared on behalf of the Corporation, as responsible for the police; Major Smith and Superintendent Forster represented the officers engaged in the inquiry.

After the jury had viewed the body, which was lying in the adjoining mortuary,

Mr. Crawford, addressing the coroner, said: I appear here as representing the City police in this matter, for the purpose of rendering you every possible assistance, and if I should consider it desirable, in the course of the inquiry, to put any questions to witnesses, probably I shall have your permission when you have finished with them.

The Coroner: Oh, certainly.

The following evidence was then called -

Eliza Gold deposed: I live at 6, Thrawl-street, Spitalfields. I have been married, but my husband is dead. I recognise the deceased as my poor sister (witness here commenced to weep very much, and for a few moments she was unable to proceed with her story). Her name was Catherine Eddowes. I cannot exactly tell where she was living. She was staying with a gentleman, but she was not married to him. Her age last birthday was about 43 years, as far as I can remember. She has been living for some years with Mr. Kelly. He is in court. I last saw her alive about four or five months ago. She used to go out hawking for a living, and was a woman of sober habits. Before she went to live with Kelly, she had lived with a man named Conway for several years, and had two children by him. I cannot tell how many years she lived with Conway. I do not know whether Conway is still living. He was a pensioner from the army, and used to go out hawking also. I do not know on what terms he parted from my sister. I do not know whether she had ever seen him from the time they parted. I am quite certain that the body I have seen is my sister.

By Mr. Crawford: I have not seen Conway for seven or eight years. I believe my sister was living with him then on friendly terms.

[Coroner] Was she living on friendly terms with Kelly? - I cannot say. Three or four weeks ago I saw them together, and they were then on happy terms. I cannot fix the time when I last saw them. They were living at 55, Flower and Dean-street - a lodging-house. My sister when staying there came to see me when I was very ill. From that time, until I saw her in the mortuary, I have not seen her.

A Juryman pointed out that witness previously said she had not seen her sister for three or four months, whilst later on she spoke of three or four weeks.

The Coroner: You said your sister came to see you when you were ill, and that you had not seen her since. Was that three or four weeks ago?

Mrs. Gold: Yes.

[Coroner] So that your saying three or four months was a mistake? - Yes. I am so upset and confused. Witness commenced to cry again. As she could not write she had to affix her mark to the deposition.

John Kelly, a strong-looking labourer, was then called and said: I live at a lodging-house, 55, Flower and Dean-street. Have seen the deceased and recognise her as Catherine Conway. I have been living with her for seven years. She hawked a few things about the streets and lived with me at a common lodging-house in Flower and Dean-street. The lodging-house is known as Cooney's. I last saw her alive about two o'clock in the afternoon of Saturday in Houndsditch. We parted on very good terms. She told me she was going over to Bermondsey to try and find her daughter Annie. Those were the last words she spoke to me. Annie was a daughter whom I believe she had had by Conway. She promised me before we parted that she would be back by four o'clock, and no later. She did not return.

[Coroner] Did you make any inquiry after her? - I heard she had been locked up at Bishopsgate-street on Saturday afternoon. An old woman who works in then lane told me she saw her in the hands of the police.

[Coroner] Did you make any inquiry into the truth of this? - I made no further inquiries. I knew that she would be out on Sunday morning, being in the City.

[Coroner] Did you know why she was locked up? - Yes, for drink; she had had a drop of drink, so I was told. I never knew she went out for any immoral purpose. She occasionally drank, but not to excess. When I left her she had no money about her. She went to see and find her daughter to get a trifle, so that I shouldn't see her walk about the streets at night.

[Coroner] What do you mean by "walking the streets?" - I mean that if we had no money to pay for our lodgings we would have to walk about all night. I was without money to pay for our lodgings at the time. I do not know that she was at variance with any one - not in the least. She had not seen Conway recently - not that I know of. I never saw him in my existence. I cannot say whether Conway is living. I know of no one who would be likely to injure her.

The Foreman of the Jury: You say you heard the deceased was taken into custody. Did you ascertain, as a matter of fact, when she was discharged? - No. I do not know when she was discharged.

[Coroner] What time was she in the habit of returning to her lodgings? - Early.

[Coroner] What do you call early? - About eight or nine o'clock.

[Coroner] When she did not return on this particular evening, did it not occur to you that it would be right to inquire whether she had been discharged or not? - No, I did not inquire. I expected she would turn up on the Sunday morning.

Mr. Crawford: You say she had no money. Do you know with whom she had been drinking that afternoon? - I cannot say.

[Coroner] Do you know any one who paid for drink for her? - No.

[Coroner] Had she on a recent occasion absented herself from you at night? - No.

[Coroner] This was the only time? - Yes.

[Coroner] But had not she left you previously? - Yes, a long time ago - some months ago.

[Coroner] For what purpose? - We had a few words, and she went away, but came back in a few hours.

[Coroner] Had you had any angry conversation with her on Saturday afternoon? - No, not in the least.

[Coroner] No words about money? - No.

[Coroner] Have you any idea where her daughter lives? - She told me in King-street, Bermondsey, and that her name was Annie.

[Coroner] Had she been previously there for money? - Yes, once last year.

[Coroner] How long have you been living in this lodging-house together? - Seven years, in the self-same house.

[Coroner] Previous to this Saturday had you been sleeping there each evening during the week? - No; I slept there on Friday night, but she didn't.

[Coroner] Did she not sleep with you? - No.

[Coroner] Was she walking the streets that night? - She had the misfortune to go to Mile-end.

[Coroner] What happened there? - She went into the casual ward.

[Coroner] What was the evening you two slept at the lodging-house during that week? - Not one.

[Coroner] Where did you sleep? - On Monday, Tuesday, and Wednesday we were down at the hop-picking, and came back to London on Thursday. We had been unfortunate at the hop-picking, and had no money. On Thursday night we both slept in the casual ward. On the Friday I earned 6d at a job, and I said, "Here, Kate, you take 4d and go to the lodging-house and I will go to Mile-end," but she said, "No, you go and have a bed and I will go to the casual ward," and she went. I saw her again on Saturday morning early.

[Coroner] At what time did you quit one another on Friday? - I cannot tell, but I think it would be about three or four in the afternoon.

[Coroner] What did she leave you for? - To go to Mile-end.

[Coroner] What for? - To get a night's shelter in the casual ward.

[Coroner] When did you see her next morning? - About eight o'clock. I was surprised to see her so early. I know there was some tea and sugar found on her body. She bought that out of some boots we pawned at Jones's for 2s 6d. I think it was on Saturday morning that we pawned the boots. She was sober when she left me. We had been drinking together out of the 2s 6d. All of it was spent in drink and food. She left me quite sober to go to her daughter's. We parted without an angry word. I do not know why she left Conway. In the past seven years she only lived with me. I did not know of her going out for immoral purposes at night. She never brought me money in the morning after being out at night.

A Juryman: Is not eight o'clock a very early hour to be discharged from a casual ward? - I do not know.

[Juryman ?] There is some tasks - picking oakum - before you can be discharged. I know it was very early.

Mr. Crawford: Is it not the fact that the pawning took place on the Friday night? - I do not know. It was either Friday night or Saturday morning. I am all muddled up. (The tickets were produced, and were dated the 28th, Friday.)

[Crawford ?] She pawned the boots, did she not? - Yes; and I stood at the door in my bare feet.

[Crawford ?] Seeing the date on the tickets, cannot you recollect when the pawning took place? - I cannot say, I am so muddled up. It was either Friday or Saturday.

The Coroner: Had you been drinking when the pawning took place? - Yes.


Frederick William Wilkinson deposed: I am deputy of the lodging-house at Flower and Dean-street. I have known the deceased and Kelly during the last seven years. They passed as man and wife, and lived on very good terms. They had a quarrel now and then, but not violent. They sometimes had a few words when Kate was in drink, but they were not serious. I believe she got her living by hawking about the streets and cleaning amongst the Jews in Whitechapel. Kelly paid me pretty regularly. Kate was not often in drink. She was a very jolly woman, always singing. Kelly was not in the habit of drinking, and I never saw him the worse for drink. During the week the first time I saw the deceased at the lodging-house was on Friday afternoon. Kelly was not with her then. She went out and did not return until Saturday morning, when I saw her and Kelly in the kitchen together having breakfast. I did not see her go out, and I do not know whether Kelly went with her. I never saw her again.

[Coroner] Did you know she was in the habit of walking the streets at night? - No; she generally used to return between nine and ten o'clock. I never knew her to be intimate with any particular individual except Kelly; and never heard of such a thing. She use to say she was married to Conway; that her name was bought and paid for - meaning that she was married. She was not at variance with any one that I know of. When I saw her last, on Saturday morning, between ten and eleven, she was quite sober. I first heard from Kelly on Saturday night that Kate was locked up, and he said he wanted a single bed. That was about 7.30 in the evening. A single bed is 4d, and a double 8d.

By a Juryman: I don't take the names of the lodgers, but I know my "regulars." If a man comes and takes a bed I put the number of the bed down in my book, but not his name. Of course I know the names of my regular customers.

Mr. Crawford: When was the last time Kelly and the deceased had slept together in your house previous to last week? - The last time the two slept at the lodging-house was five or six weeks ago, before they went to the hop-picking. Kelly slept there on Friday and Saturday, but not Kate. I did not make any inquiry about her not being there on Friday. I could not say whether Kate went out with Kelly on Saturday, but I saw them having their breakfast together. I saw Kelly in the house about ten o'clock on Saturday night. I am positive he did not go out again. I cannot tell when he got up on Sunday. I saw him about dinner time. I believe on Saturday morning Kate was wearing an apron. Nothing unusual struck me about her dress. The distance between our place and the scene of the murder is about 500 yards. Several Jurymen: Oh, more than that.

Mr. Crawford: Did any one come into your lodging-house and take a bed between one and two o'clock on the Sunday morning? - No stranger came in then.

[Crawford] Did any one come into your lodging-house about that hour? - No; two detectives came about three, and asked if I had any women out.

[Crawford] Did anyone come into your lodging-house about two o'clock on Sunday morning whom you did not recognise? - I cannot say; I could tell by my book, which can soon be produced.

By a Juryman: Kelly and the deceased were at breakfast together between ten and eleven on Saturday morning. If they had told me the previous day that they had no money I would have trusted them. I trust all lodgers I know. The body was found half a mile from my lodging-house.

The deputy was dispatched for his book, with which after an interval he returned. It merely showed, however, that there were fifty-two beds occupied in the house on Saturday night. There were only six strangers. He could not say whether any one took a bed about two o'clock on Sunday morning. He had sometimes over 100 persons sleeping in the house at once. They paid for their beds, and were asked no questions.


Edward Watkin, No. 881 of the City Police, said: I was on duty at Mitre-square on Saturday night. I have been in the force seventeen years. I went on duty at 9.45 upon my regular beat. That extends from Duke-street, Aldgate, through Heneage-lane, a portion of Bury-street, through Cree-lane, into Leadenhall-street, along eastward into Mitre-street, then into Mitre-square, round the square again into Mitre-street, then into King-street to St. James's-place, round the place, then into Duke-street, where I started from. That beat takes twelve or fourteen minutes. I had been patrolling the beat continually from ten o'clock at night until one o'clock on Sunday morning.

[Coroner] Had anything excited your attention during those hours? - No.

[Coroner] Or any person? - No. I passed through Mitre-square at 1.30 on the Sunday morning. I had my lantern alight and on - fixed to my belt. According to my usual practice, I looked at the different passages and corners.

[Coroner] At half-past one did anything excite your attention? - No.

[Coroner] Did you see anyone about? - No.

[Coroner] Could any people have been about that portion of the square without your seeing them? - No. I next came into Mitre-square at 1.44, when I discovered the body lying on the right as I entered the square. The woman was on her back, with her feet towards the square. Her clothes were thrown up. I saw her throat was cut and the stomach ripped open. She was lying in a pool of blood. I did not touch the body. I ran across to Kearley and Long's warehouse. The door was ajar, and I pushed it open, and called on the watchman Morris, who was inside. He came out. I remained with the body until the arrival of Police-constable Holland. No one else was there before that but myself. Holland was followed by Dr. Sequeira. Inspector Collard arrived about two o'clock, and also Dr. Brown, surgeon to the police force.

[Coroner] When you first saw the body did you hear any footsteps as if anybody were running away? - No. The door of the warehouse to which I went was ajar, because the watchman was working about. It was no unusual thing for the door to be ajar at that hour of the morning.

By Mr. Crawford: I was continually patrolling my beat from ten o'clock up to half-past one. I noticed nothing unusual up till 1.44, when I saw the body.

By the Coroner: I did not sound an alarm. We do not carry whistles.

By a Juror: My beat is not a double but a single beat. No other policeman comes into Mitre-street.

Frederick William Foster, of 26, Old Jewry, architect and surveyor, produced a plan which he had made of the place where the body was found, and the district. From Berner-street to Mitre-street is three-quarters of a mile, and a man could walk the distance in twelve minutes.

Inspector Collard, of the City Police, said: At five minutes before two o'clock on Sunday morning last I received information at Bishopsgate-street Police-station that a woman had been murdered in Mitre-square. Information was at once telegraphed to headquarters. I dispatched a constable to Dr. Gordon Brown, informing him, and proceeded myself to Mitre-square, arriving there about two or three minutes past two. I there found Dr. Sequeira, two or three police officers, and the deceased person lying in the south-west corner of the square, in the position described by Constable Watkins. The body was not touched until the arrival shortly afterwards of Dr. Brown. The medical gentlemen examined the body, and in my presence Sergeant Jones picked up from the foot way by the left side of the deceased three small black buttons, such as are generally used for boots, a small metal button, a common metal thimble, and a small penny mustard tin containing two pawn-tickets. They were handed to me. The doctors remained until the arrival of the ambulance, and saw the body placed in the conveyance. It was then taken to the mortuary, and stripped by Mr. Davis, the mortuary keeper, in presence of the two doctors and myself. I have a list of articles of clothing more or less stained with blood and cut.

[Coroner] Was there any money about her? - No; no money whatever was found. A piece of cloth was found in Goulston-street, corresponding with the apron worn by the deceased. When I got to the square I took immediate steps to have the neighbourhood searched for the person who committed the murder. Mr. M'Williams, chief of the Detective Department, on arriving shortly afterwards sent men to search in all directions in Spitalfields, both in streets and lodging-houses. Several men were stopped and searched in the streets, without any good result. I have had a house-to-house inquiry made in the vicinity of Mitre-square as to any noises or whether persons were seen in the place; but I have not been able to find any beyond the witnesses who saw a man and woman talking together.

Mr. Crawford: When you arrived was the deceased in a pool of blood? - The head, neck, and, I imagine, the shoulders were lying in a pool of blood when she was first found, but there was no blood in front. I did not touch the body myself, but the doctor said it was warm.

[Crawford ?] Was there any sign of a struggle having taken place? - None whatever. I made a careful inspection of the ground all round. There was no trace whatever of any struggle. There was nothing in the appearance of the woman, or of the clothes, to lead to the idea that there had been any struggle. From the fact that the blood was in a liquid state I conjectured that the murder had not been long previously committed. In my opinion the body had not been there more than a quarter of an hour. I endeavoured to trace footsteps, but could find no trace whatever. The backs of the empty houses adjoining were searched, but nothing was found.

Dr. Frederick Gordon Brown was then called, and deposed: I am surgeon to the City of London Police. I was called shortly after two o'clock on Sunday morning, and reached the place of the murder about twenty minutes past two. My attention was directed to the body of the deceased. It was lying in the position described by Watkins, on its back, the head turned to the left shoulder, the arms by the side of the body, as if they had fallen there. Both palms were upwards, the fingers slightly bent. A thimble was lying near. The clothes were thrown up. The bonnet was at the back of the head. There was great disfigurement of the face.

The throat was cut across. Below the cut was a neckerchief. The upper part of the dress had been torn open. The body had been mutilated, and was quite warm - no rigor mortis. The crime must have been committed within half an hour, or certainly within forty minutes from the time when I saw the body. There were no stains of blood on the bricks or pavement around.

By Mr. Crawford: There was no blood on the front of the clothes. There was not a speck of blood on the front of the jacket.

By the Coroner: Before we removed the body Dr. Phillips was sent for, as I wished him to see the wounds, he having been engaged in a case of a similar kind previously. He saw the body at the mortuary. The clothes were removed from the deceased carefully. I made a post-mortem examination on Sunday afternoon. There was a bruise on the back of the left hand, and one on the right shin, but this had nothing to do with the crime. There were no bruises on the elbows or the back of the head. The face was very much mutilated, the eyelids, the nose, the jaw, the cheeks, the lips, and the mouth all bore cuts. There were abrasions under the left ear. The throat was cut across to the extent of six or seven inches.

[Coroner] Can you tell us what was the cause of death? - The cause of death was haemorrhage from the throat. Death must have been immediate.

[Coroner] There were other wounds on the lower part of the body? - Yes; deep wounds, which were inflicted after death.

(Witness here described in detail the terrible mutilation of the deceased's body.)

Mr. Crawford: I understand that you found certain portions of the body removed? - Yes. The uterus was cut away with the exception of a small portion, and the left kidney was also cut out. Both these organs were absent, and have not been found.

[Coroner] Have you any opinion as to what position the woman was in when the wounds were inflicted? - In my opinion the woman must have been lying down. The way in which the kidney was cut out showed that it was done by somebody who knew what he was about.

[Coroner] Does the nature of the wounds lead you to any conclusion as to the instrument that was used? - It must have been a sharp-pointed knife, and I should say at least 6 in. long.

[Coroner] Would you consider that the person who inflicted the wounds possessed anatomical skill? - He must have had a good deal of knowledge as to the position of the abdominal organs, and the way to remove them.

[Coroner] Would the parts removed be of any use for professional purposes? - None whatever.

[Coroner] Would the removal of the kidney, for example, require special knowledge? - It would require a good deal of knowledge as to its position, because it is apt to be overlooked, being covered by a membrane.

[Coroner] Would such a knowledge be likely to be possessed by some one accustomed to cutting up animals? - Yes.

[Coroner] Have you been able to form any opinion as to whether the perpetrator of this act was disturbed? - I think he had sufficient time, but it was in all probability done in a hurry.

[Coroner] How long would it take to make the wounds? - It might be done in five minutes. It might take him longer; but that is the least time it could be done in.

[Coroner] Can you, as a professional man, ascribe any reason for the taking away of the parts you have mentioned? - I cannot give any reason whatever.

[Coroner] Have you any doubt in your own mind whether there was a struggle? - I feel sure there was no struggle. I see no reason to doubt that it was the work of one man.

[Coroner] Would any noise be heard, do you think? - I presume the throat was instantly severed, in which case there would not be time to emit any sound.

[Coroner] Does it surprise you that no sound was heard? - No.

[Coroner] Would you expect to find much blood on the person inflicting these wounds? - No, I should not. I should say that the abdominal wounds were inflicted by a person kneeling at the right side of the body. The wounds could not possibly have been self-inflicted.

[Coroner] Was your attention called to the portion of the apron that was found in Goulston-street? - Yes. I fitted that portion which was spotted with blood to the remaining portion, which was still attached by the strings to the body.

[Coroner] Have you formed any opinion as to the motive for the mutilation of the face? - It was to disfigure the corpse, I should imagine.

A Juror: Was there any evidence of a drug having been used? - I have not examined the stomach as to that. The contents of the stomach have been preserved for analysis.


Mr. Crawford said he was glad to announce that the Corporation had unanimously approved the offer by the Lord Mayor of a reward of £500 for the discovery of the murderer.

Several jurymen expressed their satisfaction at the promptness with which the offer was made.

The inquest was then adjourned until next Thursday.

Day 2, Thursday, October 11, 1888

Mr. Crawford, City Solicitor, again watched the case on behalf of the police.

Dr. G. W. Sequeira, surgeon, of No. 34, Jewry-street, Aldgate, deposed: On the morning of Sept. 30 I was called to Mitre-square, and I arrived at five minutes to two o'clock, being the first medical man on the scene of the murder. I saw the position of the body, and I entirely agree with the evidence of Dr. Gordon Brown in that respect.

By Mr. Crawford: I am well acquainted with the locality and the position of the lamps in the square. Where the murder was committed was probably the darkest part of the square, but there was sufficient light to enable the miscreant to perpetrate the deed. I think that the murderer had no design on any particular organ of the body. He was not possessed of any great anatomical skill.

[Coroner] Can you account for the absence of noise? - The death must have been instantaneous after the severance of the windpipe and the blood-vessels.

[Coroner] Would you have expected the murderer to be bespattered with blood? - Not necessarily.

[Coroner] How long do you believe life had been extinct when you arrived? - Very few minutes - probably not more than a quarter of an hour.

Mr. William Sedgwick Saunders, medical officer of health for the City, said: I received the stomach of the deceased from Dr. Gordon Brown, carefully sealed, and I made an analysis of the contents, which had not been interfered with in any way. I looked more particularly for poisons of the narcotic class, but with negative results, there being not the faintest trace of any of those or any other poisons.

Annie Phillips stated: I reside at No. 12, Dilston-road, Southwark Park-road, and am married, my husband being a lamp-black packer. I am daughter of the deceased, who formerly lived with my father. She always told me that she was married to him, but I have never seen the marriage lines. My father's name was Thomas Conway.

The Coroner: Have you seen him lately? - Not for the last fifteen or eighteen months.

[Coroner] Where was he living then? - He was living with me and my husband, at No. 15, Acre-street, Southwark Park-road.

[Coroner] What calling did he follow? - That of a hawker.

[Coroner] What became of him? - I do not know.

[Coroner] Did he leave on good terms with you? - Not on very good terms.

[Coroner] Did he say that he would never see you again, or anything of that sort? - No.

[Coroner] Was he a sober man? - He was a teetotaller.

[Coroner] Did he live on bad terms with your mother? - Yes, because she used to drink.

[Coroner] Have you any idea where Conway is now? - Not the least. He ceased to live with Eddowes entirely on account of her drinking habits.

[Coroner] Your father was in the 18th Royal Irish Regiment? - So I have been told. He had been a pensioner ever since I was eight years old. I am twenty-three now. They parted about seven or eight years ago.

[Coroner] Did your mother ever apply to you for money? - Yes.

[Coroner] When did you last see her? - Two years and one month ago.

[Coroner] Where did you live when you last saw her? - In King-street, Bermondsey.

[Coroner] Have you any brothers or sisters by Conway? - Two brothers.

[Coroner] Where are they living? - In London.

[Coroner] Did your mother know where to find either of you? - No.

[Coroner] Were your addresses purposely kept from her? - Yes.

[Coroner] To prevent her applying for money.

The Foreman: Was your father aware when he left you that your mother was living with Kelly? - Yes.

Mr. Crawford: Are you quite certain that your father was a pensioner of the 18th Royal Irish? - I was told so, but I am not sure whether it was the 18th or the Connaught Rangers. It may have been the latter.

The Coroner: That is the 88th - I do not know.

Mr. Crawford: That is so. It so happens that there is a pensioner of the name of Conway belonging to the Royal Irish, but that is not the man.

To witness: When did your mother last receive money from you?

Witness: Just over two years ago. She waited upon me in my confinement, and I paid her for it.

[Coroner] Did you ever get a letter from her? - No.

[Coroner] Do you know anything about Kelly? - I have seen him two or three times at the lodging-house in Flower and Dean-street, with my mother.

[Coroner] When did you last see them together? - About three years and a half ago.

[Coroner] You knew they were living together as man and wife? - Yes.

[Coroner] Is it the fact that your father is living with your two brothers? - He was.

[Coroner] Where are your brothers residing now? - I do not know.

[Coroner] He was always with them. One was fifteen and the other eighteen years of age.

[Coroner] When did you last see them? - About eighteen months ago. I have not seen them since.

[Coroner] Are we to understand that you had lost all trace of your mother, father, and two brothers for at least eighteen months? - That is so.

Detective-Sergeant John Mitchell, of the City police, said: I have, under instructions, and with other officers, made every endeavour to find the father and brothers of the last witness, but without success up to the present.

The Coroner: Have you found a pensioner named Conway belonging to the 18th Royal Irish? - I have. He has not been identified as the husband of the deceased. Detective Baxter Hunt: Acting under instructions, I discovered the pensioner, Conway, of the Royal Irish, and have confronted him with two sisters of the deceased, who, however, failed to recognise him as the man who used to live with the deceased. I have made every endeavour to trace the Thomas Conway in question and the brothers of Annie Phillips, but without success.

A Juror: Why did you not confront this Conway with the daughter of the deceased, Annie Phillips? - That witness had not been found then.

Mr. Crawford: The theory has been put forward that it was possible for the deceased to have been murdered elsewhere, and her body brought to where it was found. I should like to ask Dr. Gordon Brown, who is present, what his opinion is about that.

Dr. Gordon Brown: I do not think there is any foundation for such a theory. The blood on the left side was clotted, and must have fallen at the time the throat was cut. I do not think that the deceased moved the least bit after that.

The Coroner: The body could not have been carried to where it was found? - Witness: Oh, no.

City-constable Lewis Robinson, 931, deposed: At half-past eight, on the night of Saturday, Sept. 29, while on duty in High-street, Aldgate, I saw a crowd of persons outside No. 29, surrounding a woman whom I have since recognised as the deceased.

The Coroner: What state was she in? - Drunk. Lying on the footway? - Yes. I asked the crowd if any of them knew her or where she lived, but got no answer. I then picked her up and sat her against the shutters, but she fell down sideways. With the aid of a fellow-constable I took her to Bishopsgate Police-station. There she was asked her name, and she replied "Nothing." She was then put into a cell.

[Coroner] Did any one appear to be in her company when you found her? - No one in particular.

Mr. Crawford: Did any one appear to know her? - No. The apron being produced, torn and discoloured with blood, the witness said that to the best of his knowledge it was the apron the deceased was wearing.

The Foreman: What guided you in determining whether the woman was drunk or not?

Witness: Her appearance.

The Foreman: I ask you because I know of a case in which a person was arrested for being drunk who had not tasted anything intoxicating for eight or nine hours.

[Coroner] You are quite sure this woman was drunk? - She smelt very strongly of drink.

Sergeant James Byfield, of the City Police: I remember the deceased being brought to the Bishopsgate Station at a quarter to nine o'clock on the night of Saturday, Sept. 29.

[Coroner] In what condition was she? - Very drunk. She was brought in supported by two constables and placed in a cell, where she remained until one o'clock the next morning, when she had got sober. I then discharged her, after she had given her name and address.

[Coroner] What name and address did she give? - Mary Ann Kelly, No. 6, Fashion-street, Spitalfields.

[Coroner] Did she say where she had been, or what she had been doing? - She stated that she had been hopping.

Constable George Henry Hutt, 968, City Police: I am gaoler at Bishopsgate station. On the night of Saturday, Sept. 29, at a quarter to ten o'clock, I took over our prisoners, among them the deceased. I visited her several times until five minutes to one on Sunday morning. The inspector, being out visiting, I was directed by Sergeant Byfield to see if any of the prisoners were fit to be discharged. I found the deceased sober, and after she had given her name and address, she was allowed to leave. I pushed open the swing-door leading to the passage, and said, "This way, missus." She passed along the passage to the outer door. I said to her, "Please, pull it to." She replied, "All right. Good night, old cock." (Laughter.) She pulled the door to within a foot of being close, and I saw her turn to the left.

The Coroner: That was leading towards Houndsditch? - Yes.

The Foreman: Is it left to you to decide when a prisoner is sober enough to be released or not? - Not to me, but to the inspector or acting inspector on duty.

[Coroner] Is it usual to discharge prisoners who have been locked up for being drunk at all hours of the night? - Certainly.

[Coroner] How often did you visit the prisoners? - About every half-hour. At first the deceased remained asleep; but at a quarter to twelve she was awake, and singing a song to herself, as it were. I went to her again at half-past twelve, and she then asked when she would be able to get out. I replied: "Shortly." She said, "I am capable of taking care of myself now."

Mr. Crawford: Did she tell you where she was going? - No. About two minutes to one o'clock, when I was taking her out of the cell, she asked me what time it was. I answered, "Too late for you to get any more drink." She said, "Well, what time is it?" I replied, "Just on one." Thereupon she said, "I shall get a ---- fine hiding when I get home, then."

[Coroner] Was that her parting remark? - That was in the station yard. I said, "Serve you right; you have no right to get drunk."

[Coroner] You supposed she was going home? - I did.

[Coroner] In your opinion is that the apron the deceased was wearing? - To the best of my belief it is.

[Coroner] What is the distance from Mitre-square to your station? - About 400 yards.

[Coroner] Do you know the direct route to Flower and Dean-street? - No.

A Juror: Do you search persons who are brought in for drunkenness? - No, but we take from them anything that might be dangerous. I loosened the things round the deceased's neck, and I then saw a white wrapper and a red silk handkerchief.

George James Morris, night watchman at Messrs. Kearley and Tonge's tea warehouse, Mitre-square, deposed: On Saturday, Sept. 29, I went on duty at seven o'clock in the evening. I occupied most of my time in cleaning the offices and looking about the warehouse.

The Coroner: What happened about a quarter to two in the morning? - Constable Watkins, who was on the Mitre-square beat, knocked at my door, which was slightly ajar at the time. I was then sweeping the steps down towards the door. The door was pushed when I was about two yards off. I turned round and opened the door wide. The constable said, "For God's sake, mate, come to my assistance." I said, "Stop till I get my lamp. What is the matter?" "Oh, dear," he exclaimed, "here is another woman cut to pieces." I asked where, and he replied, "In the corner." I went into the corner of the square and turned my light on the body. I agree with the previous witnesses as to the position of the body. I ran up Mitre-street into Aldgate, blowing my whistle all the while.

[Coroner] Did you see any suspicious persons about? - No. Two constables came up and asked what was the matter. I told them to go down to Mitre-square, as there was another terrible murder. They went, and I followed and took charge of my own premises again.

[Coroner] Before being called by Constable Watkins, had you heard any noise in the square? - No.

[Coroner] If there had been any cry of distress, would you have heard it from where you were? - Yes.

By the Jury: I was in the warehouse facing the corner of the square.

By Mr. Crawford: Before being called I had no occasion to go into the square. I did not go there between one and two o'clock; of that I am certain. There was nothing unusual in my door being open and my being at work at so late an hour. I had not seen Watkins before during the night. I do not think my door had been ajar more than two or three minutes when he knocked.

James Harvey, City constable, 964: On the night of Saturday, Sept. 29, I was on duty in the neighbourhood of Houndsditch and Aldgate. I was there at the time of the murder, but did not see any one nor hear any cry. When I got into Aldgate, returning towards Duke-street, I heard a whistle and saw the witness Morris with a lamp. I asked him what was the matter, and he told me that a woman had been ripped up in Mitre-square. Together with Constable Hollins I went to Mitre-square, where Watkins was by the side of the body of the deceased. Hollins went for Dr. Sequeira, and a private individual was despatched for other constables, who arrived almost immediately, having heard the whistle. I waited with Watkins, and information was sent to the inspector.

[Coroner] At what time previous to that were you in Aldgate? - At twenty-eight minutes past one o'clock I passed the post-office clock.

George Clapp, caretaker at No. 5, Mitre-street, deposed: The back part of the house looks into Mitre-square. On the night of Saturday week last I retired to rest in the back room on the second floor about eleven o'clock.

The Coroner: During the night did you hear any disturbance in the square? - No.

[Coroner] When did you first learn that a murder had been perpetrated? - Between five and six o'clock in the morning.

By Mr. Crawford: A nurse, who was in attendance upon my wife, was sleeping at the top of the house. No person slept either on the ground floor or the first floor.

Constable Richard Pearce, 922 City: I reside at No. 3, Mitre-square. There are only two private houses in the square. I retired to rest at twenty minutes past twelve on the morning of last Sunday week.

[Coroner] Did you hear any noise in the square? - None at all. When did you first hear of the murder? - At twenty past two, when I was called by a constable.

[Coroner] From your bedroom window could you see the spot where the murder was committed? - Yes, quite plainly.

By Mr. Crawford: My wife and family were in no way disturbed during the night.

Joseph Lawende: I reside at No. 45, Norfolk-road, Dalston, and am a commercial traveller. On the night of Sept. 29, I was at the Imperial Club, Duke-street, together with Mr. Joseph Levy and Mr. Harry Harris. It was raining, and we sat in the club till half-past one o'clock, when we left. I observed a man and woman together at the corner of Church-passage, Duke-street, leading to Mitre-square.

The Coroner: Were they talking? - The woman was standing with her face towards the man, and I only saw her back. She had one hand on his breast. He was the taller. She had on a black jacket and bonnet. I have seen the articles at the police-station, and believe them to be those the deceased was wearing.

[Coroner] What sort of man was this? - He had on a cloth cap with a peak of the same.

Mr. Crawford: Unless the jury wish it, I do not think further particulars should be given as to the appearance of this man.

The Foreman: The jury do not desire it.

Mr. Crawford (to witness): You have given a description of the man to the police? - Yes.

[Coroner] Would you know him again? - I doubt it. The man and woman were about nine or ten feet away from me. I have no doubt it was half-past one o'clock when we rose to leave the club, so that it would be twenty-five minutes to two o'clock when we passed the man and woman.

[Coroner] Did you overhear anything that either said? - No.

[Coroner] Did either appear in an angry mood? - No.

[Coroner] Did anything about their movements attract your attention? - No. The man looked rather rough and shabby.

[Coroner] When the woman placed her hand on the man's breast, did she do it as if to push him away? - No; it was done very quietly.

[Coroner] You were not curious enough to look back and see where they went. - No.

Mr. Joseph Hyam Levy, the butcher in Hutcheson-street, Aldgate, stated: I was with the last witness at the Imperial Club on Saturday night, Sept. 29. We got up to leave at half-past one on Sunday morning, and came out three or four minutes later. I saw a man and woman standing at the corner of Church-passage, but I did not take any notice of them. I passed on, thinking they were up to no good at so late an hour.

[Coroner] What height was the man? - I should think he was three inches taller than the woman, who was, perhaps, 5ft high. I cannot give any further description of them. I went down Duke-street into Aldgate, leaving them still talking together.

By the Jury: The point in the passage where the man and woman were standing was not well lighted. On the contrary, I think it was badly lighted then, but the light is much better now.

By Mr. Crawford: Nothing in what I saw excited my suspicion as to the intentions of the man. I did not hear a word that he uttered to the woman.

[Coroner] Your fear was rather about yourself? - Not exactly. (Laughter.)

Constable Alfred Long, 254 A, Metropolitan police: I was on duty in Goulston-street, Whitechapel, on Sunday morning, Sept. 30, and about five minutes to three o'clock I found a portion of a white apron (produced). There were recent stains of blood on it. The apron was lying in the passage leading to the staircase of Nos. 106 to 119, a model dwelling-house. Above on the wall was written in chalk, "The Jews are the men that will not be blamed for nothing." I at once searched the staircase and areas of the building, but did not find anything else. I took the apron to Commercial-road Police-station and reported to the inspector on duty.

[Coroner] Had you been past that spot previously to your discovering the apron? - I passed about twenty minutes past two o'clock.

[Coroner] Are you able to say whether the apron was there then? - It was not.

Mr. Crawford: As to the writing on the wall, have you not put a "not" in the wrong place? Were not the words, "The Jews are not the men that will be blamed for nothing"? - I believe the words were as I have stated.

[Coroner] Was not the word "Jews" spelt "Juwes?" - It may have been.

[Coroner] Yet you did not tell us that in the first place. Did you make an entry of the words at the time? - Yes, in my pocket-book. Is it possible that you have put the "not" in the wrong place? - It is possible, but I do not think that I have.

[Coroner] Which did you notice first - the piece of apron or the writing on the wall? - The piece of apron, one corner of which was wet with blood.

[Coroner] How came you to observe the writing on the wall? - I saw it while trying to discover whether there were any marks of blood about.

[Coroner] Did the writing appear to have been recently done? - I could not form an opinion.

[Coroner] Do I understand that you made a search in the model dwelling-house? - I went into the staircases.

[Coroner] Did you not make inquiries in the house itself? - No.

The Foreman: Where is the pocket-book in which you made the entry of the writing? - At Westminster.

[Coroner] Is it possible to get it at once? - I dare say.

Mr. Crawford: I will ask the coroner to direct that the book be fetched.

The Coroner: Let that be done.

Daniel Halse, detective officer, City police: On Saturday, Sept. 29, pursuant to instructions received at the central office in Old Jewry, I directed a number of police in plain clothes to patrol the streets of the City all night. At two minutes to two o'clock on the Sunday morning, when near Aldgate Church, in company with Detectives Outram and Marriott, I heard that a woman had been found murdered in Mitre-square. We ran to the spot, and I at once gave instructions for the neighbourhood to be searched and every man stopped and examined. I myself went by way of Middlesex-street into Wentworth-street, where I stopped two men, who, however, gave a satisfactory account of themselves. I came through Goulston-street about twenty minutes past two, and then returned to Mitre-square, subsequently going to the mortuary. I saw the deceased, and noticed that a portion of her apron was missing. I accompanied Major Smith back to Mitre-square, when we heard that a piece of apron had been found in Goulston-street. After visiting Leman-street police-station, I proceeded to Goulston-street, where I saw some chalk-writing on the black facia of the wall. Instructions were given to have the writing photographed, but before it could be done the Metropolitan police stated that they thought the writing might cause a riot or outbreak against the Jews, and it was decided to have it rubbed out, as the people were already bringing out their stalls into the street. When Detective Hunt returned inquiry was made at every door of every tenement of the model dwelling-house, but we gained no tidings of any one who was likely to have been the murderer.

By Mr. Crawford: At twenty minutes past two o'clock I passed over the spot where the piece of apron was found, but did not notice anything then. I should not necessarily have seen the piece of apron.

[Coroner] As to the writing on the wall, did you hear anybody suggest that the word "Jews" should be rubbed out and the other words left? - I did. The fear on the part of the Metropolitan police that the writing might cause riot was the sole reason why it was rubbed out. I took a copy of it, and what I wrote down was as follows: "The Juwes are not the men who will be blamed for nothing."

[Coroner] Did the writing have the appearance of having been recently done? - Yes. It was written with white chalk on a black facia.

The Foreman: Why was the writing really rubbed out? - Witness: The Metropolitan police said it might create a riot, and it was their ground.

Mr. Crawford: I am obliged to ask this question. Did you protest against the writing being rubbed out? - Witness: I did. I asked that it might, at all events, be allowed to remain until Major Smith had seen it. Why do you say that it seemed to have been recently written? - It looked fresh, and if it had been done long before it would have been rubbed out by the people passing. I did not notice whether there was any powdered chalk on the ground, though I did look about to see if a knife could be found. There were three lines of writing in a good schoolboy's round hand. The size of the capital letters would be about 3/4 in, and the other letters were in proportion. The writing was on the black bricks, which formed a kind of dado, the bricks above being white.

Mr. Crawford: With the exception of a few questions to Long, the Metropolitan constable, that is the whole of the evidence I have to offer at the present moment on the part of the City police. But if any point occurs to the coroner or the jury I shall be happy to endeavour to have it cleared up.

A Juror: It seems surprising that a policeman should have found the piece of apron in the passage of the buildings, and yet made no inquiries in the buildings themselves. There was a clue up to that point, and then it was altogether lost.

Mr. Crawford: As to the premises being searched, I have in court members of the City police who did make diligent search in every part of the tenements the moment the matter came to their knowledge. But unfortunately it did not come to their knowledge until two hours after. There was thus delay, and the man who discovered the piece of apron is a member of the Metropolitan police.

A Juror: It is the man belonging to the Metropolitan police that I am complaining of.

At this point Constable Long returned, and produced the pocket-book containing the entry which he made at the time concerning the discovery of the writing on the wall.

Mr. Crawford: What is the entry? - Witness: The words are, "The Jews are the men that will not be blamed for nothing." [Coroner] Both here and in your inspector's report the word "Jews" is spelt correctly? - Yes; but the inspector remarked that the word was spelt "Juwes."

[Coroner] Why did you write "Jews" then? - I made my entry before the inspector made the remark.

[Coroner] But why did the inspector write "Jews"? - I cannot say.

[Coroner] At all events, there is a discrepancy? - It would seem so.

[Coroner] What did you do when you found the piece of apron? - I at once searched the staircases leading to the buildings.

[Coroner] Did you make inquiry in any of the tenements of the buildings? - No.

[Coroner] How many staircases are there? - Six or seven.

[Coroner] And you searched every staircase? - Every staircase to the top.

[Coroner] You found no trace of blood or of recent footmarks? - No.

[Coroner] About what time was that? - Three o'clock.

[Coroner] Having examined the staircases, what did you next do? - I proceeded to the station.

[Coroner] Before going did you hear that a murder had been committed? - Yes. It is common knowledge that two murders have been perpetrated.

[Coroner] Which did you hear of? - I heard of the murder in the City. There were rumours of another, but not certain.

[Coroner] When you went away did you leave anybody in charge? - Yes; the constable on the next beat - 190, H Division - but I do not know his name.

[Coroner] Did you give him instructions as to what he was to do? - I told him to keep observation on the dwelling house, and see if any one entered or left.

[Coroner] When did you return? - About five o'clock.

[Coroner] Had the writing been rubbed out then? - No; it was rubbed out in my presence at half-past five.

[Coroner] Did you hear any one object to its being rubbed out? - No. It was nearly daylight when it was rubbed out.

A Juror: Having examined the apron and the writing, did it not occur to you that it would be wise to search the dwelling? - I did what I thought was right under the circumstances.

The Juror: I do not wish to say anything to reflect upon you, because I consider that altogether the evidence of the police redounds to their credit; but it does seem strange that this clue was not followed up.

Witness: I thought the best thing to do was to proceed to the station and report to the inspector on duty.

The Juror: I am sure you did what you deemed best.

Mr. Crawford: I suppose you thought it more likely to find the body there than the murderer? - Witness: Yes, and I felt that the inspector would be better able to deal with the matter than I was.

The Foreman: Was there any possibility of a stranger escaping from the house? - Not from the front.

[Coroner] Did you not know about the back? - No, that was the first time I had been on duty there.

That being all the evidence forthcoming, The coroner said he considered a further adjournment unnecessary, and the better plan would be for the jury to return their verdict and then leave the matter in the hands of the police.

In summing up it would not be at all necessary for him to go through the testimony of the various witnesses, but if the jury wanted their memories refreshed on any particular point he would assist them by referring to the evidence on that point. That the crime was a most fiendish one could not for a moment be doubted, for the miscreant, not satisfied with taking a defenceless woman's life, endeavoured so to mutilate the body as to render it unrecognisable.

He [Coroner] presumed that the jury would return a verdict of wilful murder against some person or persons unknown, and then the police could freely pursue their inquiries and follow up any clue they might obtain. A magnificent reward had been offered, and that might be the means of setting people on the track and bringing to speedy justice the creature who had committed this atrocious crime.

On reflection, perhaps it would be sufficient to return a verdict of wilful murder against some person unknown, inasmuch as the medical evidence conclusively demonstrated that only one person could be implicated.

The jury at once returned a verdict accordingly.

The coroner, for himself and the jury, thanked Mr. Crawford and the police for the assistance they had rendered in the inquiry.

Mr. Crawford: The police have simply done their duty.

The Coroner: I am quite sure of that.

# Mary Jane Kelly

Mary Jane Kelly A.K.A.. Marie Jeanette Kelly, Mary Ann Kelly, Ginger, Fair Emma Mary Jane Kelly,

Mary Jane Kelly was approximately 25 years old at the time of her death which would place her birth around 1863. She was 5' 7" tall and stout. She had blonde hair, blue eyes and a fair complexion. "Said to have been possessed of considerable personal attractions." (McNaughten) She was last seen wearing a linsey frock and a red shawl pulled around her shoulders. She was bare headed. Detective Constable Walter Dew claimed to know Kelly well by sight and says that she was attractive and paraded around, usually in the company of two or three friends. He says she always wore a spotlessly clean white apron. Maria Harvey, a friend, says that she was "much superior to that of most persons in her position in life." It is also said that she spoke fluent Welsh. Joseph Barnett says that he "always found her of sober habits." Landlord John McCarthy says "When in liquor she was very noisy; otherwise she was a very quiet woman." Caroline Maxwell says that she "was not a notorious character."

Catherine Pickett claims "She was a good, quiet, pleasant girl, and was well liked by all of us."

History: Almost everything that is known about Mary Jane Kelly comes from Joseph Barnett, who lived with her just prior to the murder. He, of course, had all this information from Kelly herself. Some is conflicting and it may be suspected that some, or perhaps much of it, is embellished. She was born in Limerick, Ireland but we do not know if that refers to the county or the town. As a young child she moved with her family to Wales. Her father was John Kelly who worked in an iron works in either Carnarvonshire or Carmarthenshire. Mary Jane claims to have 6 or 7 brothers and one sister. She says that one brother, Henry, whose nickname is Johnto is a member of the 2nd Battalion Scots Guards. As a member of this battalion he would have been stationed in Dublin, Ireland. She also claims to Lizzie Albrook that she had a relative on the London stage. John McCarthy, landlord at Miller's Court, states that she received a letter from her mother in Ireland. Barnett says that she never corresponded with her family. Joseph Barnett and Mrs. Carthy, a woman with whom she lived at one time, say that she came from a family that was "fairly well off" (Barnett) and "well to do people" (Carthy). Mrs. Carthy also states that Kelly was "an excellent scholar and an artist of no mean degree." Mrs. Carthy is the landlady from Breezer's Hill, Ratcliffe Highway. Barnett refers to her house as "a bad house."

c. 1879: At the age of 16 she marries a collier named Davies. He is killed in an explosion two or three years later. There is a suggestion that there might have been a child in this marriage.

Kelly moves to Cardiff and lives with a cousin and works as a prostitute. The Cardiff police have no record of her. She says she was ill and spent the best part of the time in an infirmary.

She arrives in London in 1884 She may have stayed with the nuns at the Providence Row Night Refuge on Crispin Street. According to one tradition she scrubbed floors and charred here and was eventually placed into domestic service in a shop in Cleveland Street. According to Joseph Barnett, on arriving in London, Kelly went to work in a high class brothel in the West End. She says that during this time she frequently rode in a carriage and accompanied one gentleman to Paris, which she didn't like and she returned. On November 10, one day after the murder, Mrs. Elizabeth Phoenix of 57 Bow Common Lane, Burdett Road, Bow, went to the Leman Street Police Station and said that a woman matching the description of Kelly used to live in her brother-in-law's house in Breezer's Hill, off Pennington Street. Mrs. Phoenix says that "She was Welsh and that her parents, who had discarded her, still lived in Cardiff, from which place she came. But on occasions she declared that she was Irish." She added that Mary Jane was very abusive and quarrelsome when she was drunk but "one of the most decent and nice girls you could meet when sober."

A Press Association reporter who looked into the Breezer's Hill District wrote: "It would appear that on her arrival in London she made the acquaintance of a French woman residing in the neighborhood of Knightsbridge, who, she informed her friends, led her to pursue the degraded life which had now culminated in her untimely end. She made no secret of the fact that while she was with this woman she would drive about in a carriage and made several journeys to the French capital, and, in fact, led a life which is described as that "of a lady." By some means, however, at present, not exactly clear, she suddenly drifted into the East End. Here fortune failed her and a career that stands out in bold and sad contrast to her earlier experience was commenced. Her experiences with the East End appears to have begun with a woman (according to press reports a Mrs. Buki) who resided in one of the thoroughfares off Ratcliffe Highway, known as St.

George's Street. This person appears to have received Kelly direct from the West End home, for she had not been there very long when, it is stated, both women went to the French lady's residence and demanded the box which contained numerous dresses of a costly description. Kelly at last indulged in intoxicants, it is stated, to an extant which made her unwelcome. From St. George's Street she went to lodge with a Mrs. Carthy at Breezer's Hill. This place she left about 18 months or two years ago and from that time on appears to have left Ratcliffe all together. Mrs. Carthy said that Kelly had left her house and gone to live with a man who was in the building trade and who Mrs. Carthy believed would have married Kelly." c. 1886: Kelly leaves Carthy's house to live with a man in the building trades. Barnett says she lived with a man named Morganstone opposite or in the vicinity of Stepney Gasworks. She had then taken up with a man named Joseph Fleming and lived somewhere near Bethnal Green. Fleming was a stone mason or mason's plasterer. He used to visit Kelly and seemed quite fond of her. A neighbour at Miller's Court, Julia Venturney says that Kelly was fond of a man other than Barnett and whose name was also Joe. She thought he was a costermonger and sometimes visited and gave money to Kelly.

By 1886 she is living in 'Cooley's Lodging House' in Thrawl Street, Spitalfields and it is here that she meets Joseph Barnett.

Joseph Barnett is London born of Irish heritage. He is a riverside laborer and market porter who is licensed to work at Billingsgate Fish Market. He comes from a family of three sisters and one brother who is named Daniel. Barnett was born in 1858 and dies in 1926.

Julia Venturney says that Joe Barnett is of good character and was kind to Mary Jane, giving her money on occasion.

Barnett and Kelly are remembered as a friendly and pleasant couple who give little trouble unless they are drunk. She may be the Mary Jane Kelly who was fined 2/6 by the Thames Magistrate Court on September 19, 1888 for being drunk and disorderly.

Good Friday, April 8, 1887: Joseph Barnett meets Mary Jane Kelly for the first time in Commercial Street. He takes her for a drink and arranges to meet her the following day. At their second meeting they arrange to live together.

They take lodgings in George Street, off Commercial Street. Later they move to Little Paternoster Row off Dorset Street. They are evicted for not paying rent and for being drunk. Next they move to Brick Lane.

In February or March of 1888 they move from Brick Lane to Miller's Court off Dorset Street. Here they occupy a single room which is designated 13 Miller's Court.

August or early September, 1888: Barnett loses his job and Mary Jane returns to the streets. Barnett decides to leave her.

October 30, between 5 and 6 PM: Elizabeth Prater, who lives above Kelly reports that Barnett and Kelly have an argument and Barnett leaves her. He goes to live at Buller's boarding house at 24-25 New Street, Bishopsgate.

Barnett states at the inquest that he left her because she was allowing other prostitutes to stay in the room. "She would never have gone wrong again," he tells a newspaper, "and I shouldn't have left her if it had not been for the prostitutes stopping at the house. She only let them (stay there) because she was good hearted and did not like to refuse them shelter on cold bitter nights." He adds, "We lived comfortably until Marie allowed a prostitute named Julia to sleep in the same room; I objected: and as Mrs. Harvey afterwards came and stayed there, I left and took lodgings elsewhere."

Maria Harvey stayed with Kelly on the nights of November 5 and 6. She moved to new lodgings at 3 New Court, another alley off Dorset Street.

Wednesday, November 7: Mary Jane buys a half penny candle from McCarthy's shop. She is later seen in Miller's Court by Thomas Bowyer, a pensioned soldier whose nickname is "Indian Harry." He is employed by McCarthy and lives at 37 Dorset Street.

Bowyer states that on Wednesday night he saw a man speaking to Kelly who closely resembled the description of the man Matthew Packer claims to have seen with Elizabeth Stride. His appearance was smart and attention was drawn to him by his very white cuffs and rather long, white collar which came down over the front of his long black coat. He did not carry a bag.

Thursday-Friday, November 8-9: Almost every day after the split, Barnett would visit Mary Jane. On

Friday the ninth he stops between 7:30 and 7:45 PM. He says she is in the company of another woman who lives in Miller's Court. This may have been Lizzie Albrook who lived at 2 Miller's Court.

Albrook says "About the last thing she said to me was 'Whatever you do don't you do wrong and turn out as I did.' She had often spoken to me in this way and warned me against going on the street as she had done. She told me, too, that she was heartily sick of the life she was leading and wished she had money enough to go back to Ireland where her people lived. I do not believe she would have gone out as she did if she had not been obliged to do so to keep herself from starvation."

Maria Harvey also says that she was woman that Barnett saw with Mary Jane and that she left at 6:55 PM.

8:00 PM: Barnett leaves and goes back to Buller's Boarding House where he played whist until 12:30 AM and then went to bed.

8:00 PM: Julia Venturney, who lives at 1 Miller's Court goes to bed.

There are no confirmed sightings of Mary Jane Kelly between 8:00 PM and 11:45 PM. there is an unconfirmed story that she is drinking with a woman named Elizabeth Foster at the Ten Bells Public House.

11:00 PM: It is said she is in the Britannia drinking with a young man with a dark mustache who appears respectable and well dressed. It is said she is very drunk.

11:45 PM: Mary Ann Cox, a 31 year old widower and prostitute, who lives at 5 Miller's Court (last house on the left) enters Dorset Street from Commercial Street. Cox is returning home to warm herself as the night had turned cold. She sees Kelly ahead of her, walking with a stout man. The man was aged around 35 or 36 and was about 5' 5" tall. He was shabbily dressed in a long overcoat and a billycock hat. He had a blotchy face and small side whiskers and a carroty mustache. The man is carrying a pail of beer.

Mrs. Cox follows them into Miller's Court. they are standing outside Kelly's room as Mrs. Cox passed and said "Goodnight." Somewhat incoherently, Kelly replied "Goodnight, I am going to sing." A few minutes later Mrs. Cox hears Kelly singing "A Violet from Mother's Grave" (see below). Cox goes out again at midnight and hears Kelly singing the same song.

Somewhere in this time period, Mary Jane takes a meal of fish and potatoes.

12:30 AM: Catherine Pickett, a flower-seller who lives near Kelly, is disturbed by Kelly's singing. Picket's husband stops her from going down stairs to complain. "You leave the poor woman alone." he says.

1:00 AM: It is beginning to rain. Again, Mary Ann Cox returns home to warm herself. At that time Kelly is still singing or has begun to sing again. There was light coming from Kelly's room. Shortly after one, Cox goes out again.

Elizabeth Prater, the wife of William Prater, a boot finisher who had left her 5 years before, is standing at the entrance to Miller's Court waiting for a man. Prater lives in room number 20 of 26 Dorset Street. This is directly above Kelly. She stands there about a half hour and then goes into to McCarthy's to chat. She hears no singing and sees no one go in or out of the court. After a few minutes she goes back to her room, places two chairs in front of her door and goes to sleep without undressing. She is very drunk.

2:00 AM: George Hutchinson, a resident of the Victoria Working Men's Home on Commercial Street has just returned to the area from Romford. He is walking on Commercial Street and passes a man at the corner of Thrawl Street but pays no attention to him. At Flower and Dean Street he meets Kelly who asks him for money. "Mr. Hutchinson, can you lend me sixpence?" "I can't," says Hutchinson, "I spent all my money going down to Romford." "Good morning," Kelly replies, "I must go and find some money." She then walks in the direction of Thrawl Street.

She meets the man Hutchinson had passed earlier. The man puts his hand on Kelly's shoulder and says something at which Kelly and the man laugh. Hutchinson hears Kelly say "All right." and the man say "You will be all right for what I have told you." The man then puts his right hand on Kelly's shoulder and they begin to walk towards Dorset Street. Hutchinson notices that the man has a small parcel in his left hand.

While standing under a street light on outside the Queen's Head Public House Hutchinson gets a good look at the man with Mary Jane Kelly. He has a pale complexion, a slight moustache turned up at the corners (changed to dark complexion and heavy moustache in the press reports), dark hair, dark eyes, and bushy eyebrows. He is, according to Hutchinson, of "Jewish appearance." The man is wearing a soft felt hat pulled down over his eyes, a long dark coat trimmed in astrakhan, a white collar with a black necktie fixed with a horseshoe pin. He wears dark spats over light button over boots. A massive gold chain is in his waistcoat with a large seal with a red stone hanging from it. He carries kid gloves in his right hand and a small package in his left. He is 5' 6" or 5' 7" tall and about 35 or 36 years old.

Kelly and the man cross Commercial Street and turn down Dorset Street. Hutchinson follows them. Kelly and the man stop outside Miller's Court and talk for about 3 minutes. Kelly is heard to say "All right, my dear. Come along. You will be comfortable." The man puts his arm around Kelly who kisses him. "I've lost my handkerchief." she says. At this he hands her a red handkerchief. The couple then heads down Miller's Court. Hutchinson waits until the clock strikes 3:00 AM. leaving as the clock strikes the hour.

3:00 AM: Mrs. Cox returns home yet again. It is raining hard. There is no sound or light coming from Kelly's room. Cox does not go back out but does not go to sleep. Throughout the night she occasionally hears men going in and out of the court. She told the inquest "I heard someone go out at a quarter to six. I do not know what house he went out of (as) I heard no door shut."

4:00 AM: Elizabeth Prater is awakened by her pet kitten "Diddles" walking on her neck. She hears a faint cry of "Oh, murder!" but, as the cry of murder is common in the district, she pays no attention to it. Sarah Lewis, who is staying with friends in Miller's Court, also hears the cry.

8:30 AM: Caroline Maxwell, a witness at the inquest and acquaintance of Kelly's, claims to have seen the deceased at around 8:30 AM, several hours after the time given by Phillips as time of death. She described her clothing and appearance in depth, and adamantly stated that she was not mistaken about the date, although she admitted she did not know Kelly very well.

10:00 AM: Maurice Lewis, a tailor who resided in Dorset Street, told newspapers he had seen Kelly and Barnett in the Horn of Plenty public house on the night of the murder, but more importantly, that he saw her about 10:00 AM the next day. Like Maxwell, this time is several hours from the time of death, and because of this discrepancy, he was not called to the inquest and virtually ignored by police.

10:45 AM: John McCarthy, owner of "McCarthy's Rents," as Miller's Court was known, sends Thomas Bowyer to collect past due rent money from Mary Kelly. After Bowyer receives no response from knocking (and because the door was locked) he pushes aside the curtain and peers inside, seeing the body. He informs McCarthy, who, after seeing the mutilated remains of Kelly for himself, ran to Commercial Street Police Station, where he spoke with Inspector Walter Beck, who returned to the Court with McCarthy.

Several hours later, after waiting fruitlessly for the arrival of the bloodhounds "Barnaby" and "Burgho," McCarthy smashes in the door with an axe handle under orders from Superintendent Thomas Arnold.

When police enter the room they find Mary Jane Kelly's clothes neatly folded on a chair and she is wearing a chemise. Her boots are in front of the fireplace.

Post-mortem Dr. Thomas Bond, a distinguished police surgeon from A-Division, was called in on the Mary Kelly murder. His report is as follows: "The body was lying naked in the middle of the bed, the shoulders flat but the axis of the body inclined to the left side of the bed. The head was turned on the left cheek. The left arm was close to the body with the forearm flexed at a right angle and lying across the abdomen. The right arm was slightly abducted from the body and rested on the mattress. The elbow was bent, the forearm supine with the fingers clenched. The legs were wide apart, the left thigh at right angles to the trunk and the right forming an obtuse angle with the pubes. The whole of the surface of the abdomen and thighs was removed and the abdominal cavity emptied of its viscera. The breasts were cut off, the arms mutilated by several jagged wounds and the face hacked beyond recognition of the features. The tissues of the neck were severed all round down to the bone. The viscera were found in various parts viz: the uterus and kidneys with one breast under the head, the other breast by the right foot, the liver between the feet, the intestines by the right side and the spleen by the left side of the body. The flaps removed from the abdomen and thighs were on a table. The bed clothing at the right corner was saturated with blood, and on the floor beneath was a pool of blood covering about two feet square. The wall by the right side of the bed and in a line with the neck was marked by blood which had struck it in a number of separate splashes. The face was gashed in all directions, the nose, cheeks, eyebrows, and ears being partly removed. The lips were blanched and cut by several incisions running obliquely down to the chin. There were also numerous cuts extending irregularly across all the features. The neck was cut through the skin and other tissues right down to the vertebrae, the fifth and sixth being deeply notched. The skin cuts in the front of the neck showed distinct ecchymosis. The air passage was cut at the lower part of the larynx through the cricoid cartilage.

Both breasts were more or less removed by circular incisions, the muscle down to the ribs being attached to the breasts. The intercostals between the fourth, fifth, and sixth ribs were cut through and the contents of the thorax visible through the openings. The skin and tissues of the abdomen from the costal arch to the pubes were removed in three large flaps. The right thigh was denuded in front to the bone, the flap of skin, including the external organs of generation, and part of the right buttock. The left thigh was stripped of skin fascia, and muscles as far as the knee. The left calf showed a long gash through skin and tissues to the deep muscles and reaching from the knee to five inches above the ankle. Both arms and forearms had extensive jagged wounds.

The right thumb showed a small superficial incision about one inch long, with extravasation of blood in the skin, and there were several abrasions on the back of the hand moreover showing the same condition. On opening the thorax it was found that the right lung was minimally adherent by old firm adhesions. The lower part of the lung was broken and torn away. The left lung was intact. It was adherent at the apex and there were a few adhesions over the side. In the substances of the lung there were several nodules of consolidation.

The pericardium was open below and the heart absent. In the abdominal cavity there was some partly digested food of fish and potatoes, and similar food was found in the remains of the stomach attached to the intestines."

Dr. George Bagster Phillips was also present at the scene, and gave the following testimony at the inquest: "The mutilated remains of a female were lying two-thirds over towards the edge of the bedstead nearest the door. She had only her chemise on, or some underlinen garment. I am sure that the body had been removed subsequent to the injury which caused her death from that side of the bedstead that was nearest the wooden partition, because of the large quantity of blood under the bedstead and the saturated condition of the sheet and the palliasse at the corner nearest the partition.

The blood was produced by the severance of the carotid artery, which was the cause of death. The injury was inflicted while the deceased was lying at the right side of the bedstead."

## Inquest: Mary Jane Kelly

Monday, November 12, 1888

Yesterday [12 Nov], at the Shoreditch Town Hall, Dr. Macdonald, M.P., the coroner for the North- Eastern District of Middlesex, opened his inquiry relative to the death of Marie Jeanette Kelly, the woman whose body was discovered on Friday morning, terribly mutilated, in a room on the ground floor of 26, Dorset-street, entrance to which was by a side door in Miller's-court.

Superintendent T. Arnold, H Division; Inspector Abberline, of the Criminal Investigation Department, and Inspector Nairn represented the police. The deputy coroner, Mr. Hodgkinson, was present during the proceedings.

The jury having answered to their names, one of them said: I do not see why we should have the inquest thrown upon our shoulders, when the murder did not happen in our district, but in Whitechapel.

The Coroner's Officer (Mr. Hammond): It did not happen in Whitechapel.

The Coroner (to the juror, severely): Do you think that we do not know what we are doing here, and that we do not know our own district? The jury are summoned in the ordinary way, and they have no business to object. If they persist in their objection I shall know how to deal with them. Does any juror persist in objecting ?

The Juror: We are summoned for the Shoreditch district. This affair happened in Spitalfields. The Coroner: It happened within my district.

Another Juryman: This is not my district. I come from Whitechapel, and Mr. Baxter is my coroner.

The Coroner: I am not going to discuss the subject with jurymen at all. If any juryman says he distinctly objects, let him say so. (After a pause): I may tell the jurymen that jurisdiction lies where the body lies, not where it was found, if there was doubt as to the district where the body was found.

The jury having made no further objection, they were duly sworn, and were conducted by Inspector Abberline to view the body, which, decently coffined, was at the mortuary adjoining Shoreditch Church, and subsequently the jury inspected the room, in Miller's-court, Dorset-street, where the murder was committed. The apartment, a plan of which was given in yesterday's Daily Telegraph, is poorly furnished, and uncarpeted. The position of the two tables was not altered. One of them was placed near the bed, behind the door, and the other next to the largest of the two windows which look upon the yard in which the dustbin and water-tap are situated.

The Coroner (addressing the reporters) said a great fuss had been made in some papers about the jurisdiction of the coroner, and who should hold the inquest. He had not had any communication with Dr. Baxter upon the subject. The body was in his jurisdiction; it had been taken to his mortuary; and there was an end of it. There was no foundation for the reports that had appeared. In a previous case of murder which occurred in his district the body was carried to the nearest mortuary, which was in another district. The inquest was held by Mr. Baxter, and he made no objection. The jurisdiction was where the body lay.

Joseph Barnett deposed : I was a fish-porter, and I work as a labourer and fruit- porter. Until Saturday last I lived at 24, New-street, Bishopsgate, and have since stayed at my sister's, 21, Portpool-lane, Gray's Inn-road. I have lived with the deceased one year and eight months. Her name was Marie Jeanette Kelly with the French spelling as described to me. Kelly was her maiden name. I have seen the body, and I identify it by the ear and eyes, which are all that I can recognise; but I am positive it is the same woman I knew. I lived with her in No. 13 room, at Miller's-court for eight months. I separated from her on Oct. 30.

[Coroner] Why did you leave her ? - Because she had a woman of bad character there, whom she took in out of compassion, and I objected to it. That was the only reason. I left her on the Tuesday between five and six p.m. I last saw her alive between half-past seven and a quarter to eight on Thursday night last, when I called upon her. I stayed there for a quarter of an hour.

[Coroner] Were you on good terms ? - Yes, on friendly terms; but when we parted I told her I had no work, and had nothing to give her, for which I was very sorry.

[Coroner] Did you drink together ? - No, sir. She was quite sober.

[Coroner] Was she, generally speaking, of sober habits ? - When she was with me I found her of sober habits, but she has been drunk several times in my presence.

[Coroner] Was there any one else there on the Thursday evening ? - Yes, a woman who lives in the court. She left first, and I followed shortly afterwards.

[Coroner] Have you had conversation with deceased about her parents ? - Yes, frequently. She said she was born in Limerick, and went when very young to Wales. She did not say how long she lived there, but that she came to London about four years ago. Her father's name was John Kelly, a "gaffer" or foreman in an iron works in Carnarvonshire, or

Carmarthen. She said she had one sister, who was respectable, who travelled from market place to market place. This sister was very fond of her. There were six brothers living in London, and one was in the army. One of them was named Henry. I never saw the brothers to my knowledge. She said she was married when very young in Wales to a collier. I think the name was Davis or Davies. She said she had lived with him until he was killed in an explosion, but I cannot say how many years since that was. Her age was, I believe, 16 when she married. After her husband's death deceased went to Cardiff to a cousin.

[Coroner] Did she live there long ? - Yes, she was in an infirmary there for eight or nine months. She was following a bad life with her cousin, who, as I reckon, and as I often told her, was the cause of her downfall.

[Coroner] After she left Cardiff did she come direct to London ? - Yes. She was in a gay house in the West-end, but in what part she did not say. A gentleman came there to her and asked her if she would like to go to France.

[Coroner] Did she go to France ? - Yes; but she did not remain long. She said she did not like the part, but whether it was the part or purpose I cannot say. She was not there more than a fortnight, and she returned to England, and went to Ratcliffe-highway. She must have lived there for some time. Afterwards she lived with a man opposite the Commercial Gas Works, Stepney. The man's name was Morganstone.

[Coroner] Have you seen that man ? - Never. I don't know how long she lived with him.

[Coroner] Was Morganstone the last man she lived with ? - I cannot answer that question, but she described a man named Joseph Fleming, who came to Pennington-street, a bad house, where she stayed. I don't know when this was. She was very fond of him. He was a mason's plasterer, and lodged in the Bethnal-green-road.

[Coroner] Was that all you knew of her history when you lived with her? - Yes. After she lived with Morganstone or Fleming - I don't know which one was the last - she lived with me.

[Coroner] Where did you pick up with her first ? - In Commercial-street. We then had a drink together, and I made arrangements to see her on the following day - a Saturday. On that day we both of us agreed that we should remain together. I took lodgings in George-street, Commercial-street, where I was known. I lived with her, until I left her, on very friendly terms.

[Coroner] Have you heard her speak of being afraid of any one ? - Yes; several times. I bought newspapers, and I read to her everything about the murders, which she asked me about.

[Coroner] Did she express fear of any particular individual ? - No, sir. Our own quarrels were very soon over.

The Coroner: You have given your evidence very well indeed. (To the Jury): The doctor has sent a note asking whether we shall want his attendance here to-day. I take it that it would be convenient that he should tell us roughly what the cause of death was, so as to enable the body to be buried. It will not be necessary to go into the details of the doctor's evidence; but he suggested that he might come to state roughly the cause of death.

The jury acquiesced in the proposed course.


Thomas Bowyer stated: I live at 37, Dorset-street, and am employed by Mr. McCarthy. I serve in his chandler's shop, 27, Dorset-street. At a quarter to eleven a.m., on Friday morning, I was ordered by McCarthy to go to Mary Jane's room, No. 13. I did not know the deceased by the name of Kelly. I went for rent, which was in arrears. Knocking at the door, I got no answer, and I knocked again and again. Receiving no reply, I passed round the corner by the gutter spout where there is a broken window - it is the smallest window.

Charles Ledger, an inspector of police, G Division, produced a plan of the premises. Bowyer pointed out the window, which was the one nearest the entrance.

He [Bowyer] continued: There was a curtain. I put my hand through the broken pane and lifted the curtain. I saw two pieces of flesh lying on the table.

[Coroner] Where was this table ? - In front of the bed, close to it. The second time I looked I saw a body on this bed, and blood on the floor. I at once went very quietly to Mr. McCarthy. We then stood in the shop, and I told him what I had seen. We both went to the police-station, but first of all we went to the window, and McCarthy looked in to satisfy himself. We told the inspector at the police-station of what we had seen. Nobody else knew of the matter. The inspector returned with us.

[Coroner] Did you see the deceased constantly ? - I have often seen her. I knew the last witness, Barnett. I have seen the deceased drunk once.

By the Jury: When did you see her last alive ? - On Wednesday afternoon, in the court, when I spoke to her. McCarthy's shop is at the corner of Miller's-court.


John McCarthy, grocer and lodging-house keeper, testified: I live at 27, Dorset- street. On Friday morning, about a quarter to eleven, I sent my man Bowyer to Room 13 to call for rent. He came back in five minutes, saying, "Guv'nor, I knocked at the door, and could not make any one answer; I looked through the window and saw a lot of blood." I accompanied him, and looked through the window myself, saw the blood and the woman. For a moment I could not say anything, and I then said: "You had better fetch the police." I knew the deceased as Mary Jane Kelly, and had no doubt at all about her identity. I followed

Bowyer to Commercial-street Police-station, where I saw Inspector Beck. I inquired at first for Inspector Reid. Inspector Beck returned with me at once.

[Coroner] How long had the deceased lived in the room ? - Ten months. She lived with Barnett. I did not know whether they were married or not; they lived comfortably together, but they had a row when the window was broken. The bedstead, bed-clothes, table, and every article of furniture belonged to me.

[Coroner] What rent was paid for this room ? - It was supposed to be 4s 6d a week. Deceased was in arrears 29s. I was to be paid the rent weekly. Arrears are got as best you can. I frequently saw the deceased the worse for drink. When sober she was an exceptionally quiet woman, but when in drink she had more to say. She was able to walk about, and was not helpless.

Mary Ann Cox stated: I live at No. 5 Room, Miller's-court. It is the last house on the left-hand side of the court. I am a widow, and get my living on the streets. I have known the deceased for eight or nine months as the occupant of No. 13 Room. She was called Mary Jane. I last saw her alive on Thursday night, at a quarter to twelve, very much intoxicated.

[Coroner] Where was this ? - In Dorset-street. She went up the court, a few steps in front of me.

[Coroner] Was anybody with her ? - A short, stout man, shabbily dressed. He had on a longish coat, very shabby, and carried a pot of ale in his hand.

[Coroner] What was the colour of the coat ? - A dark coat.

[Coroner] What hat had he ? - A round hard billycock.

[Coroner] Long or short hair ? - I did not notice. He had a blotchy face, and full carrotty moustache.

[Coroner] The chin was shaven ? - Yes. A lamp faced the door.

[Coroner] Did you see them go into her room ? - Yes; I said "Good night, Mary," and she turned round and banged the door.

[Coroner] Had he anything in his hands but the can ? - No.

[Coroner] Did she say anything ? - She said "Good night, I am going to have a song." As I went in she sang "A violet I plucked from my mother's grave when a boy." I remained a quarter of an hour in my room and went out. Deceased was still singing at one o'clock when I returned. I remained in the room for a minute to warm my hands as it was raining, and went out again. She was singing still, and I returned to my room at three o'clock. The light was then out and there was no noise.

[Coroner] Did you go to sleep ? - No; I was upset. I did not undress at all. I did not sleep at all. I must have heard what went on in the court. I heard no noise or cry of "Murder," but men went out to work in the market.

[Coroner] How many men live in the court who work in Spitalfields Market ? - One. At a quarter- past six I heard a man go down the court. That was too late for the market.

[Coroner] From what house did he go ? - I don't know.

[Coroner] Did you hear the door bang after him ? - No.

[Coroner] Then he must have walked up the court and back again? - Yes.

[Coroner] It might have been a policeman ? - It might have been.

[Coroner] What would you take the stout man's age to be ? - Six-and-thirty.

[Coroner] Did you notice the colour of his trousers ? - All his clothes were dark.

[Coroner] Did his boots sound as if the heels were heavy ? - There was no sound as he went up the court.

[Coroner] Then you think that his boots were down at heels ? - He made no noise.

[Coroner] What clothes had Mary Jane on ? - She had no hat; a red pelerine and a shabby skirt.

[Coroner] You say she was drunk ? - I did not notice she was drunk until she said good night. The man closed the door. By the Jury: There was a light in the window, but I saw nothing, as the blinds were down. I should know the man again, if I saw him.

By the Coroner: I feel certain if there had been the cry of "Murder" in the place I should have heard it; there was not the least noise. I have often seen the woman the worse for drink.


Elizabeth Prater, a married woman, said: My husband, William Prater, was a boot machinist, and he has deserted me. I live at 20 Room, in Miller's-court, above the shed. Deceased occupied a room below. I left the room on the Thursday at five p.m., and returned to it at about one a.m. on Friday morning. I stood at the corner until about twenty minutes past one. No one spoke to me. McCarthy's shop was open, and I called in, and then went to my room. I should have seen a glimmer of light in going up the stairs if there had been a light in deceased's room, but I noticed none. The partition was so thin I could have heard Kelly walk about in the room. I went to bed at half-past one and barricaded the door with two tables. I fell asleep directly and slept soundly. A kitten disturbed me about half-past three o'clock or a quarter to four. As I was turning round I heard a suppressed cry of "Oh - murder!" in a faint voice. It seemed to proceed from the court.

[Coroner] Do you often hear cries of "Murder?" - It is nothing unusual in the street. I did not take particular notice.

[Coroner] Did you hear it a second time? - No.

[Coroner] Did you hear beds or tables being pulled about? - None whatever. I went asleep, and was awake again at five a.m. I passed down the stairs, and saw some men harnessing horses. At a quarter to six I was in the Ten Bells.

[Coroner] Could the witness, Mary Ann Cox, have come down the entry between one and half-past one o'clock without your knowledge ? - Yes, she could have done so.

[Coroner] Did you see any strangers at the Ten Bells ? - No. I went back to bed and slept until eleven.

[Coroner] You heard no singing downstairs ? - None whatever. I should have heard the singing distinctly. It was quite quiet at half-past one o'clock.


Caroline Maxewell, 14, Dorset-street, said: My husband is a lodging-house deputy. I knew the deceased for about four months. I believe she was an unfortunate. On two occasions I spoke to her.

The Coroner: You must be very careful about your evidence, because it is different to other people's. You say you saw her standing at the corner of the entry to the court ? - Yes, on Friday morning, from eight to half-past eight. I fix the time by my husband's finishing work. When I came out of the lodging-house she was opposite.

[Coroner] Did you speak to her ? - Yes; it was an unusual thing to see her up. She was a young woman who never associated with any one. I spoke across the street, "What, Mary, brings you up so early ?" She said, "Oh, Carrie, I do feel so bad."

[Coroner] And yet you say you had only spoken to her twice previously; you knew her name and she knew yours ? - Oh, yes; by being about in the lodging-house.

[Coroner] What did she say ? - She said, "I've had a glass of beer, and I've brought it up again"; and it was in the road. I imagined she had been in the Britannia beer-shop at the corner of the street. I left her, saying that I could pity her feelings. I went to Bishopsgate-street to get my husband's breakfast. Returning I saw her outside the Britannia public-house, talking to a man.

[Coroner] This would be about what time ? - Between eight and nine o'clock. I was absent about half-an-hour. It was about a quarter to nine.

[Coroner] What description can you give of this man ? - I could not give you any, as they were at some distance.

Inspector Abberline: The distance is about sixteen yards.

Witness: I am sure it was the deceased. I am willing to swear it.

The Coroner: You are sworn now. Was he a tall man ? - No; he was a little taller than me and stout.

Inspector Abberline: On consideration I should say the distance was twenty-five yards.

The Coroner; What clothes had the man ? - Witness: Dark clothes; he seemed to have a plaid coat on. I could not say what sort of hat he had.

[Coroner] What sort of dress had the deceased ? - A dark skirt, a velvet body, a maroon shawl, and no hat.

[Coroner] Have you ever seen her the worse for drink ? - I have seen her in drink, but she was not a notorious character.

By the Jury: I should have noticed if the man had had a tall silk hat, but we are accustomed to see men of all sorts with women. I should not like to pledge myself to the kind of hat.

Sarah Lewis deposed: I live at 24, Great Pearl-street, and am a laundress. I know Mrs. Keyler, in Miller's-court, and went to her house at 2, Miller's-court, at 2.30a.m. on Friday. It is the first house. I noticed the time by the Spitalfields' Church clock. When I went into the court, opposite the lodging-house I saw a man with a wideawake. There was no one talking to him. He was a stout-looking man, and not very tall. The hat was black. I did not take any notice of his clothes. The man was looking up the court; he seemed to be waiting or looking for some one. Further on there was a man and woman - the later being in drink. There was nobody in the court. I dozed in a chair at Mrs. Keyler's, and woke at about half- past three. I heard the clock strike.

[Coroner] What woke you up ? - I could not sleep. I sat awake until nearly four, when I heard a female's voice shouting "Murder" loudly. It seemed like the voice of a young woman. It sounded at our door. There was only one scream.

[Coroner] Were you afraid ? Did you wake anybody up ? - No, I took no notice, as I only heard the one scream.

[Coroner] You stayed at Keyler's house until what time ? - Half-past five p.m. on Friday. The police would not let us out of the court.

[Coroner] Have you seen any suspicious persons in the district ? - On Wednesday night I was going along the Bethnal-green-road, with a woman, about eight o'clock, when a gentleman passed us. He followed us and spoke to us, and wanted us to follow him into an entry. He had a shiny leather bag with him.

[Coroner] Did he want both of you ? - No; only one. I refused. He went away and came back again, saying he would treat us. He put down his bag and picked it up again, saying, "What are you frightened about ? Do you think I've got anything in the bag ?" We then ran away, as we were frightened.

[Coroner] Was he a tall man ? - He was short, pale-faced, with a black moustache, rather small. His age was about forty.

[Coroner] Was it a large bag ? - No, about 6in to 9in long. His hat was a high round hat. He had a brownish overcoat, with a black short coat underneath. His trousers were a dark pepper-and- salt.

[Coroner] After he left you what did you do ? - We ran away.

[Coroner] Have you seen him since ? - On Friday morning, about half-past two a.m., when I was going to Miller's-court, I met the same man with a woman in Commercial-street, near Mr. Ringer's public-house (the Britannia). He had no overcoat on.

[Coroner] Had he the black bag ? - Yes.

[Coroner] Were the man and woman quarrelling ? - No; they were talking. As I passed he looked at me. I don't know whether he recognised me. There was no policeman about.


Mr. George Bagster Phillips, divisional surgeon of police, said: I was called by the police on Friday morning at eleven o'clock, and on proceeding to Miller's-court, which I entered at 11.15, I found a room, the door of which led out of the passage at the side of 26, Dorset-street, photographs of which I produce. It had two windows in the court. Two panes in the lesser window were broken, and as the door was locked I looked through the lower of the broken panes and satisfied myself that the mutilated corpse lying on the bed was not in need of any immediate attention from me, and I also came to the conclusion that there was nobody else upon the bed, or within view, to whom I could render any professional assistance. Having ascertained that probably it was advisable that no entrance should be made into the room at that time, I remained until about 1.30p.m., when the door was broken open by McCarthy, under the direction of Superintendent Arnold. On the door being opened it knocked against a table which was close to the left-hand side of the bedstead, and the bedstead was close against the wooden partition. The mutilated remains of a woman were lying two-thirds over, towards the edge of the bedstead, nearest the door.

Deceased had only an under- linen garment upon her, and by subsequent examination I am sure the body had been removed, after the injury which caused death, from that side of the bedstead which was nearest to the wooden partition previously mentioned. The large quantity of blood under the bedstead, the saturated condition of the palliasse, pillow, and sheet at the top corner of the bedstead nearest to the partition leads me to the conclusion that the severance of the right carotid artery, which was the immediate cause of death, was inflicted while the deceased was lying at the right side of the bedstead and her head and neck in the top right-hand corner.

The jury had no questions to ask at this stage, and it was understood that more detailed evidence of the medical examination would be given at a future hearing.

An adjournment for a few minutes then took place, and on the return of the jury

the coroner said: It has come to my ears that somebody has been making a statement to some of the jury as to their right and duty of being here. Has any one during the interval spoken to the jury, saying that they should not be here to-day ?

Some jurymen replied in the negative.

The Coroner: Then I must have been misinformed. I should have taken good care that he would have had a quiet life for the rest of the week if anybody had interfered with my jury.

Julia Vanturney [Van Turney], 1, Miller's-court, a charwoman, living with Harry Owen, said: I knew the deceased for some time as Kelly, and I knew Joe Barnett, who lived with her. He would not allow her to go on the streets. Deceased often got drunk. She said she was fond of another man, also named Joe. I never saw this man. I believe he was a costermonger.

[Coroner] When did you last see the deceased alive ? - On Thursday morning, at about ten o'clock. I slept in the court on Thursday night, and went to bed about eight. I could not rest at all during the night.

[Coroner] Did you hear any noises in the court ? - I did not. I heard no screams of "Murder," nor any one singing.

[Coroner] You must have heard deceased singing ? - Yes; I knew her songs. They were generally Irish


Maria Harvey, 3, New-court, Dorset-street, stated: I knew the deceased as Mary Jane Kelly. I slept at her house on Monday night and on Tuesday night. All the afternoon of Thursday we were together.

[Coroner] Were you in the house when Joe Barnett called ? - Yes. I said, "Well, Mary Jane, I shall not see you this evening again," and I left with her two men's dirty shirts, a little boy's shirt, a black overcoat, a black crepe bonnet with black satin strings, a pawn-ticket for a grey shawl, upon which 2s had been lent, and a little girls white petticoat.

[Coroner] Have you seen any of these articles since? - Yes; I saw the black overcoat in a room in the court on Friday afternoon.

[Coroner] Did the deceased ever speak to you about being afraid of any man ? - She did not.


Inspector Beck, H Division, deposed that, having sent for the doctor, he gave orders to prevent any persons leaving the court, and he directed officers to make a search. He had not been aware that the deceased was known to the police.

Inspector Frederick G. Abberline, inspector of police, Criminal Investigation Department, Scotland-yard, stated: I am in charge of this case. I arrived at Miller's-court about 11.30 on Friday morning.

[Coroner] Was it by your orders that the door was forced ? - No; I had an intimation from Inspector Beck that the bloodhounds had been sent for, and the reply had been received that they were on the way. Dr. Phillips was unwilling to force the door, as it would be very much better to test the dogs, if they were coming. We remained until about 1.30 p.m., when Superintendent Arnold arrived, and he informed me that the order in regard to the dogs had been countermanded, and he gave orders for the door to be forced. I agree with the medical evidence as to the condition of the room. I subsequently took an inventory of the contents of the room. There were traces of a large fire having been kept up in the grate, so much so that it had melted the spout of a kettle off. We have since gone through the ashes in the fireplace; there were remnants of clothing, a portion of a brim of a hat, and a skirt, and it appeared as if a large quantity of women's clothing had been burnt.

[Coroner] Can you give any reason why they were burnt ? - I can only imagine that it was to make a light for the man to see what he was doing. There was only one small candle in the room, on the top of a broken wine-glass. An impression has gone abroad that the murderer took away the key of the room. Barnett informs me that it has been missing some time, and since it has been lost they have put their hand through the broken window, and moved back the catch. It is quite easy. There was a man's clay pipe in the room, and Barnett informed me that he smoked it.

[Coroner] Is there anything further the jury ought to know ? - No; if there should be I can communicate with you, sir.

The Coroner (to the jury): The question is whether you will adjourn for further evidence. My own opinion is that it is very unnecessary for two courts to deal with these cases, and go through the same evidence time after time, which only causes expense and trouble. If the coroner's jury can come to a decision as to the cause of death, then that is all that they have to do. They have nothing to do with prosecuting a man and saying what amount of penalty he is to get. It is quite sufficient if they find out what the cause of death was. It is for the police authorities to deal with the case and satisfy themselves as to any person who may be suspected later on. I do not want to take it out of your hands. It is for you to say whether at an adjournment you will hear minutiae of the evidence, or whether you will think it is a matter to be dealt with in the police-courts later on, and that, this woman having met with her death by the carotid artery having been cut, you will be satisfied to return a verdict to that effect. From what I learn the police are content to take the future conduct of the case. It is for you to say whether you will close the inquiry to-day; if not, we shall adjourn for a week or fortnight, to hear the evidence that you may desire.

The Foreman, having consulted with his colleagues, considered that the jury had had quite sufficient evidence before them upon which to give a verdict.

The Coroner: What is the verdict:

The Foreman: Wilful murder against some person or persons unknown.

3635830R00141

Printed in Great Britain
by Amazon.co.uk, Ltd.,
Marston Gate.